The Protestant Movement in Bolivia

Hurst Memorial Library
Pacific Christian College
Long Beach, Calif.

The Protestant Movement in Bolivia

C. Peter Wagner

Hurst Memorial Library
Pacific Christian College
Long Beach, Calif.

William Carey Library
South Pasadena, California

© Copyright 1970 by the William Carey Library.
All rights reserved.
No part of this book may be used or reproduced in any manner whatsoever without written permission, except in the case of brief quotations embodied in critical articles and reviews.

International Standard Book Number: 0-87808-402-9
Library of Congress Catalog Number: 76-126079

If your order is accompanied by full payment (U.S. check only) single copies may be obtained by sending $4.25 (i.e. retail price of $3.95 plus 30¢ postage and handling) to MARC/DOC, 919 W. Huntington Drive, Monrovia, California 91016, or from your bookstore. All quantity orders should be directed to the publisher, William Carey Library, 533 Hermosa St., South Pasadena, California 91030.

PRINTED IN THE UNITED STATES OF AMERICA

To

George Allan

Verne D. Roberts

Joseph S. McCullough

The distinguished succession of General Directors of the Andes Evangelical Mission, 1909 - 1969

Contents

ILLUSTRATIONS ix
TABLES xi
FOREWORD xiii
PREFACE
ABBREVIATIONS

1 SOIL OF BOLIVIA 1
    Bolivian Geography 2
    Bolivian Economics 6
    Bolivian People 6
    Bolivian History 10
    Religious Liberty 13

2 SEEDS OF PROTESTANTISM 16
    In Neighboring Countries 16
    Beginnings in Bolivia 19

3 PIONEER CHURCH-PLANTERS 24
    Brethren Assemblies 27
    Bolivian Baptist Union 33
    The Methodist Church in Bolivia 52
    The Evangelical Christian Union 72
    Seventh Day Adventists 87

4 SECOND SOWING OF MISSIONS 93
Union Bible Seminary and Bolivian Friends Holiness Mission 93
Swedish Free Mission 96
Salvation Army 97
Oregon Yearly Meeting of Friends Church 97
South America Indian Mission and New Testament Missionary Union 108
International Church of the Foursquare Gospel 112
Other Groups 113

5 CHACO WAR AND POST-WAR INFLUENCES 114
Bolivia's Defeat 114
A Tide of Progress 115
The War and the Churches 116
New Missions Enter Bolivia 117

6 NATIONAL REVOLUTION 1952 121
The Rise of the MNR 123
René Barrientos O. 127

7 THIRD SOWING OF MISSIONS 133
New Tribes Mission 133
World Gospel Mission 135
Church of the Nazarene 136
Church of God (Holiness) 138
Brazilian Baptists 140
Assemblies of God 141
Bolivian Holiness Mission 147
Bethesda Missions 152
Midnight Call Mission 152
Maranatha Baptists 152
Other Smaller Groups 153

8 PROTESTANT COOPERATION 154
Regional Conference for Bolivia 154
Comity Agreements 155
Conference of National Evangelical Workers 156
Task-oriented Versus Conciliar Cooperation 157
Local United Churches 159
The Formation of ANDEB 161

Contents

8 PROTESTANT COOPERATION, cont.
    Evangelism-in-Depth 164
    Cooperation in Theological Education 175
    Cooperation in Social Service 176
    Hymnology 177

9 DENOMINATIONAL COMPARISONS 179
    Growth Rates 188

10 REGIONAL CHURCH GROWTH 192
    The Lowlands and the Jesuit Reductions 192
    Urbanization and the Church 195
    Migration from Mountains to Tropics 197

11 ETHNIC CHURCH GROWTH 199
    Quechuas and Aymaras 199
    The Chipayas 201
    The Okinawans 205

12 STRATEGY FOR FUTURE HARVEST 205
    Further Research is Needed 206
    Completing the Aymara Harvest 208
    Saturating the Colonies with Churches 209
    Multiplying Congregations in Urban Areas 210
    Renewed Efforts to Win the Quechuas 212
    Missionary and National Workers Should be Mobile 212
    Training the Ministry for a Growing Church 213
    Allowing Regional and Ethnic Autonomy 213
    Maintaining a Social Witness 214
    Developing Bolivian Hymnology 215
    Conclusion 215

APPENDIX 217
BIBLIOGRAPHY 221

Illustrations

1 Departments and Capital Cities; Regions of Bolivia 3
2 Density of Population by Department 4
3 Brethren Assemblies 32
4 Seven Local Churches of Bolivian Baptist Union 43
5 Bolivian Baptist Union Membership Growth 53
6 Canadian Baptist Mission in Bolivia 54
7 Methodist Church in Bolivia 59
8 Locations of Principal Methodist Churches 67
9 Historical Development of the Evangelical Christian Union 74
10 Locations of Principal Stations of AEM 80
11 Evangelical Christian Union 86
12 Seventh-day Adventists 90
13 Historical Development of Friends' Holiness Mission 94
14 Oregon Yearly Meeting of Friends 99
15 Historical Development of South America Indian Mission and New Testament Missionary Union 109
16 World Mission Prayer League 120
17 Old Social Structure 130
18 New Social Structure 131
19 Church of the Nazarene 137
20 Church of God (Holiness) 140
21 Assemblies of God 142
22 Assemblies of God Comparison of Regional Growth 143
23 Assemblies of God Total and Regional Rates of Growth 144
24 Bolivian Holiness Church 150

25 Rates of Growth in Relation to Evangelism-in-Depth   166
26 Comparative Growth Rates of Twelve Major Bolivian
   Denominations   182
27 Population Compared with Protestant Church Growth   184
28 Twelve Major Bolivian Denominations   185
29 Church Growth According to CGRILA Classification   189
30 Church Growth According to Ecclesiastical Tradition   190

Tables

1. Language Distribution of Bolivia 9
2. Ethnic Division of Bolivia 9
3. Brethren Assemblies 31
4. Bolivian Baptist Union 39
5. 1929 Canadian Baptist Membership 45
6. Guatajata Church Attendance and Increase in Schools 48
7. Membership of Individual Methodist Churches 61
8. The Methodist Church in Bolivia 65
9. Evangelical Christian Union 82
10. Seventh Day Adventists 91
11. Union Bible Seminary and Friends' Holiness Mission 95
12. Oregon Yearly Meeting of Friends Church 100
13. INELA Regional Church Growth 102
14. South America Indian Mission and New Testament Missionary Union 112
15. World Mission Prayer League 120
16. World Gospel Mission 135
17. Church of the Nazarene 136
18. Church of God (Holiness) 139
19. Regional Statistics of Assemblies of God 146
20. Assemblies of God 147
21. Comparison of Thirty-Four Bolivian Holiness Churches 148
22. Bolivian Holiness Church Annual Membership 151
23. Church Growth in Eight Denominations Before, During, and After Evangelism-in-Depth 165
24. Current Denominational Membership 179

25 Church Growth According to Ecclesiastical Tradition 181
26 Ecclesiastical Groupings of Bolivian Denominations 186
27 Theological Groupings 187
28 Church Growth According to CGRILA Classification 188
29 Possible Regional-Ethnic Combinations 207

Foreword

There is now little question that the recent series of books dealing with every aspect of church growth, flowing from the pens of Donald McGavran and his growing circle of disciples, constitutes one of the most important and stimulating innovations in the field of modern missions. The group of missionary scholars and students which clusters around "the apostle of church growth" at the School of Missions in Pasadena, California, is vigorously attempting to restudy the history of missions as well as to restate their theological and biblical bases.

C. Peter Wagner, Associate General Director of the Andes Evangelical Mission, is one of the younger men who has recently cast his lot with the church growth team. While a student at the School of Missions in 1967-1968, he took a long, hard look at the history of missions in his own country, Bolivia, and as a result has written the first history of the Protestant Church of that Andean republic.

The Protestant Movement in Bolivia is not a dry, stogy history book. It tells the story from the times of the early pioneers to the present with a sense of emotional involvement, sprinkled with an urgency to accelerate the spread of the Gospel in the future. Already the Protestant Church in Bolivia is growing at a rate eight times that of the general population growth, but Wagner feels that improved methods can make it grow even faster.

Without an attempt to be iconoclastic, Wagner examines such movements as Evangelism-in-Depth with the keen eye of a diagnostician rather than with the rose-colored spectacles of a public relations man. His conclusions are rather disturbing, and have been commented on at some length by Malcolm Bradshaw in his recent book *Church Growth Through Evangelism-in-Depth*.

This is typical of the style of the book. The author does not dodge such questions as: Why don't Pentecostals grow as fast in Bolivia as in other Latin American countries? Why have the Seventh-Day-Adventists become Bolivia's largest denomination? What tensions between ecumenicals and non-ecumenicals did the formation of Bolivia's fellowship of churches (ANDEB) cause? In which areas and among which peoples is the Protestant Church most likely to grow in the near future?

Apparently, the Bolivians themselves were happy to see a book like this written. Bolivia's ranking secular publisher, Los Amigos del Libro, has translated it into Spanish and is including it in the fifty-volume Bolivian Encyclopedia series.

CLYDE W. TAYLOR
Executive Secretary,
Evangelical Foreign Missions Association

Preface

   This book takes its place in one of the most significant series of missionary studies ever conducted. Under the auspices of the Fuller Theological Seminary School of World Mission, career missionaries from all parts of the world are researching and analyzing the development of the churches on their fields from the point of view of church growth. This particular school of missionary thought is convinced that faithfulness to God implies multiplying churches in receptive populations, thus bringing multitudes to redeeming faith in Jesus Christ as Lord and Savior. "Making disciples of all nations" (Matthew 28:19) is God's directive to the Church in all ages, and His constant imperative for strategy and action.
   These studies are not ends in themselves. They are source materials which will form the basis for a reevaluation of missionary strategy worldwide. Under the distinguished leadership of Dean Donald A. McGavran, the influence of the type of church growth thinking characteristic of the School of World Mission is growing to a rather astonishing degree in many geographical areas of the world and among missionaries of a wide range of theological persuasions.
   The present study of Bolivia's Protestant Church comes as a result of the author's first-hand experience which began when he arrived there as a missionary in 1956. The research project itself was started in 1967, when arrangements for graduate study at the School of World Mission during the

academic year 1967-1968 were finalized. As a preliminary step, the author published three numbers of a Bolivian *Church Growth Bulletin*, in Spanish, designed to make church and missionary leaders aware of both church growth theory and the specific research which was being undertaken. The first number consisted of a Spanish translation of the article in the Fall, 1966, issue of the *Evangelical Missions Quarterly* by John T. Seamands entitled, "The Significance of McGavran's Church Growth Thesis." The second number was a directory of all Protestant denominations in Bolivia, sent to the leaders for their revision and correction. The third was a master plan for the research to be carried out over a period of two years.

In the meantime the author made extensive use of the libraries of Fuller Theological Seminary (including the Church Growth Research in Latin America library and archives) and the University of California at Los Angeles, digging out the information which provided the historical background for the study. A large volume of correspondence was carried on with church leaders on the field. Excellent cooperation was received from the Canadian Baptists, Seventh-day Adventists, Methodist Church, Andes Evangelical Mission, Oregon Yearly Meeting of Friends, Assemblies of God, and Bolivian Holiness Mission. Other groups either had not kept statistical accounts of their work or for some other reason failed to provide the desired information.

The courses taken at the School of World Mission under Professors McGavran, Alan R. Tippett and Ralph D. Winter, were invaluable in providing the theoretical framework for this study. The cumulative effect of their theological, anthropological and historical emphases made this year of study the most rewarding academic experience of the author's career. Even if all the data were on hand, this book could not have been written without the insights gathered from the class work.

The task is not finished. This book is a preliminary work, a foundation supplied for future studies. Before this is completed, denominational leaders will have to go over their respective sections to check for accuracy, statistical gaps will have to be filled, and ideally a nationwide church growth seminar for Bolivia should be held. At this time suggestions for future strategy will be pooled and refined.

The author wishes to express special appreciation to his major advisor, Dr. Ralph D. Winter, for his creative suggestions throughout all phases of this research; to his professor, Donald A. McGavran, for the theoretical framework in which this book is cast; to his wife, Doris, for willingly undertaking the arduous and painstaking task of typing the manuscript; and to his field colleagues, Joseph S. McCullough, Peter Savage, Kenneth Fowler, and Pamela Toomey, who helped gather the data upon which the study is based.

Abbreviations

ACE	Asociación Cristiana Evangélica (Santa Cruz)
AEBET	Asociación Evangélica Boliviana de Educación Teológica
AEM	Andes Evangelical Mission
AG	Assemblies of God
ALFALIT	Alfabetización y Literatura (Lit-Lit)
ANDEB	Asociación Nacional de Evangélicos de Bolivia
ANE	Asociación Nacional de Evangélicos (La Paz)
ASAM	Australasia South American Mission
BBU	Bolivian Baptist Union
BIM	Bolivian Indian Mission
CALA	Committee for Aymara Literature and Literacy
CBFMB	Canadian Baptist Foreign Mission Board
CGRILA	Church Growth Research in Latin America
COMBASE	Comisión Boliviana de Acción Social Evangélica
COMIBOL	Bolivian Mining Corporation
DIA	Difusiones Interamericanas
ECU	Evangelical Christian Union
EFMA	Evangelical Foreign Missions Association
EID	Evangelism-in-Depth
EOS	*Echoes of Service*
EUSA	Evangelical Union of South America
IFMA	Interdenominational Foreign Missions Association
INELA	Iglesia Nacional Evangélica Los Amigos (Oregon Friends)
ISAL	Iglesia y Sociedad en América Latina
LAM	Latin America Mission

LEAL	Literatura Evangélica para América Latina
MEC	Movimiento Estudiantil Cristiano
Meth.	Methodist Church
MNR	Movimiento Nacionalista Revolucionario
NTM	New Tribes Mission
NTMU	New Testament Missionary Union
Naz.	Church of the Nazarene
NCC	National Council of Churches (USA)
OYM	Oregon Yearly Meeting of Friends Church
SAIM	South America Indian Mission
SAMS	South American Missionary Society (Anglican)
SDA	Seventh-day Adventists
UBS	Union Bible Seminary
UNELAM	Comisión Provisional Pro-Unidad Evangélica Latinoamericana
USAID	United States Agency for International Development
UWM	United World Mission
WCC	World Council of Churches
WCH	*World Christian Handbook*
WGM	World Gospel Mission
WMPL	World Mission Prayer League

1

Soil of Bolivia

If the landlocked country of Bolivia, which occupies the heart of the South American continent, does not literally defy description, she at least presents a formidable challenge to word-coining authors. Jesuits Bannon and Dunne have chosen to call Bolivia the "poor little rich girl," (1947:599) probably taking the cue from the classical "beggar on the throne of gold" attributed to French explorer Alcides d'Orbigny. After his second visit, John Gunther described the republic as "the nation where almost anything can happen and everything does" (1967:389). Some Bolivians tend to be more cynical than the foreign observers. Alcides Arguedas, for example, writes about his country as the pueblo enfermo, the sick people.

Although Bolivia might have had her times of illness such as under the tyrannical dictator, Mariano Melgarejo (1864-1871), today, and especially since the revolution of 1952, she shows definite signs of good health. If the economy of Bolivia is relatively poor today, it is no doubt in part because she has been unjustly exploited by foreigners throughout her history. Her huge store of gold, skillfully worked into native art forms, was sacked and melted down by Pizarro and his conquistadores. Her fabulously rich silver mountain of Potosí yielded some 30,000 tons of the metal to the benefit of Spanish colonizers. When the mines were in full production toward the end of the sixteenth and into the seventeenth centuries, Bolivia was the wealthiest country in the hemisphere and Potosí the largest city of the Americas. The Jesuits exported large quantities of wealth from Bolivia's tropical areas until they themselves were expelled in 1767. Chile took Bolivia's nitrate deposits and her outlet to the sea in 1876. Then in the twentieth century, the United States as the "Colossus of the North" has been accused of economic imperialism, although steps are being taken that may correct that impression.

BOLIVIAN GEOGRAPHY

Politically, Bolivia is divided into nine departments (see Figure 1). Her 424,000 square miles include an area about the size of Texas and California combined. The departments of La Paz and Oruro include the great Altiplano or high plateau. This flat, brown, cold, windswept area is home to some 50 percent of Bolivia's 3,900,000 inhabitants (Alonso 1962:156; Population Reference Bureau 1968), qualifying it as the most densely populated region of the nation (see Figure 2). The Altiplano spreads southeast from Lake Titicaca, at 13,000 feet the world's highest navigable body of water. Although rainfall is a perennial problem for the farmers, it is slightly heavier near the lake and therefore the density of population increases as one approaches it. Figure 2 indicates the population density of each department.

The departments of Cochabamba, Chuquisaca, Potosí and Tarija are mountainous, with their inhabitants clustered in numerous valleys. In general, rainfall is slightly heavier in the valleys than on the Altiplano. Most Bolivians are farmers, and one of their chief crops is the potato. Few people know that the Altiplano is the birthplace of the potato and that the Spaniards found over two hundred varieties of this strange tuber when they arrived. Perhaps the most typically Bolivian food is the chuño, potatoes dehydrated by allowing them to freeze at night, then squeezing out the excess moisture by treading on them in bare feet during the day.

As the Andes mountains drop off to the north and east, the vast tropical lowlands are formed, comprising the departments of Pando, Beni and Santa Cruz. Whereas 16 percent of the country is Altiplano, and 14 percent valleys, 70 percent is tropical lowland. But only approximately 30 percent of the population lives in the lowland area. The hot valleys on the edge of the mountain range are called the Yungas. There the

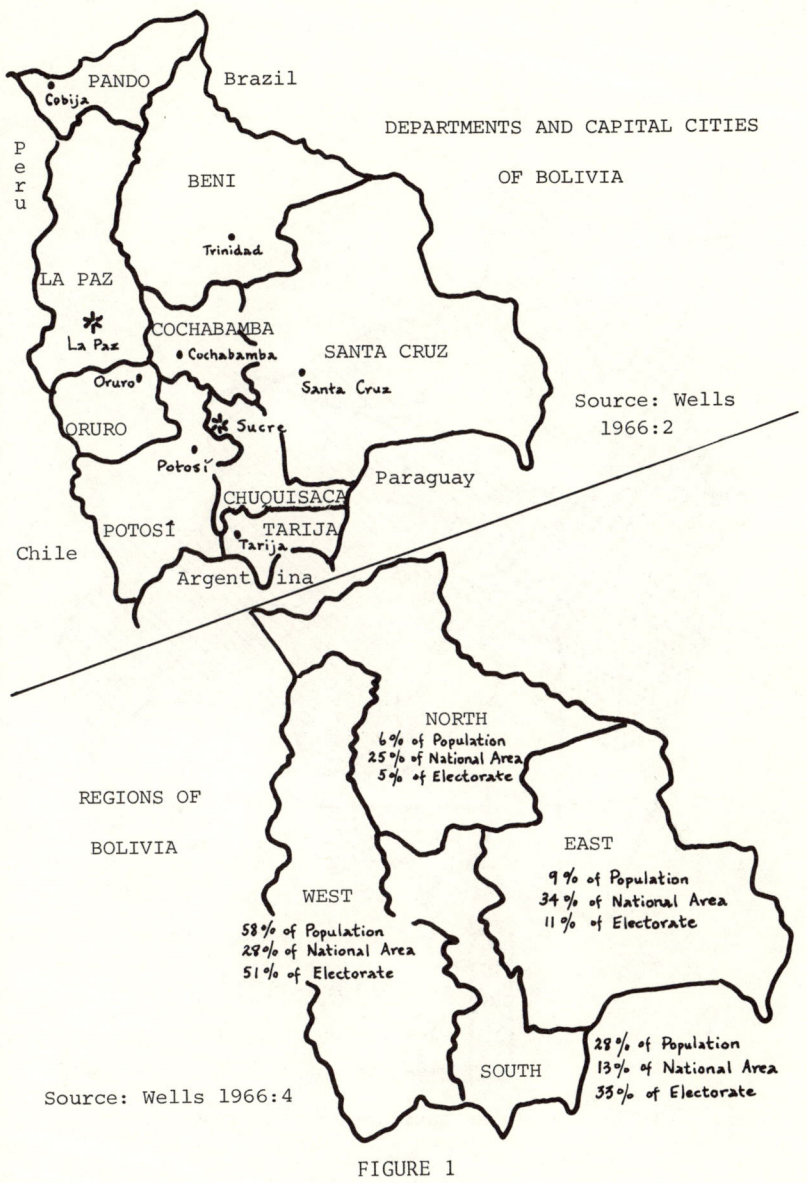

FIGURE 1

BOLIVIA: DENSITY OF POPULATION BY DEPARTMENT

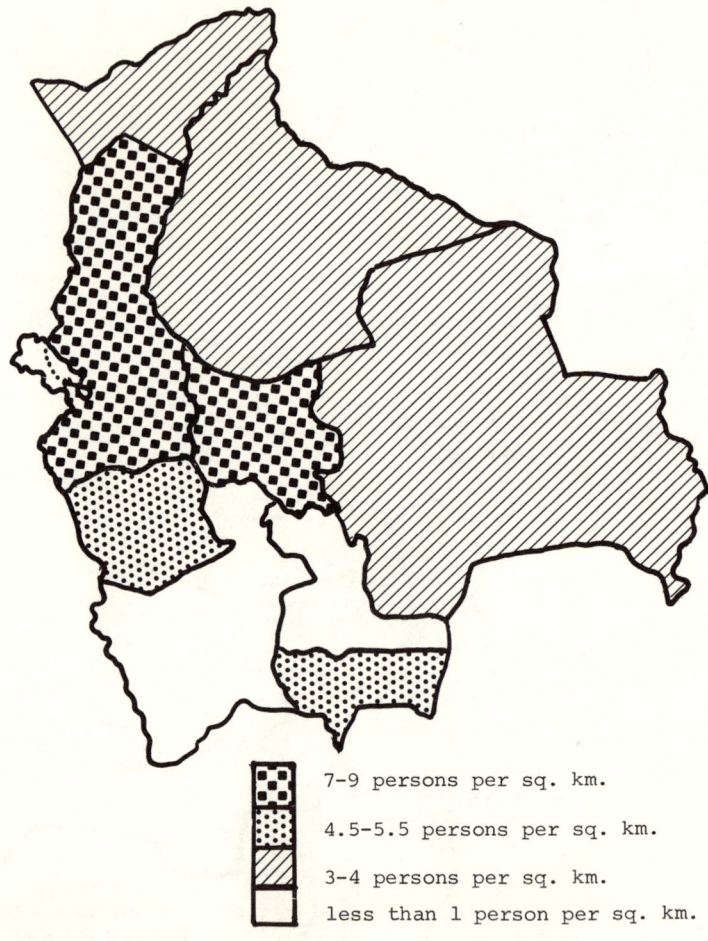

Data taken from Bolivian National Census, 1950

FIGURE 2

coca leaf is grown. Coca, the source of cocaine, is constantly chewed by most of the highland peasants who depend on its mild narcotic effect to relieve them from hunger pangs and the dullness of peasant life. The department of the Beni, crisscrossed by meandering rivers, which eventually empty into the Amazon, is a patchwork of vast pampas and islands of dense jungle. Torrential summer rains make it virtually one vast lake for three or four months of the year. The western side of Santa Cruz resembles the Beni, but as one moves east and crosses from the Amazon watershed to the Paraguay watershed, the Chaco, as it is called, becomes more like a desert than a jungle. With the exception of occasional palm groves, the vegetation is low, brown, thorny trees barely existing on the sandy soil.

The three principal cities in Bolivia are La Paz (460,936), Cochabamba (115,989), and Santa Cruz (80,522), which are the prominent capital cities of their respective departments. These are connected by frequent air and bus schedules. Oruro (90,407), Potosí (65,690), and Chuquisaca's capital city of Sucre (57,608), are connected to La Paz and Cochabamba by rail and bus services. Tarija and Trinidad (Beni) have populations of 24,217 and 15,446 respectively, and far-away Cobija (Pando) is only a village of 2,478. Beni and Pando are isolated with only air transportation to the interior of the country. Although the railroad between Santa Cruz and Cochabamba is still on the drawing boards, Santa Cruz is connected by rail to Brazil on the east and Argentina on the south.

Each department is divided into several provinces. Of the provinces, Keith Hamilton, in his excellent pioneer study, *Church Growth in the High Andes*, says:

> Within each State are counties (provincias), each with its county seat town. Each county corresponds closely to the basin which from time immemorial has been the home of a certain tribe. The county seat town is not merely an administrative center - it is the chief town of a tribal area. The larger the proportion of Indians in a county, the more important this factor becomes ... Thus, in addition to the civic spirit known in other lands which leads to competition between neighboring towns for roads, markets, political spoils, and schools, there is throughout the Highlands a racial or tribal rivalry (1962:17).

Hamilton underscores the importance of this local loyalty for church growth. Peasants are concerned about what happens in their own province, but they might even react against what happens in a neighboring province, just because their enemies are involved.

BOLIVIAN ECONOMICS

Although 70 percent of Bolivians work in agriculture, only 5 percent of her land is arable and 2 percent of her total area is under cultivation. The agricultural potential of the country is still immense. As the highland peasants increasingly respond to the government's urging them to migrate into the tropical regions, many of these resources will be developed. The future of Bolivia is undoubtedly in the tropical region, not only from agriculture, but also from the petroleum reserves that are just beginning to be tapped.

Until agriculture and petroleum are developed, mining will continue to be the principal source of foreign exchange for Bolivia. At present Bolivian mines produce 14 percent of the free world's tin, 12 percent of the antimony, 6 percent of the tungsten, and smaller amounts of lead, zinc, copper, and silver. Gulf Oil Company is exporting petroleum and Bolivia has recently been assigned a USA sugar quota.

The economy of Bolivia is improving, but nevertheless her inhabitants live on perhaps the lowest per capita income in Latin America. According to the 1950 census it was $82.00 per year. Today it is $122.30, according to the U.N. Economic Commission for Latin America, with Haiti next up the list at $149.20 and Argentina in the lead with $799.00 (Rycroft and Clemmer 1963:68). The standard of living, however, is "higher than income indicates because of the high percentage of persons engaged in agriculture" (Wells 1966:3).

BOLIVIAN PEOPLE

While Bolivia's birth rate is relatively high at 43-45 per 1000, her annual rate of population increase, set by the Population Reference Bureau (1968) at 2.4 percent, is below that of Latin America in general which is 3.0 percent. One cause is a very high rate of infant mortality in the mountain areas of Bolivia, estimated by one Peace Corps physician at 60 percent. Emigration is another cause of low population increase. Large numbers of agricultural workers (braceros) have moved to the sugar cane fields of northern Argentina, and the Bolivian community there is placed at some 600,000, many of them functionally monolingual Quechua or Aymara. In addition, many middle and upper class professionals have moved to Brazil, Peru and the United States where they command higher salaries for their skills.

Two-thirds of Bolivia's population is rural lower class, and they in turn constitute the majority of the illiterates who number somewhere around 63 percent (Wells 1966:3). Although the economic level of the cities is higher than the country, probably one-third of the city dwellers are of the lower class. Of the remaining 20 percent of the inhabitants perhaps 15 percent are in what could be called a middle class and 5 percent in the upper class.

The people who inhabit Bolivia's three most characteristic geographical regions exhibit quite distinct personality traits. Llosa describes the peasant of the Altiplano as "sultry, introverted, active and Stoic"; the valley dweller as "cheerful, sociable, decisive and a lover of beauty"; those of the tropics as "masters of the primitive forces of nature, calm and enjoyers of life" (1966:28).

The highland peoples are descendants of the ancient Incas. Ethnically they are divided between Quechua and Aymara. In the country areas the dress of all Bolivian peasants is simple, with the most visible regional distinction being the women's hats. Men wear homespun trousers made from sheep wool, open sandals, and in places distinctive vests or ponchos. Women fix their hair in long pigtails and wear attractively embroidered blouses over multiple layers of full, homespun skirts called polleras. Those who retain their native dress used to be known as Indians (indios), but since the revolution of 1952 the word has taken on a derogatory implication. They are now called peasants (campesinos).

Social mobility depends more on language and dress than upon race or economic status. Racially, the dividing line between a pure-blooded Quechua or Aymara and one who has supposedly been mixed with Spanish blood and is called therefore a mestizo is undiscernible in most cases. Homespun clothing and a rather unkempt appearance characterize the peasants. When they move to the city, the men soon obtain clothing sewn from factory-made cloth, and look rather like the lower middle class men. The women retain similar clothing style, but wear colorful cotton or satin skirts, gold jewelry, and they comb their hair more often. This upper-lower class is called the cholo class.

The movement from the cholo class into the lower middle class is usually an evolutionary process for men, but a more radical change for the women. Women must make the decision to cut their braids and exchange their polleras for dresses (cf. Leons 1966:225-226). This step involves knowing Spanish, and women who have not learned this language will not usually remove their native clothing. Many chola women have become relatively affluent, often as merchants in the open market, and although they may know Spanish, other cultural features associated with the cholo class make them conservative enough not to choose to advance socially.

The lowland people are predominantly criollo (pure Spanish descent) and true mestizo. So different are they from the highland folk that for centuries Bolivia was almost two countries. The lowlanders referred to the highlanders by the sometimes derogatory term "Collas" (a misnomer derived from the Inca name for the region inhabited by the Aymaras, Collasuyo), and the highlanders called the lowlanders by the equally derogatory term "Cambas." Their accents are as distinct as those of Long Island and Georgia. The asphalt highway connecting Cochabamba with Santa Cruz, opened in 1954, has increased commerce and social interchange between Santa Cruz and the highlands, and has done much to reduce the tension between the two groups and unify the nation.

Another important sociological factor which is helping to unify the country is the program of government-encouraged internal migration from the barren highlands to the areas of the tropical region which hold high agricultural potential. This program will undoubtedly continue to pick up in tempo, and will cause significant changes in Bolivia's social and economic patterns. Potato production, for example, hitherto unknown in the tropical region, is now growing rapidly due to the introduction of new varieties.

In spite of the fact that internal migration is taking place from the highlands to the tropical colonies, Bolivia is not following the most common Latin American migratory pattern, that of rapid urbanization. The growth of the cities in Bolivia has not been appreciably larger than the population growth in general.

According to Alonso, the language distribution of Bolivia is as shown on Table 1.

TABLE 1

Language Distribution of Bolivia

Quechua	36.5%	
Aymara	24.6	
Guaraní, others	2.5	
Total indigenous languages		63.6%
Spanish		35.9
Foreign languages combined		.5
		100.0%

Source: Alonso 1962:101

Approximately one-third of Bolivians are monolingual, most of these being Quechua or Aymara.

Basing his figures on data supplied from the Ministry of the Treasury of Bolivia as of 1962, Juan Comas breaks down the Bolivian population ethnically as seen in Table 2.

TABLE 2

Ethnic Division of Bolivia

Non-Indian	1,281,202	(37%)
Quechua	1,190,251	
Aymara	868,137	
Jungle Dwellers	83,360	
	2,141,748	(63%)

Source: Comas 1962:13-17

His figure on the jungle dwellers would include those who have settled down in the villages and who are acculturated to the Bolivian way of life as well as those aboriginal peoples who still live in a savage state. My own estimate would be that the savage jungle Indians total something around 10,000.

BOLIVIAN HISTORY

No one knows when civilization in the Bolivian region first appeared. Her written traditions date back only to the Spanish conquest since the Incas had no system of writing. The earliest center of culture has been identified as Tiahuanacu, just south of Lake Titicaca. When the Incas conquered this so-called Colla civilization, probably in the fourteenth century, the inhabitants of the region had forgotten their own origins. The magnificent monolithic sculptures, including the famous "Gateway of the Sun," meant nothing to them.

Before the Incas consolidated the peoples of the Andes into their empire by means of what has been called "the most tremendous political event in the history of native America" (Steward and Faron 1959:112), the whole region was split up into autonomous states.

> The total number of independent political units is not known ... most of the provinces probably had their own language or dialect and many had distinguishing cultural features (Steward and Faron 1959:113).

As far as possible, the Incas imposed the Quechua language upon all the conquered peoples, and the Spaniards encouraged this effort for linguistic unity.

The most stubborn resistance to this forced acculturation of the Incas came from the Aymaras. While they accepted the political domination of the Inca overlords, they refused to change either their language or their culture. This independence and determination still characterizes the Aymara people today.

Keith Hamilton states that when the Spaniards arrived, most of the highland peasants were Aymara-speaking, with only four tribes of Quechua-speakers. The Aymaras, including some who lived in modern Peru, were made up of a total of thirteen tribes.

After Pizarro had invaded Tahuantinsuyu (as the Incas called their own empire), captured and executed the Inca ruler Atahualpa in 1532, extracted $22,000,000 worth of ransom (Clark and Clark 1909:236), and gained solid control over Peru by 1535, he paused and took stock of what he had won. He found an efficient and useful political structure for his administration. Whereas one hundred years previously the land had been divided into "an almost unbelievable number of small political units, for many of which we do not even have the name," Pizarro found that the Inca had successfully imposed his own Quechua language on almost all of his realm (Rowe 1963:185). This, combined with the magnificent roads and communication system, had prepared the Inca Empire for Catholic Christianity much as the Roman Empire had been prepared in the first century.

Steward says that, once they were established in the New World, the colonist, the conquistador and the missionary were one in desiring "to exploit the native peoples through a system of tribute, which soon amounted to mass labor" (1963:763ff). While this may be true, and through forced labor in the mines the Indian population of the Audiencia of Lima and Charcas dropped from 1,490,000 in 1561 to 612,000 in 1754 (Collier 1947), the folk culture, language and social structure were left fairly well intact. Bennett and Bird are somewhat misleading when they say that "the Spanish superimposed a new culture, a different language and a contrasting physical type on the indigenous inhabitants of the Central Andes" (1960:240). This would only be true of those who lived in close proximity to the Spaniards and criollos in the cities, but not so for the bulk of peasants on the Altiplano and through the valleys.

Once political control was established, the priests who accompanied Pizarro had little difficulty in establishing Christianity as the state religion. The Incas were accustomed to taking the religion offered to them by the head of the state, so they accepted the new forms with little resistance. But Christianity had scant influence on their deeper religious beliefs. Shamanism, sorcery, the more covert local practices, and local shrines and deities survived (Steward 1963:763ff).

The highland peasants today are remarkably solemn, serious and fatalistic. Whether they were like this before coming up against the "unprecedented and nerve-shattering ferocity of the Europeans" (Hyams and Ordish 1963:8), is a point warmly debated by students of ancient cultures. Some of the Andes valleys are so remote even today, that it is possible that during the sixteenth century their inhabitants did not even hear that the conquistadores had come.

In 1542 Spain established the Viceroyalty of Lima, and in 1559 divided the Audiencia of Charcas from the Audiencia of Lima as two political jurisdictions of the Viceroyalty. Charcas, or "Upper Peru," was roughly the territory that later became Bolivia. The capital of Charcas was La Plata, whose name was later changed to Chuquisaca and then to Sucre. In

1776 Charcas was taken from the Viceroyalty of Lima and placed under the Viceroyalty of Buenos Aires.

The move for independence began in 1809 and ended with the victory of Simon Bolivar's General Antonio José de Sucre over the Spanish forces at Ayacucho in 1825. Since independence, Bolivia's political history has been turbulent with 179 changes of government in 126 years (Gunther 1967:397).

While Bolivia's energy was being consumed on her internal political problems, her neighbors voraciously lopped off huge chunks of her land. Today she has less than 50 percent of her original territory. The worst blow came in 1879 when Chile took the Department of Litoral which contained rich nitrate deposits and Bolivia's only outlet to the sea. Becoming a landlocked country has caused a profound psychological mood to settle over Bolivians. Incumbent President René Barrientos Ortuño once called it a "jailbird complex." Regaining an outlet to the sea is the most emotionally charged political slogan in Bolivia and is used by all parties. Chile could become one of the bright stars of twentieth-century nations if she would recognize the validity of Bolivia's claims for a seaport.

A very small but extremely powerful upper class ruled Bolivia from independence until 1952. The oligarchy, the army and the Church controlled the government in typically Latin American fashion. Frequent revolutions did little to change the social and economic conditions of the common man, but simply shifted the power patterns of the elite.

The two outstanding events in Bolivia's twentieth-century history were the Chaco War with Paraguay (1932-35) and the Revolution of 1952. Since both of these affected the growth of the Protestant Church, they will be treated in separate chapters.

Today Bolivia is under a civilian government, strongly oriented toward the military. President Barrientos resigned his post as head of the Bolivian Air Force to become Vice-President in 1964, and later that year overthrew Victor Paz Estenssoro, the engineer of the 1952 revolution, with the help of his good friend and close associate General Alfredo Ovando Candia, Armed Forces Chief of Staff. Paz Estenssoro, strongly influenced by Marxist Juan Lechín, was charged with becoming tyrannical and allowing too much corruption into his political machine. Barrientos and Ovando are good friends of the United States. They are encouraging the entrance of foreign capital, and are using the Alliance for Progress to the advantage of the country.

RELIGIOUS LIBERTY

Bolivia today enjoys complete religious liberty, more so than many Latin American countries. No restrictions of any kind are imposed on religious activities, and religious propaganda may be diffused by any means. It was not always this way, however.

The first governments which came into power after the Latin American republics had secured their independence from Spain and Portugal in the early nineteenth century were conservative. Not only was the Roman Catholic Church the official state Church in Bolivia, but the practice of any other religion was prohibited by law. Simón Bolívar, after whom the country is named, represented the liberal current of the age that did not gain full strength until later in the century. In a letter to General Sucre who was helping Bolivia write her first constitution, Bolívar said:

> Legislators! I will mention one article that my conscience has caused me to omit. A political constitution should not prescribe a religion; because according to the best doctrines of fundamental law, constitutions are guarantees of political and civil rights, and since religion is not involved in any of these rights it is by nature indefinable in the social order and belongs to that which is moral and intellectual. Religion governs man in his home, his office, and within himself, and it is subject to examination by his most intimate conscience. Laws, on the other hand, deal with superficial things, they only govern outside the citizen's house. Applying these considerations, can the State control the conscience of its subjects, enforce religious laws, and give rewards or punishment when the courts are in heaven and when God is the judge?
>
> Religion is the law of the conscience. Any law imposed over that anulls it, because by making duty requirement, it removes all merit from the faith which is the basis of religion. Sacred laws and dogmas are useful, illuminating, and based on metaphysical evidence; we all ought to profess them. But this is a moral, not a political duty.
>
> Then again, in this world, what are man's rights in religious matters? These are found in heaven; there the courts reward merit and dispense justice according to the law book of the Legislator. Since all this falls under divine jurisdiction, it seems to me at first glance to be a

sacrilege to mix our laws with the Lord's commandments. The legislator has no right to prescribe a religion because he must then fix punishments for infractions of the laws in order that they are not taken only as suggestions. Since there is no temporal punishment nor judges to apply it, the law ceases to be law.
... Parents should not neglect their religious obligations to their children. Spiritual shepherds are obligated to teach the science of heaven; the example of the true disciples of Jesus is the most eloquent teacher of His divine morality; but morality cannot be imposed and he who attempts to impose it is no teacher, nor can force be employed in giving counsel (Bolivar 1950:769-770).

During the wars of independence the Bolivian Roman Catholic hierarchy was unswerving in its loyalty to Spain. Archbishop Moxo of Chuquisaca (Sucre) and Bishop La Santa of La Paz fought bitterly against the liberal tendencies (Mecham 1966: 179). Some priests, however, such as José Medina and Muñecas joined with the patriots. After the war the hierarchy switched its allegiance to the new republic and was successful in promoting conservative ideas. Bolivia's first constitution contains the following clause:

The Roman Catholic Apostolic religion is the religion of the Republic to the exclusion of all other public cults. The government protects it and insures it respect, recognizing the principle that there is no human power over conscience (Mecham 1966:179).

As the Liberal Party rose in power toward the end of the nineteenth century, it advocated the separation of Church and state, freedom of religion, the sovereignty of the state over the Church, lay education, the abolition of judicial privileges for clergy, and civil marriage (Pattee 1951:60). The Liberals finally won power under General Pando in 1898, the same year that the great pioneer of Bolivian Protestantism, Archibald Reekie, arrived in Oruro. The Liberals were in power until 1920, and during this time they succeeded in bringing religious liberty to Bolivia. A Catholic writer looks at this period in this way:

These twenty years, rich in works of material progress, constitute the darkest and most difficult period that the Church and Catholicism have had to face in all the course of Bolivian history (Pattee 1951:60).

The Protestants who were already in the country, the Plymouth Brethren from England and the Baptists from Canada, influenced the government and spurred the liberals on in their campaign for freedom. The Baptists had close personal contact with lawmakers in La Paz, while in Sucre missionary Will Payne took on the Archbishop himself in the Supreme Court. His wife, Lizzie, wrote from Sucre on June 29, 1901:

> The Archbishop here has again been the loser in Supreme Court and was condemned to costs. Many long for liberty of worship and were glad that the "evangelists" did not suffer; indeed the news was telegraphed to other parts and "congratulations to the Protestants" were published in a liberal paper. There is a movement on foot in several towns to sign a petition which will be presented to Congress in August asking libertad de cultos (*Echoes of Service* Sept. 1901:338).

While these lawsuits had their influence and, as Will Payne himself wrote, "The presence of the Canadian Baptist Missionaries and their excellent schools must have had a good effect" (Payne and Wilson 1904:139), probably the strongest force was that of the United States government. President McKinley, in a message to Congress on December 5, 1899, began the pressure (Lee 1907:195). In 1894 John Lee had been named to head up a Methodist committee in Chicago, which did some successful lobbying in Washington. Lee describes his efforts and quotes correspondence between the governments of Bolivia and the United States with dates of 1900, 1901, 1902, 1904, and 1905. On August 19, 1905, an amendment which would "permit the public exercise of all cults" was passed by the lower house of the Bolivian Congress, it went through the Senate on September 4, 1905, and was finally passed by a full Congress on August 6, 1906 (Lee 1907:en loc). August 6 is the anniversary of the opening of the doors of the country to the Gospel of Christ.

Before the advent of religious liberty, the Bolivian soil had been impenetrable to the gospel message. Seed fell from time to time, but the birds came and ate it up, as Jesus' parable suggests. Religious liberty did not make Bolivia receptive to the Gospel, but it did open the way for more extensive seed-sowing. Five pioneer missions entered to sow the seed; today thirty-five are reaping the harvest.

2

Seeds of Protestantism

Most historians regard the first permanent Protestant mission to Latin America that of Fountain E. Pitt, who arrived in Río de Janeiro in 1835. He was sent there by the Methodist Episcopal Church of the USA. There were, however, some noteworthy previous attempts at Protestant missions in Latin America.

FIRST IN NEIGHBORING COUNTRIES

Huguenots. The first known Protestant entrance into the New World was the heroic attempt of the French Huguenots to establish a colony on an island in the bay of Río de Janeiro in 1555 (Beach 1916:64). The plan was conceived by the vice-admiral of Brittany, Seigneur de Villegagnon (also known as Nicolás Durand), who proposed the colony to Admiral Coligny. Coligny personally directed the movement "with the hope that his persecuted brother Protestants, the Huguenots, might find a refuge in the new country, peacefully grow into the proportions of a Protestant commonwealth, and, at the same time, convert the South American Indians" (Neely 1909:190). This mention of a definite evangelistic purpose on the part of the Protestants is most unusual for this historical period, and sets the effort apart from some of the other projects of colonization in the New World. Even more striking is the fact that John Calvin himself took interest in the second expedition to what became known as "Coligny Island," and sent two

ministers and fourteen of his students there. Whether these
clergymen were only to be chaplains to the French colonists,
or whether they had a missionary mandate to evangelize the
Indians is a fascinating question for further study. Speer
(1915) indicates that Parkman's *Pioneers of France in the New
World* contains a chapter on the details of this enterprise,
but I have not been able to locate a copy of it.

In any case, the colony came to a tragic end through the
crimes of Villegagnon himself who became a ruthless tyrant,
converted to Roman Catholicism, and allowed the community to
disintegrate. Some of the colonists fled to the mainland
where they became Catholics, some escaped to other ships and
returned to France, and some were massacred when the
Portuguese, instigated by the Jesuits, wiped the colony out in
1567. At this time, ten thousand additional Huguenots were
making preparations to emigrate to the New World, but they
naturally had to change their plans. Neely remarks:

> France lost an opportunity as also did Protestantism, but
> by these losses South America, and especially Brazil, lost
> infinitely more. With a strong Protestantism at that early
> day, the history of the Brazilians and the South American
> people would have been far different and immeasurably
> better (1909:193).

Like the Jewish dispersion from Jerusalem, however, this
breakup of the Huguenot colony launched forth the man who is
in all probability the first bona fide Protestant missionary
to the South American natives, Jean de Bioleau. One of the
survivors of the Jesuit massacre, he fled from Coligny Island
into the Brazilian jungles. He and two companions began
efforts to win the Indians to Christ. But they were discovered by the Jesuits and taken prisoner. After years of
imprisonment and trials they were finally executed. Jesuit
José de Anchieta personally tied the noose around Bioleau's
neck to demonstrate to the executioner how "to dispatch a
heretic as quickly as possible" (Neely 1909:194).

Dutch Reformed. The Dutch Reformed Church sent missionaries to the Brazilian Indians in the seventeenth century
after capturing Bahía in 1624 and proclaiming religious
liberty there. While most of the ministers were sent from
Holland as chaplains to the colony and thus were not what we
call missionaries, some did work among the Indians and
registered a number of conversions. They even advanced to the

point where they had prepared a catechism in the Indian language. However, the Portuguese recaptured the colony in 1654, and wiped out what they considered to be the Protestant heresy. Nothing survived (Neely 1909:195).

Moravians. The efforts of the Moravians in British Guiana in 1735 are called by Glover the beginning of the modern evangelical effort in Latin America (1960:354). But this could hardly be classified as a mission since the Indians were not even permitted near the British settlement. In 1738 they moved over into Dutch Guiana where John Guttner and Christopher Dahne began to evangelize the Arawak Indians. By 1748 they had baptized forty-one of them (Neely 1909:196). Commenting on this effort, Gustav Warneck says, "Special blessing attended the work of Missionary Schumann (d.1760), who was the author of an Arawak grammar and dictionary" (1906: 182). Later, however, the work switched from the Arawaks to the negroes who were imported as slaves, and this mission has continued. In 1906 Warneck reported 15,000 Christians (1906: 183).

Henry Martyn. The next Protestant missionary to set foot on Latin American soil was Henry Martyn, the well-known missionary to India, whose ship stopped for a time in Bahía, Brazil in 1805. With the Vulgate in his hand, he preached the Gospel to the priests there and "gained alike the love of the wealthy planter and poor slave" (Neely 1909:199).

Anglicans. The London Missionary Society began work among the slaves of British Guiana in 1807 (Warneck 1906:183), the Church Missionary Society made a brief attempt to evangelize the Indians of the Essequibo and Potaro rivers there, and the Society for the Propagation of the Gospel in Foreign Parts also began a work among the negroes in British Guiana in 1835 (Neely 1909:198).

James Thomson. There is some question as to whether James Thomson, a Scottish Baptist from the University of Glasgow, was primarily a missionary or an educator. Before leaving the British Isles he had made contact with Joseph Lancaster, an advocate of a new type of pedagogy in which the professor would teach the brightest students who in turn would teach the other pupils. Thomson arrived in Buenos Aires as an educator in 1818 and introduced the Lancasterian system there. He later was invited to Chile and Peru, making personal friends with such illustrious persons as Bernardo O'Higgins, José de San Martín and Simón Bolivar.

While in Lima, Thomson made contacts with the British and Foreign Bible Society and acted as their unofficial agent as he traveled north (Browne 1859:354). He was later appointed agent for Mexico (Browne 1859:358), and finished his career in this work. His biography was written by Argentine Juan Varetto (1918), and a recent critical study of his work has been made by Donald Mitchell in a Princeton Seminary Ph.D. dissertation. David Phillips says, "This great precursor opened the pathways to the Gospel in all of the republics and colonies. Thomson should be recognized as the great prototype of the evangelical worker in Latin America" (n.d.:n.p.).

BEGINNINGS IN BOLIVIA

Luke Matthews. While James Thomson never visited Bolivia, nor did the second British and Foreign Bible Society agent, Rev. Armstrong (Browne 1859:354), the third did. His name was Luke Matthews, and he traveled through Bolivia selling Bibles in 1827 and 1828. He visited Cotagaita, Caiza, Potosí, Oruro, Chuquisaca (Sucre) (BFBS 1828:112-116), Cochabamba, and La Paz (BFBS 1829:84-89). Matthews says that in Sucre "The grand Marshall Sucre, President of the Republic, as well as the other principal authorities, honoured me, indeed, with their notice and patronage; but my object made no impression on the people" (BFBS 1829:84). In all, Matthews' work was not outwardly successful, and the Committee in London reported that they "cannot but express their entire approbation of their agent, notwithstanding his letters do not present any splendid details" (BFBS 1828:lxxxv). Matthews reached Bogotá in 1829, left there for Mompox, but was never heard from again. His death remains a mystery, although it is probable that he was murdered and robbed by his guides (Browne 1859: 372-373).

Allen Gardiner. Captain Allen Gardiner, founder of the South American Missionary Society, is remembered chiefly for his tragic death in the cold wastelands of Patagonia. His first effort at establishing a missionary work, however, was undertaken in Bolivia in 1846 (Phillips n.d.:n.p.). Gardiner, an Anglican, first went to Bolivia with a young assistant, paying all his own expenses. Concerning his trip to Potosí, he wrote, "We have traveled 1061 miles on the

worst roads perhaps in the world" (Daniels 1916:113). He was
interested primarily in reaching the Indian peoples, and after
making a trip to La Paz to visit government officials,
received permission to establish a mission under the condition
that he minister only to the Indians and not proselytize
Catholics. He left his fellow worker, González, in Potosí and
returned to London to recruit more workers. The SAMS was prepared to send a Spanish Protestant named Robles to join
González in Potosí, when the Bolivian government suddenly
changed and put a stop to the project (Phillips n.d.:n.p.).
This was the first attempt to start a permanent church-
planting work in Bolivia.

Joseph Monguiardino. The first Protestant to lay down his
life for the sake of the Gospel on Bolivian soil was Joseph
Monguiardino. As an agent of the British and Foreign Bible
Society, he embarked on what R. Kilgour called "the greatest
colportage journey yet made in South America" in 1876
(Browning 1930:173-174). Monguiardino did not visit Bolivia
until his next trip the following year. He passed through
many previously unvisited places, and sold over one thousand
copies of Scripture in Spanish (Browning 1930:174). On his
way back to Argentina for more Bibles, he was attacked near
Santiago de Cotagaita by two men who killed him with stones,
tied a large boulder around his neck, and threw his body into
the river. The civil authorities discovered the crime, took
the criminals prisoner and forced them to carry the dead man
two leagues back to Cotagaita. There the priest refused to
allow the body to be buried within the town limits. In his
account of the martyrdom, Penzotti states that a strange thing
happened. The murderers were allowed to go free at the urging
of the priest, but soon afterward one was horribly dragged to
death by a mule and the other killed by lightning (1916:13).

Francisco Penzotti. Francisco Penzotti is probably the
best-known of all the nineteenth-century colporteurs in Latin
America. The United Bible Societies today call their training
workshops "Penzotti Institutes," in his memory. According to
his autobiography, Penzotti was born in Italy of staunch Roman
Catholic parents in 1851. When he was thirteen, he was taken
to Montevideo by a brother and a sister. In 1875 he heard the
preaching of Methodist John F. Thompson (distinguished as
having been the first missionary to Latin America to begin
regular preaching services in Spanish in 1867) and was deeply
impressed. It remained for Thomas B. Wood and Andrew Milne to

Seeds of Protestantism

lead him to a complete faith in Jesus Christ in 1876. He dedicated his life to God and became a Methodist evangelist to the Waldensian colony in Uruguay from 1879 to 1886. As an evangelist he was invited to accompany American Bible Society agent Andrew Milne on a trip to Bolivia in 1883. When they reached Monguiardino's grave outside the town of Cotagaita, they removed their hats and rededicated themselves to the evangelization of South America (Neely 1909:217). Daniels writes concerning the trip:

> Traveling in Bolivia in those days meant riding on muleback over abominable roads or no roads at all. There were no inns; no hospitable friends waiting to welcome him; often nothing but the bare ground to sleep on after a hard day; and no extra money for comforts of any kind (1916:207-208).

During this trip they distributed between 5000 and 6000 Bibles and portions, visiting Tupiza, Potosí, Sucre, Oruro, La Paz, and other towns (Barclay 1957:775).

Penzotti began his second journey to Bolivia in June, 1884, this time accompanied by Juan Pedro Geymonat and Paulino Ocáriz. Geymonat, who could not stand the privations, turned back when they arrived at Sucre. Ocáriz and Penzotti settled there for a time, rented a house, and held the first Sunday School recorded in Bolivian history. The Archbishop tried to get rid of them, and the town was divided in opinion (Penzotti 1916:20). Two children made decisions for Christ, then their mothers came to the Lord. Penzotti says "that hovel became a center of light" (Penzotti 1916:22). These were the first recorded Protestant conversions of Bolivians.

Moving on to Oruro, then to Cochabamba, the colporteurs ran into "a wasps' nest" (Penzotti 1916:23). Penzotti says, "It is probable that at no other time in my life was I in so much danger as there; my life hung by a thread" (Penzotti 1916:22). Nevertheless, they were able to stay a month and sell three or four boxes of Bibles and portions. From there they moved on to Punata, Cliza, Arani, and La Paz.

In 1887 Penzotti was named agent for the American Bible Society on the Pacific Coast, and with residence in Callao he traveled occasionally to Bolivia. He had just returned from a trip to Bolivia when he was thrown into prison in Callao on July 26, 1890, and his trial became somewhat of a cause célébrè in Peru.

Thomas Wood. Thomas B. Wood, the man who led Penzotti to the Lord, describes the conditions in Bolivia rather extensively in his report of 1883. This will help us to get a clear picture of the resistance of Bolivia to the Gospel and to the Protestant faith in the latter part of the nineteenth century:

> The darkest spot on the American Continent is Bolivia. It has rejected the Gospel by its national constitution which forbids religious toleration and by its malicious priestcraft which murdered José Monguiardino and burned the Bibles he took there in 1877. Since that date no attempt has been made to penetrate the region until the present year. The first installment of books was confiscated, but the effort was persistently and prudently followed up with great success and at the time of this writing (October, 1883), Brothers Milne and Penzotti are canvassing the chief cities of Bolivia ...
>
> A few years ago an influential Bolivian, residing in the Argentine capital as Minister of his nation, became acquainted with the Gospel work in the La Plata regions. Brother Andrew Milne formed his acquaintance and received from him assurances that the civil authorities in Bolivia would look with favor on the introduction of the Gospel. Now, in the evolution of Bolivian politics, that man has come to occupy the most influential post in the Bolivian national cabinet. This providential ... fact has facilitated the present movements of Bros. Milne and Penzotti ...
>
> The year 1883 will be notable in the history of this mission as the one in which the last corner of the field was penetrated. It marks a new epoch in the history of Bolivia's redemption, and shows new proof that the moral regeneration of all South America is speedily approaching (Methodist Episcopal Church, *Annual Report* 1883:50).

McCleary mentions the visit of another colporteur, Henricksen, who was "turned back by force," but nothing more concerning him is known at this writing (1965:1).

J. B. Arancet. The next Protestant to move into Bolivia was American Bible Society agent J. B. Arancet, living in La Paz from 1890 to 1892. Reports of his work were sent out by Methodist John F. Thompson, who toured Bolivia in 1890 giving public lectures on religion in all the major cities. When Thompson arrived in La Paz he found Arancet and his family

Seeds of Protestantism

"prosecuting his work quietly and successfully" (Methodist Episcopal Church, *Annual Report* 1891:56). He was not only selling Bibles, but he was holding meetings in his house. Thompson cooperated in the meetings and encouraged Arancet. Then,

> as a means of preparing the way for elementary religious instruction of the Indians, a little company of the liberal young men of the city was organized into a Society for the Promotion of Indian Sunday Schools (Barclay 1957:785).

This was probably the first Protestant organization in the country.

From 1892 to at least 1893, a Methodist named Orellana was "still carrying on the Bible work in Bolivia with increasing success and encouragement," as Thomas B. Wood wrote from Lima (Methodist Episcopal Church, *Annual Report* 1892:266). Wood goes on to say:

> In our Lima congregation we have several Bolivians, one of whom has expressed the earnest desire to prepare himself as a messenger of the Gospel to his native city, Cochabamba.

Regions Beyond Missionary Union. Before moving on to the beginning of the permanent work which has resulted in enduring churches being planted in Bolivia, mention should be made of two other pioneers. The first is Robert Lodge, an English missionary who went to Bolivia under the Regions Beyond Missionary Union in 1896. He traveled from Arequipa, Peru to La Paz, but took ill and died of typhoid fever (Stillwell n.d. 92-93). Lodge became the second Protestant to lay down his life in Bolivia. Another missionary who accompanied Lodge left the country, and the Regions Beyond Missionary Union has never returned although they have a work in the neighboring country of Peru.

Writing in 1909, Thomas Neely tells of a Dane named Karl Hanson who entered Bolivia "in recent years" (1909:218-219). He moved through Bolivia with a supply of Bibles in a basket. When he entered a town he simply would play his harmonica in the public plaza, gather a crowd, then uncover his Bibles and offer them for sale. In one town he was jailed, but he sold his entire supply of Bibles to fellow prisoners. With this brief note, Karl Hanson seems to disappear from the scene in Bolivia.

3

Pioneer Church-planters

None of the early colporteurs who entered Bolivia found a ripened harvest field. From the time Luke Matthews sold his first Bible in 1827 through the rest of the century, a conversion was rarely recorded and no continuing churches were planted or organized. Since Bolivia was the next-to-last South American republic to receive resident, church-planting missionaries (Ecuador was the last), it is not overly strange that in some respects the development of the Protestant Church has lagged behind other nearby republics such as Brazil and Argentina.

Factors of Resistance. Four important factors combined to produce a strong resistance to Protestantism in nineteenth-century Bolivia. The first was an ecclesiastical factor. Since the Protestant Reformation had made little impact in Spain, being ruthlessly stamped out by the Inquisition, it would be expected that Bolivia's clergy, predominantly Spanish, would have little appreciation for Protestantism. The clergy considered Protestantism a heresy, and indoctrinated Bolivian Catholics with this negative idea. The illiteracy and lack of education of most of the Bolivian people in those days made them gullible, and the priests told them tales of Protestant atrocities such as requiring converts to go into a dark room and whip images of Christ and the Virgin. Thus it was possible to convince many people that Protestants were devils.

A second factor was a sociological factor. A very small but

powerful elite controlled the country in the traditional Latin American pattern. This was the political oligarchy, the army and the Church. These three units were interdependent and for their own enrichment were able to maintain the Bolivian peasants in a feudal state. The complexities of the interrelationship did not leave room for introducing a foreign element such as a Protestant church. Since the rulers in general did not know what the Protestant Church was, they were not sure they could handle it if it were to enter the scene. It might have upset a very comfortable power structure. As long as this upper class could maintain the status quo, they resisted any innovation which might affect their sociological pattern.

The third factor was a political factor. A wave of liberal thinking was penetrating Latin America in the second half of the nineteenth century, and Bolivia was not without its core of young liberals who had high principles. A liberal-minded government was in power when Allen Gardiner secured permission to begin a mission among Indians in 1846. But when it fell victim to a conservative coup, his permission was withdrawn. From independence to 1898 the liberals never were able to control the power structures of Bolivia's politics. When they did come into power, however, this probably was the most important event leading to eventual church growth in the history of the nation. In other words, a political change was the first secular factor used by God to begin to transform Bolivia from a stubborn, resistant, stony field to one which would receive the seed of the Gospel and bring forth some fruit.

The fourth factor of resistance was what might be called an anthropological factor. The Indian communities were tightly structured, and decisions were taken as a group. The upper classes lived in closely knit families. Individual conversion from such a society would have been unlikely. In Bolivia at that time there was no way in which a person could become a Protestant without breaking with his society. Until an Aymara, for example, could become a Protestant and still remain culturally an Aymara, little church growth could be expected among them or any of the other ethnic groups.

Rise of the Liberal Government. In 1898 the political scene changed, but the ecclesiastical, sociological and anthropological conditions remained the same. The result was a degree of receptivity to the Gospel, but not the whitened harvest field that came when the other factors of resistance were eventually altered. In the providence of God, the first

resident missionaries were on hand and prepared when the
liberal influence in Bolivia began to rise. Chapters 3 and 4
will be concerned about them and others who quickly entered
through the newly opened doors.

Dates of Origin. The matter of dates of the origin of each
denomination needs to be discussed before we begin to describe
the several missionary societies which entered Bolivia to
evangelize the country. Several criteria, such as unbroken
continuity of the particular denomination or the time of the
first exploratory visit could be used. I have chosen to use
the date of arrival and settling down of the first missionary
to come with his family (if he had one) for the ultimate
purpose of planting churches. This excludes colporteurs,
explorers and adventurers. The presence of women and children
lends a dimension of permanence to a Protestant missionary
enterprise.

Major Historical Divisions for Church Growth. As we consider the history of each missionary group to enter Bolivia, it will be helpful to recall the following historical breakdown. For the purposes of this church growth survey, these divisions should be kept in mind:

1895-1919. This period starts with the entrance of the particular mission and ends with the fall of the liberals and the resurgence of conservative power. It includes the amendment of the Bolivian Constitution to permit religious freedom. It also includes World War I, during which the sending countries radically curtailed their missionary activities.

1920-1935. This is the period of conservative rule, and in many cases records strong persecution of the Protestant Church. It includes the difficult period of the Chaco War, and on the home front the worst years of the great depression when missionary resources were again reduced.

1936-1945. This period includes the reconstruction of Bolivia after the defeat of the Chaco War, and then World War II.

1946-1951. This period is characterized by the post-war resurgence of North American foreign missionary activity in all of Latin America, and also in Bolivia by the events leading up to the Revolution of 1952.

1952-1967. The social revolution engineered by the MNR party in 1952 (see Chapter 6) is the major factor in Bolivian life during this final period, and more than any other secular event in recent times has prepared the way for rapid church

Pioneer Church-planters

growth.

Five Protestant groups entered Bolivia between the years 1895 and 1907 for a permanent, church-planting ministry. No others came until after World War I, leaving a period of twelve years with no new work. It is therefore rather simple to separate the true pioneers of the Bolivian Protestant Church from those who came later. This chapter will be concerned with them: the Brethren Assemblies, the Canadian Baptists, the Methodists, the Andes Evangelical Mission, and the Seventh-day Adventists.

BRETHREN ASSEMBLIES
(Hermanos Libres)

William Payne. The traditional date for the beginning of the Protestant work in Bolivia has been given as 1898 when Archibald Reekie of the Canadian Baptists entered. While this was the beginning of the first uninterrupted work, William Payne is the man who qualifies as the first missionary who brought his family and settled down with the purpose of planting churches. The Paynes were "commended" by the Brethren Assembly in Dublin, Ireland, in 1895 (*Echoes of Service* January 1966; cf. Beach 1916:73; Goddard 1967:152), but it is not clear where they settled at first. McCleary claims that Payne and Wilson were "asked to leave" in 1895, but details are fuzzy (1965:1). *Echoes of Service,* the official publication of their missionary society, known as Christian Missions in Many Lands, Inc., carries letters from both Will and Lizzie Payne written from Sucre in 1900, and it is likely that until this time the bulk of their pioneer work had been done in Sucre (*Echoes of Service* 1900:191,239). Will Payne writes of arriving in Sucre on March 17 of that year after riding 500 miles on muleback from Argentina. Lizzie Payne describes their efforts in these words:

> The work will go forward slowly in this dark city ... Our work consists in speaking to souls, and giving out papers where it is wise to do so ... nobody seems worthy of trust, and many spies are about (*Echoes of Service* 1900:239).

In 1901 Payne moved to Oruro, then to Cochabamba in September of 1902. There the Roman Catholic priests instigated a fierce attack, and Payne nearly became Bolivia's second martyr. His life was saved by soldiers but he was forced to leave (*Echoes of Service* January 1966). This may be the event Penzotti refers to when he says that the persecutors burned all of Payne's possessions, and tried to drag the missionary himself into the bonfire of furniture and books (1916:28). Writing in 1924, H. E. Stillwell of the Canadian Baptists gives another account of the incident which shows it in perhaps a more realistic light:

> Another flaming evangelist, a member of the Plymouth Brethren, came to the city [Cochabamba] with the openly avowed purpose of making it hot for the priests who, thus forewarned, made it hot for him. In six fiery public addresses, in which he mercilessly flayed the Catholic Church, he created a great stir ... The authorities, fearing for his life, compelled him to leave the city ... The whole city was now placed under military law ... and around the home of the Mitchells [Canadian Baptist missionaries], a military police guard stood incessantly for several weeks (1924:145).

Stillwell's opinion is that this incident had such deep repercussions that it turned the city staunchly against Protestantism for years to come. Whether this is true or not, Payne's intentions were good, and his method perhaps not too different from that of many other Protestant pioneers to Latin America. Will Payne finished his days on Bolivian soil, dying in Santa Cruz in 1924 (*Echoes of Service* January 1966). Apparently his efforts of seed sowing resulted in little harvest.

George Hamilton. Dr. George Hamilton, a New Zealand physician, and his wife went to Sucre in 1911, where he set out to qualify for the Bolivian medical examinations before beginning his missionary work as such (*Echoes of Service* October 1911). In 1917 the Hamiltons moved to Potosí; in 1922 they moved to Santa Cruz; and later went to Tupiza. In every place he worked, Hamilton planted a continuing church which in each case was the first Protestant church (Brown 1965). In 1916 Hamilton baptized the first native of Sucre to become a church member (*Echoes of Service* January 1917).

Brethren Today. From this beginning, the Brethren work in Bolivia has developed to a "conservative estimate of between 450 and 500 in fellowship in the various assemblies in Bolivia where New Testament principles are practised" (*Echoes of*

Service January 1966). The 1968 *Prayer Handbook* (*The Fields* 1966:28) lists twenty-nine workers from Britain, New Zealand and Australia in nine locations, with three commended national workers. This would give a ratio of one worker to every sixteen believers, or subtracting 40 percent for married women missionaries, a ratio of about 1:27.

Brethren assemblies are now found in the cities and towns of La Paz, Cochabamba, Oruro, Sucre, Montero, Potosí, Uyuni, Tupiza, Tarija, Villa Montes, Santa Cruz, and Cobija (*Echoes of Service* January 1966). In 1960, sixteen assemblies were recorded (Harlow and Smart 1960:43), which would make the average membership per assembly about thirty.

Church Quality, not Quantity. The emphasis of the Brethren work in Bolivia is strongly on perfecting the churches, and high standards of separation from worldly practices are required for membership. Little doctrinal deviation is permitted. With a minimal emphasis on growth and a maximum emphasis on quality of the Church, it would be expected that few statistics of growth would be available. In 1929, for example, Eric F. Smith writes from Uyuni: "The Indian work is prospering, and though we fear none have been saved so far, God has encouraged my heart" (*Echoes of Service* October 1929: 235). To Smith at this stage of his work, numerical growth was not associated with prosperity of his mission.

Radio Ministry. A radio ministry was carried on by Dr. Percy Hamilton, son of pioneer George Hamilton, in the city of Potosí. Evangelistic programs were broadcast twice a week for thirteen years from 1947 to 1960. The rather surprising fact about these radio programs is that while literature was offered to the listeners, Hamilton did not receive a single request for it during this period. The reasons for this lack of response would be important for a general study of the value of radio work to the growth of the Protestant Church in Bolivia. The low rate of literacy in the Potosí area would be one factor. Another might be the lack of a generalized habit of "writing in" for something on the part of the Bolivians. As an innovation, "writing in" has not yet been accepted.

Growth in Argentina Compared to Bolivia. In neighboring Argentina, as Arno Enns points out in his excellent study, *Profiles of Argentine Church Growth* (1967), the Brethren Assemblies have experienced remarkable growth. For some time it was the largest denomination in Argentina, and recently has been surpassed only by the Pentecostals. But while the Brethren count some 25,000 communicants in Argentina, they remain one of Bolivia's smallest denominations with 500. Why this difference in growth? Some of the Argentine Brethren attribute their growth there to the application of "New Testament" methods, but the same methods have been rigorously applied in Bolivia and have not brought comparable results. The doctrine and spiritual dedication of the missionaries is the same in both countries. An absence of responsiveness of the Bolivian people is not the difference, since the latest figures show the Bolivian Protestant Church as a whole to be growing at a rate of 11.5 percent per year (1960-1967) as compared to Argentina's 5 percent (CGRILA 1967).

Enns sets forth four major reasons for Brethren growth in Argentina: 1) the high British influence and prestige especially through the railroads; 2) the fellowship and intercommunication between assemblies through Bible conferences; 3) the effective use of laymen resulting in hundreds of Brethren lay preachers; and 4) the absence of a large foreign mission organization which would stand over against the national Church. The missionaries, in fact, became members of the churches and many earned their living through self-employment in Argentina (1967:187-190).

None of these factors could effectively come into play in Bolivia. There was some British influence and the British built the Bolivian railroads, but the segment of Bolivian population to which they could serve as an effective bridge was small. Since Argentines are mostly of European descent and Bolivians mostly of Indian descent, it is understandable why the British would come into a more intimate contact with residents there. In Bolivia there was little opportunity for Europeans to take gainful emplyment such as many did in Argentina because of the low economic condition of the country in general. The missionaries, therefore, received their support from abroad in the ordinary manner. An exception to this may have been Dr. George Hamilton, although it is not known how much he earned through his medical practice. The fact that his son, also a physician, is now practicing in Argentina and not in Bolivia, however, may be significant.

Even if the missionaries had been able to earn their own living, they would have had a difficult time being accepted by the Bolivian people socially, since Bolivia does not have the large middle class that Argentina does. To compensate, the Brethren generally moved with those Bolivians who were nearest to them socially, the upper middle or upper class. This at once put them to a disadvantage as far as church growth is concerned, since in this stratum the reservoir of potential converts was very small, and that particular class of Bolivians is known to be the most resistant and the most unwilling to leave the Catholic Church in the country. It is notable that the Brethren have not trained outstanding Bolivian leaders in comparison to other denominations, nor have they been able to mobilize the laity as they have in Argentina.

The factor of the Bible conference ministry, of course, depends to a large extent on the momentum that a work has already gained because of other factors. Bible conferences will be a help in a rapidly growing Church such as existed in Argentina, but perhaps not so much in a static Church such as was found in Bolivia.

At this writing, the preliminary statistics for the Brethren Assemblies are found on Table 3 and diagrammed on Figure 3.

TABLE 3

Brethren Assemblies 1895 - 1967

Date	Foreign Workers	National Workers	Churches	Baptized	Total Members	Source
1901	2	-	-	none	none	*EOS* Sept. 1901
1916	4	-	-	-	20	Beach 1916:73; *EOS* March 1916
1918	-	-	-	-	31	*EOS* May 1918
1925	7	-	-	-	-	Beach 1925
1930	-	-	-	-	30	Read 1967
1938	15	-	-	-	-	Parker 1938:119
1940	-	-	-	-	60	Read 1967
1950	-	-	-	-	100	Read 1967
1960	-	-	-	-	140	Read 1967
1966	27	3	16	500	-	*EOS* Jan. 1966; *The Fields* 1966:28

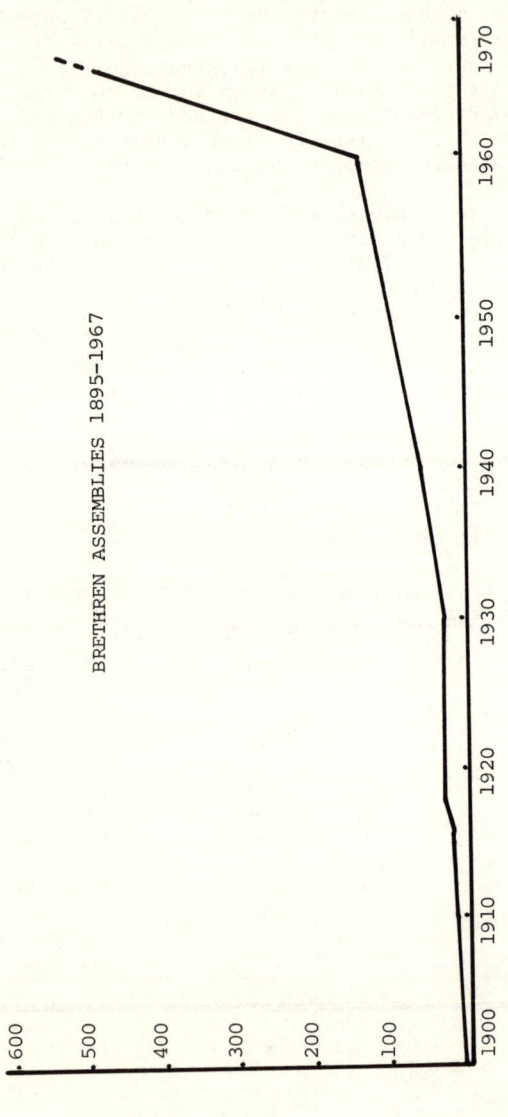

FIGURE 3

BOLIVIAN BAPTIST UNION
(Unión Bautista Boliviana)

The Bolivian Baptist Union is the denomination established by the Canadian Baptist Mission to Bolivia. This group is considered by many as the true pioneer of Protestantism in Bolivia, perhaps because the total membership of the Brethren Assemblies is small today and not too much is known about them or their history since they do not freely associate with other Protestant groups in Bolivia.

1898 - 1919

Archibald Reekie. Archibald Reekie, whom we have already met, established the work of the Canadian Baptists in Bolivia in 1898. As a student at McMaster University in Toronto, he became burdened for the evangelization of Bolivia through reading *The Neglected Continent* (Millard and Guinness 1894). The same book coincidentally influenced the man who was to become Reekie's close friend and founder of the Andes Evangelical Mission (then called the Bolivian Indian Mission), George Allan (Phillips n.d.:n.p.). The reference to Bolivia comments:

> an enormous inland State ... with a population of 1,450,000 has received one or two passing visits from colporteurs of the noble American Bible Society, but has no resident Protestant missionary (1894:76).

In 1894, when the book was written, there were no resident missionaries in either Bolivia or Ecuador, the last two countries in Latin America to receive church-planting missionaries.

Stillwell says that Reekie applied to "an Interdenominational Mission in Toronto now extinct," but the mission "did not feel that Reekie with his closed communion views could work with them to the extent their principles required" (1924: 81). The mission referred to by Stillwell would likely be the South American Evangelical Mission of Toronto (Goddard 1967:601), the very mission that accepted George Allan from New Zealand and charged him with establishing their Australasian Council.

In 1896, while yet a student, Reekie paid a visit to Bolivia, spending one week in La Paz. One of the financial

contributors to this exploratory venture was Charles Mitchell, a fellow student, who later joined Reekie as a missionary and laid down his life in Bolivia (Stillwell 1924:83). Reekie's report stirred the Canadian Baptists to adopt Bolivia as a mission field, adding this to their already existing work in India. Reasons given for the choice of Bolivia can be summarized as follows:
1. India's climate was very hard on the health of Canadians.
2. The Pacific Coast countries of South America were mountainous and probably a good climate for Canadians.
3. Chile had missionaries already.
4. Bolivia "being wholly inland and less in touch with the outside world than the others, it would probably from the religious point of view be the most needy" (Stillwell 1924:83).

Reekie chose the city of Oruro as the place in Bolivia to begin his work. Oruro lies on the eastern side of the Altiplano at some 13,000 feet of altitude. It is a dry, brown area which was said not to have a single tree at the time Reekie arrived. The center of Bolivia's most important mining region, Oruro probably had around 20,000 inhabitants at that time. But Reekie chose Oruro because it was "the single spot in the republic that took some civic pride in its liberal outlook" (Dabbs 1952:46). In a day when the death penalty technically could have been applied to a Protestant, this was a most important consideration. Eight months after Reekie arrived, the liberal party came into power and relieved tensions considerably.

Reekie's two closest contacts when he reached his destination were the Scotch Protestant families of the Pennys and the Philps, both well-to-do and both more than willing to help the new missionary. Reekie stayed with them at times, held meetings in their homes, and they contributed to the financial needs of the mission (Stillwell 1924:122). The only soil which was ready to receive the seed of the Gospel at that time was the expatriate community. Reekie's first baptisms in 1902, for example, included an Englishman, a Scotsman and his Bolivian wife (Stillwell 1924:130). This woman, who had already broken from her native culture by marrying the foreigner, was probably the first Bolivian to be baptized into the Protestant Church, with the exception of those Bolivians who had become Protestants in neighboring countries. Reekie took his first furlough in 1905, having won a total of six souls in his first seven and one-half years (Stillwell 1924:133).

Pioneer Church-planters 35

School Approach. Since the public preaching of the Gospel was prohibited by law, it seemed to Reekie that the most practical way to begin his work would be to open a school. This he did when he finished his basic language study. There was good response to the school, but little response to the Gospel. As Stillwell observes, the schools "did much to win the sympathy and confidence of the people, especially of the better classes and of men in public life" (1924:121). While Reekie and the other missionaries distributed Christian literature, established Sunday Schools, and even held gospel services when it could be done discreetly, they must have felt that being tied down to the institutions was hindering them in the concentrated evangelistic work they felt they had been called to do. While Stillwell says that the schools were "reluctantly given up" (1924:121), it is doubtful that the missionaries themselves felt reluctant. In 1902, for example, Brethren missionary Will Payne wrote from Oruro:

> These [Canadian Baptist] missionaries, having acquired the language and gained the confidence of the people, are now desirous of being set free from school ties, to engage entirely in visiting and preaching, and hope that soon some school teachers may come and relieve them (Payne and Wilson 1904:104).

In 1908 the Canadian Baptist Mission Board resolved "that the school work be discontinued at present and that our missionaries devote their time to evangelization" (Dabbs 1952: 74). It would be reasonable to surmise that Reekie had recommended this action when he went to Canada on furlough in 1905.

In his book *Dawn Over the Bolivian Hills,* Norman Dabbs takes strong exception to the Board's decision. Since the value of the school approach is of vital interest to those who analyze church growth, it is well to set forth Dabbs' point of view here. He calls the resolution a "serious blunder" (1952:74). Dabbs defends school work as the "handmaid of evangelism," and explains that

> in every instance where the Canadian Baptist missionaries opened a school they also began a preaching service. But the gospel meetings were always on the margin of the law and depended on the good-will of the authorities for their continuance. The officials were tolerant towards them because they were conducted by men and women who sought the

betterment of Bolivia (Dabbs 1952:51).

Here Dabbs is undoubtedly right in his appraisal of the school approach in the days before the decree of religious liberty in 1905. The reasons for schools as here stated, however, largely disappear in the atmosphere of religious liberty. The 1908 resolution to discontinue schools was undoubtedly taken largely on that basis.

But Dabbs sets forth some other arguments in opposition to the resolution. He says that the resolution

> really meant that the training of a Bolivian native pastorate be discontinued; that work among the upper class children of Bolivian society be discontinued; that the salvation of the future leaders in Bolivian political and professional life be discontinued (1952:75).

What Dabbs is saying here is not that schools are needed to break down religious intolerance, but that even in an atmosphere of religious liberty, the schools are a good mission approach for church growth. This is open to serious question.

In the first place it should not be assumed that Christian ministers need to be trained in Christian schools. Recent experiments such as that of the Presbyterian Seminary in San Felipe, Guatemala, have shown that ministerial training can be provided to potential pastors of widely varying degrees of previous schooling. Whereas many fine Protestant pastors have been trained through Protestant elementary and secondary schools, this is by no means true of the majority of Protestant pastors serving in Bolivia today, or other parts of Latin America. A study of the educational background of Bolivia's approximately eight hundred evangelical pastors would be revealing and useful for planning this important area of church work. In recent years the Bolivian Baptist Union has been harder hit than other groups by pastors emigrating to the United States. Many of these were trained in the Baptist primary and secondary schools. It is possible that they were trained out of their own denomination. In the United States, most are active Baptists and at least three are in the ministry.

Secondly, neither the school approach nor any other has been successful in reaching Bolivia's upper class, the political leaders, or the professional people. No one has done as outstanding a job as the Methodists in establishing educational institutions, but the professionals and upper class people who have been discipled by them are very few. The theory that upper class parents can be reached through their children has not been proven in Bolivia. A survey of graduates of Protestant schools would undoubtedly show that of those who made professions of faith in school, a high percentage have reverted to Catholicism or became indifferent to all religion when they returned to their families and stepped out into society. The direction of influence in the Bolivian family structure does not usually extend from the children to the parents, but vice-versa.

Religious Liberty. The declaration of religious liberty in 1905 was the most important event for future church growth during the 1898-1919 period. Undoubtedly the Canadian Baptist missionaries had a good deal to do with influencing this decision. Given events in Latin America in general at this time, it is probable that the decision would have come inevitably, but at the same time it is possible that the presence of the missionaries and their unusually close contact with key leaders was not only a catalytic factor, but also one of the reasons why Bolivia's freedom of religion has been much more complete than that of some other Latin American republics. A mission report states the following:

> The liberals came into power ... There was a breaking with the past and the forward march was begun. The changes have been rapid and revolutionary ... Toward all these revolutionary changes our missionaries have been a factor far beyond what their numbers might indicate ... To the missionaries is due much of the credit for the religious reforms indicated. It was they who furnished most of the ammunition for many of the greatest speeches in the Senate and the House of Deputies when the Bills for religious liberty and other reform measures were passed (CBFMB 1914: 26-27).

Two of the outstanding contacts were the close friendship of the Routledges in La Paz with a very influential lawyer, Severino Campuzano, and the providential visit of the Prefect of Oruro to a Protestant service in Oruro. As has already been mentioned, he rose high in the government later and consistently took the side of the Protestants.

TABLE 4

Bolivian Baptist Union (Canadian Baptists) 1898 - 1967

Date	Foreign Workers	National Workers	Churches	Baptized	Total Members	Source
1911	4	–	2	20	50	Dennis 1911:97
1914	–	3	–	60	–	CBFMB
1915	–	3	–	80	–	CBFMB
1916	10	3	3	80	–	CBFMB; Beach 1916
1917	–	3	–	100	–	CBFMB
1918	–	3	–	53	178	CBFMB
1919	–	3	–	63	213	CBFMB
1920	–	3	–	73	206	CBFMB
1921	–	3	–	76	–	CBFMB
1922	–	3	–	89	–	CBFMB
1923	–	3	–	94	–	CBFMB
1924	–	–	–	100	–	CBFMB
1925	18	2	4	88	–	CBFMB; Beach 1925
1926	–	–	–	–	–	
1927	–	4	–	118	–	CBFMB
1928	–	6	–	175	–	CBFMB
1929	–	5	–	174	–	CBFMB
1930	–	5	–	212	–	CBFMB
1931	–	5	–	249	–	CBFMB
1932	–	5	–	287	–	CBFMB
1933	–	–	–	312	–	CBFMB
1934	–	–	–	300	–	CBFMB
1935	–	–	–	355	–	CBFMB
1936	–	7	–	345	–	CBFMB
1937	–	7	–	380	–	CBFMB
1938	16	9	7	389	–	CBFMB; Parker 1938
1939	–	–	–	378	–	CBFMB
1940	–	8	–	436	–	CBFMB
1941	–	–	–	471	–	CBFMB
1942	–	–	–	500	–	CBFMB
1943	–	–	–	500	–	CBFMB
1944	–	–	–	500	–	CBFMB
1945	–	–	–	–	–	

TABLE 4, cont.

Date	Foreign Workers	National Workers	Churches	Baptized	Total Members	Source
1946	-	10	-	487	-	CBFMB
1947	-	12	-	524	-	CBFMB
1948	-	18	-	651	-	CBFMB
1949	18	21	22	651	-	CBFMB; *WCH* 1949
1950	-	22	-	700	-	CBFMB
1951	-	22	-	750	-	CBFMB
1952	25	22	22	750	-	CBFMB; *WCH* 1952
1953	-	22	-	750	-	CBFMB
1954	-	25	-	800	-	CBFMB
1955	-	34	-	1218	-	CBFMB
1956	-	-	-	-	-	
1957	42	39	56	954	-	CBFMB; *WCH* 1957
1958	-	40	-	1101	-	CBFMB
1960	-	39	-	1303	-	CBFMB
1961	-	46	-	1546	-	CBFMB
1962	-	-	40	-	-	*WCH* 1962
1967	37	90	39	1133	3435	*WCH* 1967

La Paz. Robert Routledge and his wife arrived in Oruro shortly after Archibald Reekie in 1898, then transferred to La Paz the following year. They started a school there and in the early days the Mitchells and the Bakers, all of whom arrived in 1900, joined them. Routledge was not in favor of the school approach, however, and on this basis resigned in 1905. Stillwell comments on this as follows:

> It had not been discovered to the Routledges as clearly as it was later that in South America school work is one of the most far-reaching and ultimately fruitful forms of evangelism (1924:140).

Around 1902 Father Eloy Rodriguez, a Roman Catholic priest, was converted and baptized in La Paz. One of the other highlights of this pioneer work was the brief visit of the fiery Austrian (Dabbs says Yugoslav) evangelist, Maximiliano Rohrsetzer, who was also a colporteur of the British and Foreign Bible Society. When he preached he invariably drew standing-room crowds. Routledge says, "had we been able to inject a little more of Rohrsetzer enthusiasm into our mission work, greater results, I believe, would be attained" (Stillwell 1924:139). In 1905 Baker took sick and Routledge resigned, so the La Paz station was temporarily closed.

Cochabamba. Mitchell, in the meantime, had gone to Cochabamba in 1901 to open the third mission station. His school there attracted eighty pupils from the upper class. In 1904 they baptized the first two believers with George and Mary Allan, founders of the Andes Evangelical Mission, present (Stillwell 1924:143). Mrs. Mitchell fell ill in 1905 and they had to leave on furlough. With no one else from their mission available, they were forced to leave the converts, the school and the house in the hands of Allan, described as "an immersed Presbyterian missionary" (Stillwell 1924:148).

From 1905, when the missionary force hit a low, to 1919, only ten new workers who remained five years or more came to Bolivia.

Resistance to the Gospel. As Table 4 shows, the Baptist churches counted 63 members in 1919. Bolivia was still a resistant field.

Commenting on a loss of eight members in 1915-1916, Mitchell writes:

> Another discouraging surface fact is that we had no baptisms during the year. All these things look bad, but in spite of them we have had one of the most successful years in the history of our work. The pastor can now look into the faces of a good number in the congregation and feel that they are living right, that they will always be in their places in every service of the church, that they take a genuine interest in the work, that they are growing in knowledge and grace, and that they really form a secure basis for future prosperity (CBFMB 1916:31).

Mitchell is somewhat of an optimist, seeing some good in the midst of slow growth. Reekie writes more realistically, stating that

> The visible spiritual results are disappointing, and when we ask why, we seem to hear the Master say, "because of

your little faith" ... more prayer is needed ... we trust
the day of larger reaping is not far off (CBFMB 1918:48-49).

While the government no longer opposed the preaching of the
Gospel, nothing seemed to penetrate the hearts of the people.
Harry Strachan, who later founded the Latin American Mission,
drew "great crowds" for his evangelistic meetings in 1916,
but no visible enduring results were recorded (CBFMB 1917:37).
Even the Seventh-day Adventists, the only denomination
which showed considerable growth between 1920 and 1950, did
not grow much in this early period. The message was clear;
the missionaries preached "the absolute and unchallengable
authority of the Lord Jesus our Redeemer over the thought and
life of the individual," "liberty of conscience," "personal
faith in ... Jesus as the basis of conversion and membership
in the church," "Jesus as the only mediator between God and
man" (Stillwell 1924:119-120), and other doctrines which
should have appealed to nominal Catholics. Stillwell blames
it largely on the low moral and religious state of both the
clergy and the laity of the Catholic Church. The people had
"no thought of direct touch with God ... only the feeblest
moral sense ... they were superstitious and believers of
magic ... exceedingly inflammable ... they exercised no
private judgment in religion ... the Bible was under ban to
them" (Stillwell 1924:106-110). The situation was discour-
aging enough without the added blow of the loss of the
liberal government's power, but the missionaries realized
that with no persistent sowing there would be no abundant
reaping in the future, so they continued courageously.

1920 - 1935

With a conservative government in power, it was decided to
resume the school approach, discontinued in 1908. Under the
leadership of Alexander Haddow, Reekie School was opened in
Oruro in 1923. Today this continues with full primary and
secondary divisions, and is regarded as one of Bolivia's
outstanding schools. Only four primary grades were opened in
1923.

Mining Centers. In 1921 a very important move was made
into the mining town of Llallagua. Eventually this and other
mining towns in the Oruro area gave good results. Hamilton
concludes that these mining districts were fertile fields
"probably because of freedom from both Roman Catholic pressure

and village ties" (Hamilton 1962:57).

The Guatajata Farm Project. Undoubtedly the most significant aspect of the Canadian Baptist work in this period was the purchase of the Guatajata hacienda. Stillwell (1924), Dabbs (1952), and Hamilton (1962) all tell the story of its purchase in great detail, so a summary will suffice at this point. An Italian immigrant, Antonio Chiriotto, made a fortune in a winery in Los Angeles, California, then was soundly converted in the Peniel Mission there. He gave his life as a missionary to Argentina, then moved to La Paz as an old man at the invitation of an independent Methodist missionary, Dr. Foster. He died in La Paz in 1911 and left $30,000 to the "Peniel Hall Society." Two Methodists and one Baptist served on the Board of Directors, which was self-perpetuating. The following year this Board purchased the hacienda of 800-1000 acres, sold, like all properties in those days, with its 275 Aymara Indian serfs as part of the deal. After rather unsuccessful Methodist efforts to manage the farm, the Canadian Baptists agreed to take the responsibility of it in 1920. On October 15, 1927, six men and women were baptized and the church was organized. Membership rose to 90 in 1932 and stayed at this level or below for several years (see Figure 4). When Stillwell visited the farm in 1921 he found the children singing with the missionaries in "newly acquired Spanish" (1924:229). At the same time, however, the missionaries were making attempts to learn the Aymara language, recognizing that the people could not be reached properly except in their own tongue. Whereas the missionaries were successful in interesting the children in Christ, their parents soon took all ideas of conversion from their minds.

In a stimulating and incisive analysis of the Guatajata hacienda work, Hamilton (1962:59-63) points out that the bulk of church growth up until 1936 was from the free Aymaras who lived on other lands, not from the Guatajata serfs. For one thing, the serfs, "while treated with great kindness and justice, they remained serfs who had to work the mission land" (1962:59). For the oppressed masses the distinction between a white absentee overlord and a white resident missionary was not too great.

Individual Approach in a Communal Society. The evidence also points to another difficulty. The missionaries of that day were probably using the individual approach to evangelism

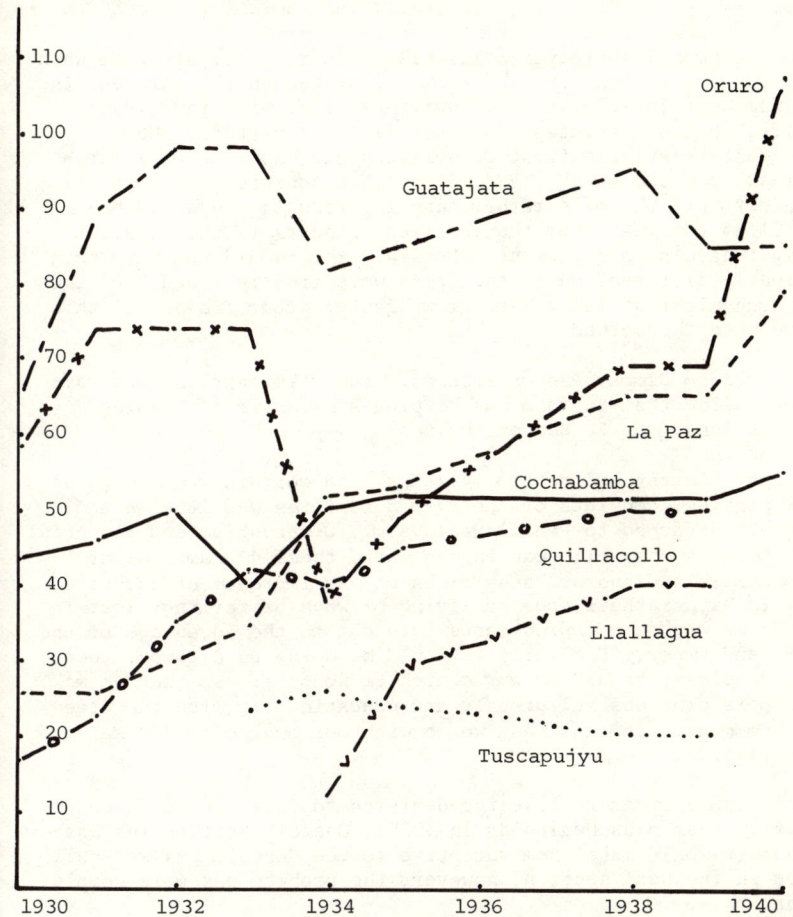

BOLIVIAN BAPTIST UNION 1930-1940
GROWTH COMPARISON OF SEVEN LOCAL CHURCHES

FIGURE 4

in a communal society. Stillwell reflects their attitude when he reports accurately "the communal system on the farm and the consequent interlocking of individual life with individual life," but his strategy does not fit this pattern. He suggests that "the first conversions and baptisms call for a break from the mass" (1924:233). If a conscious attempt were made to win the mass rather than individuals who would be willing to break from the mass, one wonders if the results might have been different. Possibly they would not have been greatly different until the serfs were finally freed, but the church might at least have grown faster *after freedom* if this had been the method.

Serfdom Blocks Responsiveness. The missionaries soon came to realize that serfdom was keeping Aymaras from becoming Christians. F. F. Bennett writes:

> Our biggest obligation, perhaps, and certainly our biggest problem, consists of the 47-odd families who live on and are attached to Peniel Hall Farm. Distrustful and resentful towards the white man in the past, these 47 families of Aymara Indians are suspicious of any improvement suggested in either their mode of living or ways of farming, lest in some way such improvements turn out to the advantage of the land owner. Similarly it would be doing us a favor, they consider, to attend our church or schools: so that we make more progress religiously and educationally with the free community Indians than we do with our own peons (CBFMA 1935:3).

This caused them to take the decision to free the serfs under a five-year plan beginning in 1935. One of the theories was that it would make them receptive to the Gospel. As we shall see in the next section, however, the problem was more complex than this.

Reconsideration of Methods. The slow growth in the denomination as a whole gave rise to much critical reconsideration of methods. Stillwell was so impressed with the hardness of the Bolivian Indians in 1924 that he wrote: "There is no more difficult and unresponsive Mission work among any people with the exception of the Mohammedans" (1924:75). Even those who responded had problems living up to the moral demands of Christianity. Persecution was common in these days under the conservative government and there was little street preaching. The Baptists used the personal approach, holding classes with women, running schools in Guatajata and Oruro, farming and healing. In 1929, the five Canadian Baptist stations showed the membership statistics seen in Table 5.

TABLE 5

1929 Canadian Baptist Membership

Oruro/Llallagua	63
La Paz	26
Cochabamba	41
Quillacollo	17
Guatajata	27

Alexander Haddow was convinced that the methods being used were good. He reported:

> I am quite well aware there is sometimes a tendency to question our method of work in the Mission as a whole, but, facing all facts, I am more sure than ever that we are on the right road, that we have the right ideals, and that we ought to have the patience and perseverance to give God a chance to work out something with the human material at hand ... I have seen since I have been in Bolivia a good many things work out on the principle of "little by little". I am far from being alarmed about the "one by one" method in saving souls ... we are making progress undreamed of by the pioneers of the Mission (CBFMB 1928:25).

Curiously, the Protestants in this period seemed to be ignorant of the activities of the Seventh-day Adventists, who had begun to grow in 1920 and who had almost 3000 members in 1934. The Canadian Baptists, with approximately double the number of missionaries, could count only one-tenth that number of members.

Pieces of the Ethnic Mosaic. The difference was in the ethnic groups that each mission was harvesting. The Baptist chapel on the Prado in La Paz was the finest Protestant building in the country, but church growth was slow there. In 1920 all 73 Baptist church members were mestizos. But the report states that by 1931 fully one-half of the 249 members were Indians - Aymaras in Guatajata and Quechuas in Llallagua and Quillacollo. This means that the Indian population was turning responsive, whereas the mestizo cities were remaining resistant. Good church growth strategy might have shifted resources into the responsive areas. H. S. Hillyer saw the picture clearly in 1933. He pointed out that city evangelism had not been successful. Among other efforts to which he may have referred was the second campaign of Harry Strachan, accompanied this time by Argentine Juan Varetto, who had preached in Oruro, Cochabamba and La Paz in 1927. Strachan stated that he had never visited a place in which he found it so difficult to preach the Gospel as Bolivia (Phillips n.d.: n.p.). Hillyer observed, "Beyond all doubt the fruits of evangelism among these two Indian tribes, the Aymara and the Quechua, are the most promiseful of all our Mission undertaking in Bolivia" (CBFMB 1933:8). Although the opportunity was clear, there is no evidence that the mission was mobile enough to shift the resources significantly.

The Chaco War. Dabbs reports that the Chaco War (1932 - 1935) had devastating effects on the Baptist Church. The government took men of combat age, as well as those over and under age. From the Oruro church alone, 50 men were fighting on the front. The Cochabamba congregation counted 5 women for each man during the war, whereas before the war there were 5 men for each woman. Some congregations lost every last man (Dabbs 1952:144).

The curious fact is, however, that the total membership of the Baptist denomination during the period 1930-1935 increased at the rate of 130 percent per decade, which is a good rate of growth. The fact that the rate decreased from the 282 percent per decade of 1925-1930 is due largely to the relatively small over-all figures involved at that time. In spite of the Chaco War, then the churches were growing in 1935. Figure 4 shows that the churches of La Paz, Quillacollo and Llallagua showed no significant decline during the war. Guatajata, Oruro, Cochabamba, and Tuscapujyu declined, but with the exception of the small church of Tuscapujyu, the others began a healthy comeback before the war ended. The severe drop in the Oruro church was probably due in part to membership transfer to the Llallagua church.

1936 - 1945

The Bolivian Baptist Union. During the period following the Chaco War, three major developments took place in the work of the Canadian Baptist Mission. The war itself, as we shall see in more detail in Chapter 5, stimulated the feelings of nationalism among the Bolivian people, and this in turn spurred the mission to create Bolivia's first national church organization. Dabbs says, "Perhaps the most important fruit of the Chaco War ... was a clearer understanding of the place and function of the indigenous church" (1952:146). The process of formation was instituted by the missionaries, not at that time demanded by the nationals. But the missionaries were clear-thinking and far-sighted enough to realize that if nationals were not given the responsibility of the work on the initiative and with the approval of the missionaries, serious dissent would inevitably arise as the spirit of nationalism in the country continued to increase. Thus during the Carnival holidays of 1936, the first Convention of the Bolivian Baptist Union (Unión Bautista Boliviana) was called. Missionary Johnson Turnbull, who had come to Bolivia with George Allan's Andes Evangelical Mission and then transferred to the Canadian Baptists with Allan's approval in 1910, was the moving force (Dabbs 1952:151). The Union was to become the employer of all Bolivian workers, handling all the obligations to them instead of the mission. Since the churches were not able to carry the financial load, the mission agreed to subsidize the BBU cutting their subsidy 5 percent per year (Dabbs 1952:154). Macedonio Montaño became the first Bolivian worker under the new organization.

Home Missions. The second major development arose out of the first. With the formation of the BBU and the hiring of national workers, home missions were stressed in a stronger way. The Bolivian Church was taught that it must take the responsibility for extension within its own country. The first effort was among the Quechua population of Llallagua, originally opened in 1921, and the second in 1937 to the Aymaras of Viacha (CBFMB 1937).

Freeing the Serfs. The decision to free the Guatajata serfs was the third major development. It was not an entirely new concept, since field minutes of the mission dating as far back as 1929 indicate dissatisfaction with the feudal structure (Phillips n.d.:n.p.). When the decision was taken in

1936, only 25 percent of the church members and only 3 of the 25 school pupils were from the hacienda. The rest came in from the nearby communities of free Indians. The title of Dabbs' book is taken from his comment on the freeing of the peasants: "Dawn was coming up over the stone-gray hills of Bolivia" (1952:187-188). Church growth did not begin on the hacienda with the announcement of the five-year plan, however. In fact, church membership in Guatajata in 1940 was the same as in 1935 (see Figure 4). Freedom was finally granted in 1942, amidst much excitement and rejoicing.

Why Growth Slowed Down. In his evaluation of the period 1936-1945, Dabbs indicates that it is a period of much growth and unusual responsiveness. He attributes the growth to two causes: the freedom of the serfs and the increase in schools in the Guatajata area as shown on Table 6.

TABLE 6

Guatajata Increase in Schools and Church Attendance

Year	Schools	Attendance
1940	2	200
1945	6	500
1946	8	700

Dabbs says that 1943-1944 was a time of "vigorous growth," and of the awakening of the Aymara Indian (1952:198-201).

In spite of Dabbs' impression, the per decade growth rate for the period was only 45 percent. This could be contrasted to the 82 percent of the following period and the 130 percent of the preceding period. In other words, this period shows a definite slackening in vigor as far as the Church is concerned. While the establishment of the BBU, the stress on home missions, and the freeing of the serfs were all commendable moves, and undoubtedly did much to pave the way for future church growth, none of them were immediate causes of growth. Why, then, did Dabbs and others think that "there was a rising tide in spiritual things" (Hamilton 1962:61)? Hamilton does a good job in analyzing the problem:

Few were baptized. This optimistic language applies to mission work, not to church growth. Teaching and preaching were expanded to a forty-mile district, but in all this district were only 147 members - including those at the mission station of Guatajata. The evangelist was a "welcome guest;" but that was all. The Indian who "was convinced," was convinced of the advantages of an education. He was not converted.

We can rejoice in this degree of opening, but see it as a preliminary stage. This kind of friendship, welcome, spread of "work" and conviction was not and is not the goal. That remains the establishment of churches of confessed baptized Christians (1962:61).

Missionary Alexander Haddow, in his report to Canada, was realistic in his appraisal of the work in 1939. He said, "The slowness of the growth of the work in Bolivia is common to all Missions working in the Republic and does not mean that we are on the wrong track, but that we are on a stiff grade with plenty of short curves" (CBFMB 1939:2). This picture was true, even of the Seventh-day Adventists who were at that time in their period of great decline.

Neither the commencement of radio evangelism in Oruro and La Paz nor the founding of the Baptist Theological Seminary (Seminario Teológico Bautista) as the Cochabamba Bible College in 1941, immediately turned the growth of the Church upward. This caused the missionaries to see their work in terms of "quality" rather than "quantity," a dangerous mentality for a Church or a mission which has growth as its goal. Hindrances which were named in 1945 were persecution, prejudices, typhus, and financial problems (CBFMB 1945:1-2). My impression would be that the financial problems were probably the strongest determent to the work during the period. The Chaco War impoverished Bolivia and made the problem of finding enough for the family to eat more acute than ever. Then the effects of the depression in Canada still would have been felt, at least in the beginning of the period. The Second World War also would have cut down resources. The demoralization caused by these several factors was felt across the board by all churches in Bolivia.

1946 - 1952

The Canadian Baptist missionary staff numbered eighteen in 1940, twenty-three in 1945 and twenty-five in 1950. In spite of this small increase, church membership rose from 500 to 750, and the per decade growth rose from 45 percent to 82 percent.

Massacre of Melcamaya. The tragic massacre of Melcamaya in 1949 set the Baptist work back severely. A mob of drunken Indians, incited by a priest named Tumiri (Phillips n.d.:n.p.) attacked a truck full of Baptist Christians with stones, and succeeded in murdering eight. Among the dead were Norman Dabbs, whose book we have been referring to and who had been appointed Director of the Baptist Theological Seminary in Cochabamba; Carlos Meneses, perhaps the most outstanding young pastor of the denomination; and Francisco Salazar, President of the Bolivian Baptist Union (Dabbs 1952:250-258).

Radio Ministry. The Southern Cross Radio Station (Radio la Cruz del Sur), was set up by the Canadian Baptists when they purchased Radio Nacional in La Paz for $14,500 (Dabbs 1952: 263). This is Bolivia's only Protestant radio station, and has served the Christian community well. From 1964 to January 1968, it was jointly administered by the Baptists and Methodists, but this arrangement has been discontinued. The Methodists built a retransmitting plant in Montero so that the station could be heard on standard broadcast in the Santa Cruz area. In other parts of the country besides La Paz and Santa Cruz it is heard on short wave. Just to what extent the Southern Cross has contributed to church growth is not known. No one questions its contribution to Bolivian culture. Protestants and non-Protestants all over the republic are appreciative of it, and some say that it is the only station with absolutely reliable news broadcasts. The operation of the station has caused some friction recently, as the question of whether it should be preserved as strictly a mission project or turned over to the BBU has been debated.

Upward Social Mobility. Writing a conclusion to Dabbs' book, H. S. Hillyer sums up the state of the work in 1952 as being most successful among Aymaras around Lake Titicaca. He indicates certain good results among the Quechuas in Oruro and Cochabamba, but says that the cholos (mestizos) in La Paz, Oruro and Cochabamba are "the backbone of our churches and from them have come some of our finest national pastors and most devoted Christians" (Dabbs 1952:258). What this means is that Hillyer evaluated the Baptist Church as ideally a middle-class Church, a Church which depended on the mestizos in the

cities for its future growth. There is little question that
this represents the predominant viewpoint in the denomination.
While it is true that the Baptists perhaps have been the most
successful of all groups in winning the middle-class, urban
residents, it is not yet certain that these have helped the
Church grow in other segments of the ethnic mosaic of the
country. Although the Baptist Theological Seminary has been
an excellent institution for ministerial training, the
denomination has had more of a problem than have other groups
of its pastors and capable laymen emigrating from Bolivia to
the USA and other countries. At this writing there are at
least four graduates of the Baptist seminary in Los Angeles
County alone. This is partially due to the emphasis placed on
middle-class status and on the upgrading of the ministry.
Making the Cochabamba Seminary the prerequisite for the
ministry has contributed to this. Some have been so upgraded
that they have no longer felt comfortable in Bolivian society,
particularly for economic reasons. More study needs to be
done as to the present locations and employment of the
graduates of the seminary. However, the recently founded
Aymara Bible Institute in Oruro should help this multicultural
problem, but one questions whether an urban institution will
satisfactorily prepare a rural ministry.

This is not to say that segregation is practiced in the
Baptist denomination. Quite the contrary. It might well be
that one of the reasons the BBU has not grown quite as rapidly
as other denominations in Bolivia is that it is in some ways
overly integrated. The BBU President elected in 1968 was
Justino Quispe, a graduate of the Baptist Theological Seminary
and a full-blooded Aymara. While Quispe has unquestionably
high qualifications for his position, one wonders if a
denomination which has built up a middle-class "backbone" will
function as efficiently as possible under this kind of leadership. This experiment will bear close watching. Quispe's
unusual leadership ability was amply demonstrated when he led
the Aymara department of Evangelism-in-Depth in 1965,
conducting an impressive Aymara Protestant Congress which
brought together 7,000 Aymaras. Whether this ability can be
transferred to a multicultural structure, and how it will
affect future growth, remains to be seen.

Ministerial Professionalism. Another point which is
significant is the economic dependency of the BBU on the
foreign mission. With the desire to do all in proper order,
the BBU, as has been mentioned, from the beginning acted as

the employer of the national pastors. This employer-employee relationship necessitated compliance with all Bolivian laws regarding secular labor and the BBU pastors have insisted on their full social benefits from their employer. As long as the foreign mission subsidized this program, few problems were encountered, except for the rather professional and commercial attitude toward the ministry which some BBU pastors have taken. In 1967 the Canadian Baptist Mission decided (against an official protest of the BBU in their 1967 Convention) to eliminate the foreign subsidy over a five-year period. In 1972 no more subsidy is to be given for pastors' salaries. In the light of what other more rapidly growing denominations have done, this seems like sound procedure.

1952 - 1967

The 1967 *World Christian Handbook* places the membership of the BBU at 3435. Baptist statistics, taken from official Canadian Baptist Foreign Mission Board reports, are found on Table 4. The denominational graph of growth is found on Figure 5. A map showing the centers of Bolivian Baptist Union ministry in 1963 constitutes Figure 6.

THE METHODIST CHURCH IN BOLIVIA
(Iglesia Metodista)

Many earlier writers have dated the origin of the Methodist Church in Bolivia as 1906, the year when the first missionaries sent from the United States arrived in Bolivia to begin their work. A more accurate reading of the records, however, is reflected in Copplestone's article in *The Encyclopedia of Modern Christian Missions,* which states that "Karl G. Beutelspacher opened a mission in Bolivia in 1901" (1967: 409). Diffendorfer (1923:153) also sets the date for the beginning of the work at 1901. This means that the Methodist Church is the third Church chronologically to be planted in Bolivia.

Methodist interest in Bolivia dates further back than 1901. Francisco Penzotti, Andrew Milne, Thomas Wood, John Thompson, and Bible agent Orellana were known Methodists, and it is likely that others of the early colporteurs and missionary explorers mentioned in Chapter 2 were Methodists also. As a denomination, the Methodists were the true pioneers of the Protestant work in the southern cone of South America. The

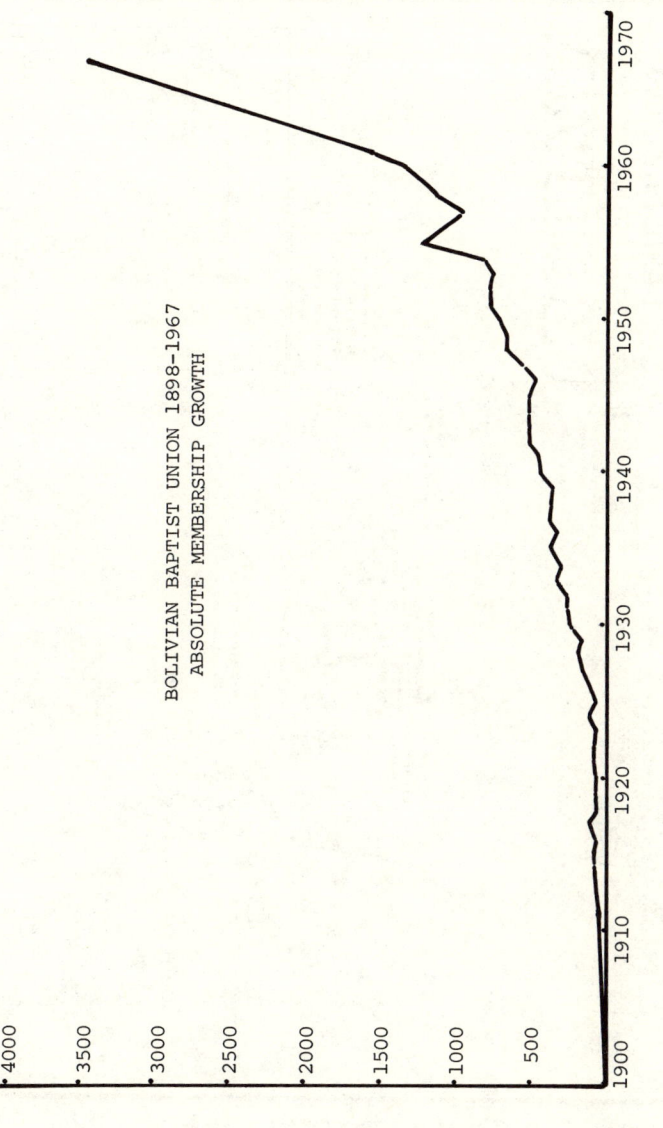

FIGURE 5

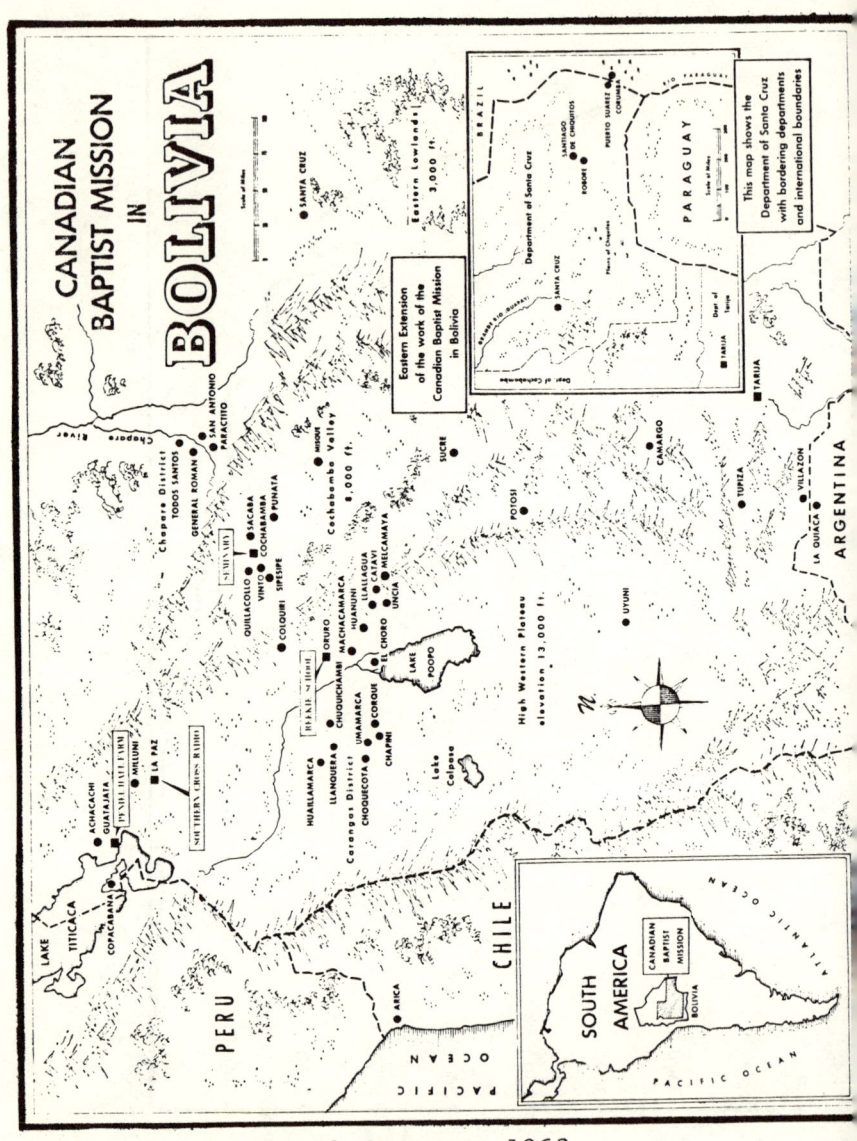

Source: *The Church Overseas 1963*

FIGURE 6

burden that Thomas Wood had for Bolivia is evident in his reports to his mission board. In 1883 he jubilantly announced that "Bolivia is at last penetrated" (M.E.C. *Annual Report* 1883:50); and then four years later, "Dr. Goodfellow started Bro. Milne at the house-to-house work in 1884 in the form of the sale of books. In that form we have penetrated Bolivia through and through" (M.E.C. *Annual Report* 1887:62). Journeys by Methodists into Bolivia are reflected in reports from Argentina, Peru, and Chile.

Karl Beutelspacher. Permanent Methodist work among Spanish-speaking people in Chile began in 1888 (Kessler 1967: 100), and from there the Church was extended into Bolivia in a permanent form. In that same year, Karl Beutelspacher, a converted German sailor, arrived in Antofagasta, which had been a Bolivian seaport until the War of the Pacific in 1879 when Chile took it over. Beutelspacher supported himself by working in the railroad shops in Antofagasta. He started an English-language church, then changed to Spanish. By 1896 he had a very good and solid congregation (Barclay 1957:800).

In 1901 Bishop McCabe of Chile sent Beutelspacher to Bolivia as the Superintendent of the new Bolivia district. The railroad had been completed, linking Antofagasta and Oruro, and already some of the Methodist laymen who worked and traveled on the railroad had carried their Christian witness to Oruro and some of the railroad towns. The Chile mission was on self-support, so it had no funds to help Beutelspacher. The Bolivian district consequently separated from the Chile mission and united with the "North Andes Mission Conference" so he could receive funds from North America. He was appointed to the Bible Society and served under that organization also between 1902 and 1905 (Arms 1921:168-169).

By 1902 organized classes were reported at Uyuni with a Brother Barbosa, and at Oruro with Brothers Petie and Carlos A. Reyes, all members of the Antofagasta church (M.E.C. *Annual Report* 1902:353). The 1903 report describes the work in these terms:

> It is marvellous how the brethren have been able to raise up large congregations along the Antofagasta and Oruro railway. Working all day in the mines and on the railway, they preach the Gospel in the evening and on Sundays. The members that go out from the Antofagasta church all seem to be preachers. Wherever they go a church is organized (M.E.C. *Annual Report* 1903:399).

La Paz' 12,000-foot altitude became too much for Beutelspacher's health, and he had to leave Bolivia in 1905 (Lewis 1960:258-259).

Francis Harrington. What Paul McCleary calls "the first permanent work of the Methodist Church in Bolivia" began the following year with the arrival of Francis and Mary Harrington from the USA (1965:2). Harrington had previously been director of the Methodist English College in Iquique, Chile. He had contracted tuberculosis there, and it was thought that his health could improve in the drier La Paz climate (Barber 1965:12).

Harrington was in La Paz when the constitutional amendment for religious liberty was passed in 1906, and just as the Brethren claim some credit for Payne's influence and the Baptists for Routledge and Baker's, the Methodists claim that Harrington was also one of the engineers of the law. Natalie Barber says, for example:

> Right from the beginning of his work in La Paz, Harrington was faced with many problems. He discovered an old, semi-forgotten clause in the constitution that prescribed death for anyone who "preached or practiced any other religion except Roman Catholicism." As he had a good knowledge of law, he set out to have this changed, and within a year the word "permitted" was substituted for "prohibited" and Francis was free to start a school (1965:12).

As we have seen in Chapter 1, President McKinley had begun to pressure the Bolivian government for religious liberty back as far as 1899, and the amendment had already been passed by both houses of the Bolivian Congress before Harrington arrived in Bolivia. There is little doubt, however, that Harrington moved freely with the liberals who were pushing the bill which finally became law on August 6, 1906, and favorably influenced them.

The Institutional Approach. In spite of the new law, the Methodists still felt that the "situation called for discreet evangelism" (McCleary 1965:2), and Harrington followed the lead of the Baptists in using the school approach. He established excellent rapport with government officials, and could report in 1906:

> The Bolivian government has offered me an annual subsidy of

15,000 Bolivian dollars to establish a high grade school in La Paz. This school is to be under the control and direction of our Mission Board in New York ... In addition to the above, the President of the Republic, Ismael Montes, through his Minister of Justice and Instruction, J. M. Saracho, has placed at my disposition 25,000 Bolivian dollars to organize and supply with a principal and teachers, the government high school in Oruro, the railway center of Bolivia ... Should the Oruro school prove to be a success, it will give us great prestige in Bolivia, and the Minister of Instruction hinted that they would place the schools of the country in our hands (M.E.C. *Annual Report* 1906:358-359).

With Harrington as principal, the American Institute opened its doors in La Paz in February of 1907 (McCleary 1965: 2). One hundred and thirty students were enrolled (Barber 1965:12). Unfortunately, tuberculosis returned with full force, and Harrington died before he had finished his first year of directing the school.

By establishing the American Institute and tying into the Bolivian government through subsidies, Harrington had set the course of the development of the work of the Methodist Church for the next half century. From the point of view of education, the Methodists have made an outstanding contribution to the development of the Bolivian nation. This has been recognized by the awarding of the "Condor of the Andes" medal to more Methodists than all other Protestant missionaries combined. The award has gone to Dr. Frank S. Beck, Dr. Bell, Miss Helen Rusby, Mr. Murray Dixon, and Mr. Legrand B. Smith, all educators (although Beck also distinguished himself through medical work). The Methodists pioneered co-education in Bolivia by admitting girls to the American Institute in 1910. In 1912 Beck, who had been directing the La Paz Institute, moved to Cochabamba and founded the American Institute there. These two schools, which now run from kindergarten through high school, are universally recognized as among Bolivia's top educational institutions.

With their deep involvement in institutional work from the beginning, the Methodists, perhaps inadvertently, restricted their church-planting activities. Although they did some church work, they remained an institution-centered mission until the late 1950's. The establishment of the highly successful American Clinic (now the Pfeiffer Memorial Hospital) in La Paz by Frank Beck, who had returned to the USA at the age of thirty-five to earn his M.D., further tied the mission to institutions.

In 1924, Stillwell of the Canadian Baptists evaluated the Methodist school work in these terms: "Unfortunately, no religion could be taught. The school, thus handicapped, had a liberalizing, though not a directly evangelizing, influence" (1924:187).

The Struggle for Existence. The Methodists had become so deeply committed to the schools that when the Roman Catholic Church regained enough influence to pressure the government in 1916, and government support of the Methodist educational work was withdrawn, the Methodist Church "entered a long period of crisis which was a struggle for existence" (McCleary 1965:3).

> Work started among the indigenous population during this period had also been lost to the Church during the same period due to the lack of funds and personnel. Names of communities on the Altiplano and in the Yungas appeared in early appointment lists and are now silent reminders of the sacrificial efforts of others which bore no fruit (McCleary 1965:3).

The major problem undoubtedly was not so much the unavailability of funds and personnel as the commitment of resources to institutions. When a mission has taken upon itself the responsibility of educational and medical institutions, with the large investment of capital funds on one hand and moral responsibility to those who are served by the institutions on the other hand, the die is cast for any time of crisis. When a church-planting program is carried side by side with an institutional program, priorities must eventually be set. During periods of prosperity in the sending countries, available resources are abundant and little difficulty is experienced in maintaining the institutions as well as sending others to plant churches at the same time. But in times of economic crisis such as war or depression in the homelands, resources are cut back, and some part of the work on the field has to be curtailed. Inevitably the cutback first seems to come in the church work because commitment of funds and personnel is less and because missionaries who are in church work are usually more mobile than those involved in institutions.

A glance at Figure 7 which shows the growth of the denomination as a whole will reveal significant dips during

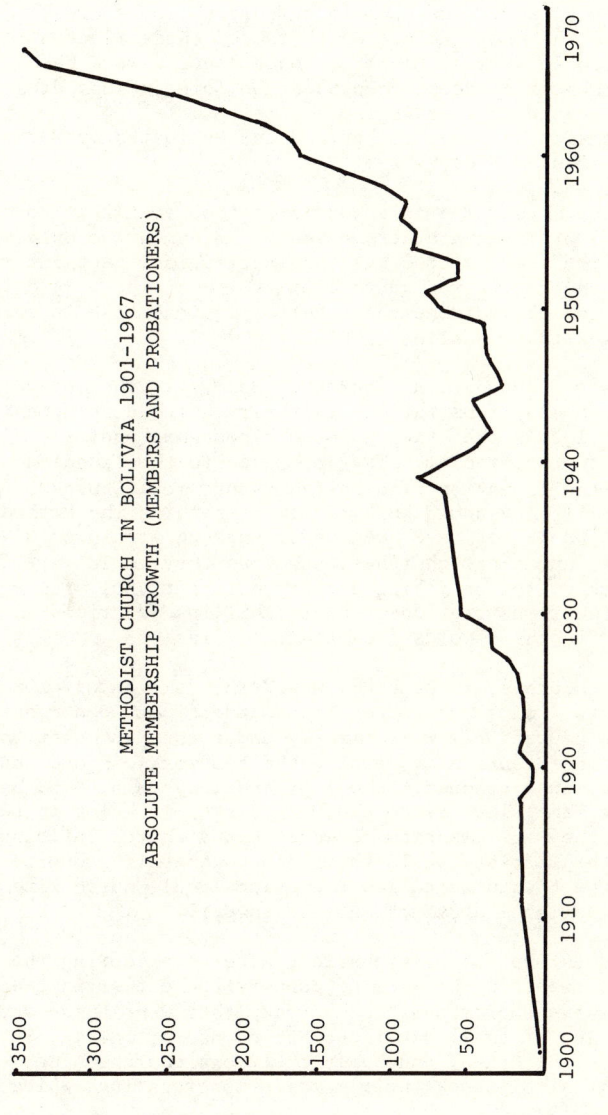

FIGURE 7

the depression of the early thirties and during World War II, both times of worldwide cuts in resources. Of course, these may not be the only factors which caused these fluctuations, but they could well be the major ones since a work based on institutions is so deeply dependent on foreign subsidies for the maintenance of the program.

The tension has been recognized and evaluated by Methodist leaders. Paul McCleary says:

> the church took the only form or method available to her to express or incarnate her message. At times the only congregation that existed was the institution. But interestingly enough, it was quite clear to those who worked in education or medicine that their principal task in being here was to evangelize (1965:3).

The United Evangelical Church of Bolivia. The Methodists suffered so many frustrations in their church development in the early 1920's that they adopted a somewhat radical solution to the problem. They proposed to the Canadian Baptists the formation of a United Evangelical Church of Bolivia. If they could work together in this, the Methodists obviously would not have been under so much pressure to evangelize and plant churches, and thus they could more fully have concentrated on making a contribution to Bolivian society through their institutions. David Phillips describes the encounter in these words (translated): In 1923

> the Methodists, through Mr. Washburn, make an offer to the Baptists: of close cooperation between both denominations in the educational work already under the Methodist Church with the intention of merging the two works in one and developing a graduate school of theology on a 50-50 basis. At the same time, since the Methodists own a lot in La Paz where they are planning to construct a church building, that the Baptists build their church on this property and that the church be called the Evangelical Church with no denominational distinction (n.d.:n.p.).

The Canadian Baptist missionaries, after considering the proposal, rejected the idea of cooperation either in the church or the educational work. They then went ahead and bought a lot of their own in La Paz on one of the major boulevards, El Prado, and built their own church. The Methodists simply took their mestizo congregation, which was

Pioneer Church-planters

meeting on the Prado also, and merged it with the Baptists. Some thirty-two members were involved in the transfer (McCleary 1968). Table 7 shows this move. The Methodist congregation in Cochabamba went to the Calle Calama Baptist Church, and the work in Viacha ceased.

TABLE 7

Membership of Some Individual Methodist Churches

Year	La Paz Prado, Reforma	La Paz Redentor	La Paz Obrajes	Cochabamba, Salvador	Ancoraimes	Trinidad	Corocoro	Viacha	Cholumani
1916	65			14				14	28
1918	63			12			14	4	23
1919				12			18	4	30
1920				12			18		30
1921	32			12			38		30
1922	32			12			39		30
1925	0	37		15			64		
1926		66							
1927		151					61		
1928		231			*		73		
1929		264					75		
1930		414					90		
1931		410							
1933		384							
1934		348							
1935		309		10					
1939		250							
1941		360		12					
1942				18					
1944		386		28	70				
1945			16	28	95				
1947		256	10	37	95				
1950	29	442		35					
1951	44	174		72					

TABLE 7, cont.

Year	La Paz Reforma	La Paz Prado	La Paz Redentor	La Paz Obrajes	Cochabamba, Salvador	Ancoraimes	Trinidad
1952	45	222	13	49	250		
1953	67	222	17	42	231	2	
1954	120	289	21	75	349		
1955	131	269	38	59	310	19	
1956	167	294	45	57	341	27	
1957	194	259	46	52	313	24	
1958	217	271		77	278	34	

*
Some members of the Ancoraimes church are reported by Hamilton (1962:54).

To illustrate the "credibility gap" which often exists between the promotional efforts of the home board and the actual conditions on the field, the following quotation is taken from a report to the Methodist public in the United States in 1923:

> From the day of the opening of the American Institutes in La Paz and Cochabamba they have been outstanding successes ... "The school," says a veteran missionary, "is the most effective evangelizing agency in Bolivia. By means of Bible classes and the Christian example of its teachers, the students are brought to a knowledge of the Christian life. Even though many of them have not linked themselves definitely with the church, they are leading Christian lives, and exerting a wide influence" (Diffendorfer 1923: 154-155).

While there is no question that the institutions were doing a fine job in helping to educate the children of Bolivia's upper classes, graduation from a Christian school should never be confused with commitment to Christ and membership in His

Body. The simple fact is that at that time the institutions were not producing a church nor church growth.

At this time the Baptists agreed to leave the institutional work to the Methodists, and with the exception of the Colegio Reekie in Oruro, they concentrated on evangelization rather than institutions. Nevertheless, it is to be expected that the Colegio Reekie absorbed a disproportionate amount of funds and personnel, thus depriving many of the opportunity of direct church-planting work. Evidently, the combination of congregations in La Paz had begun to cause some friction since in the Canadian Baptist missionary conference of January 1929, Percy Buck said:

> It is not only desirable, but imperative that we discontinue the agreement. The Methodists now have a missionary and a native pastor, and it would be more desirable for each to form its own church with its own doctrines and policies in all honesty (Phillips n.d.:n.p.).

The Methodist mestizo congregation in La Paz, however, did not begin its independent existence again until 1950 (see Table 7).

Before leaving this subject of institutionalism, it would be well to mention the similar frustration which descended upon the Methodist Church in Bolivia during and just after World War II. "The economic crisis in the United States placed in jeopardy its existence" (McCleary 1965:3). In 1942 the United States government accepted the responsibility of the American Institute in La Paz as a last resort to avoid bankruptcy. This arrangement continued until 1949 (Phillips n.d.:n.p.).

Methodism's Nadir. The state of the Methodist Church deteriorated to its lowest point in 1948 when "the Methodist Board of Missions seriously considered an offer to sell Bolivian Methodism to the Lutheran Church" (McCleary 1965:3).

Today, twenty years later, the wisdom of not pulling out is evident to all. It is not only one of the largest and most vigorous Churches in Bolivia, but "the church has grown more rapidly than any other Methodist Church in Latin America" (Methodist Church 1966:363). The reason for this is now evident: "After many years during which large educational and medical institutions dominated the Bolivian Methodist scene, the emphasis has clearly shifted to the development of the church" (Methodist Church 1966:363).

Current Institutional Commitments. Before moving on to describe the recent, exciting growth of the Church, it would be well to mention the institutions other than the American Institutes and the Pfeiffer Memorial Hospital which the Church still operates. They include:

Primary schools: 26 (with 25 around Lake Ancoraimes)
Secondary schools: 1
Student centers: University Student Center and Hostel, Sucre. University Student Center, La Paz. Student work at Warisata government teacher training school.
Community centers: Community center program at Santa Cruz. Merubia Community at Cochabamba.
Agricultural centers: Instituto Rural, Montero. Agricultural Center, Carabuco, Altiplano. Community Development Project, Alto Beni.
Literature centers: Bookstore in La Paz. Distribution and Publication Center, Cochabamba. Literacy program, Santa Cruz. Literacy program, Ancoraimes.
Hospitals and Clinics: School of Nursing, La Paz. Frank S. Beck Clinic, Ancoraimes. Clinic and Medical program, Caranavi. Clinic and Medical program, Montero and colonies.
Seminary: Wesley Seminary, Montero (Methodist Church 1966:363-364).

This list shows that in spite of the shifting of the emphasis from institutions to church, the institutional commitment of the Methodist Church continues to be very deep. Little pulling back in this area is contemplated, since the current request for funds to develop the institutions listed is $437,000 (Methodist Church 1966:367-370). Whereas this type of program can be successful in times of economic prosperity, a change in the world situation, such as a war or depression, may retard not only the institutional work, but the church work as well, since workers will once again need to be pulled out of the church-related ministries to staff the institutions if a personnel shortage presents itself. Sixty-seven missionaries were listed in 1966 (Methodist Church 1966:365).

Church Growth Analyzed

Membership statistics in the Methodist Church will be calculated as the total of full members and probationary members so as to make a meaningful basis of comparison to the other Churches in the country. In many of the other churches in Bolivia, the Christians counted as probationary members of the Methodist Church would be regarded as full members, and in some they would have been baptized. Total membership figures are given in Table 8, and the growth of the Church plotted on Figure 7. The location of the principal Methodist centers is shown on Figure 8.

TABLE 8

The Methodist Church in Bolivia 1901 - 1967

Date	Foreign Workers	National Workers	Churches	Full Members	Total Members	Source
1910	-	-	-	34	-	CGRILA
1911	-	1	3	34	136	Dennis 1911:97
1916	23	3	6	78	113	M.E.C.;Beach 1916:73
1918	-	-	6	56	116	M.E.C.
1919	-	-	5	14	64	M.E.C.
1920	-	-	4	14	60	M.E.C.
1921	-	-	4	56	112	M.E.C.
1922	-	-	4	45	113	M.E.C.
1925	34	3	3	58	116	M.E.C.;Beach 1925
1926	-	-	3	137	169	M.E.C.
1927	-	-	3	205	212	M.E.C.
1928	-	-	3	256	304	M.E.C.
1929	-	-	3	291	339	M.E.C.
1930	-	-	3	450	504	M.E.C.
1938	17	59	7	334	643	Parker 1938:119
1939	-	-	-	294	833	M.E.C.
1941	-	-	-	172	450	M.E.C.
1942	-	-	-	150	350	M.E.C.
1944	-	-	-	215	484	M.E.C.
1945	-	-	-	253	295	M.E.C.
1947	-	-	-	347	395	M.E.C.

TABLE 8, cont.

Date	Foreign Workers	National Workers	Churches	Full Members	Total Members	Source
1949	17	4	7	347	398	WCH 1949
1950	-	-	-	342	676	M.E.C.
1951	-	-	-	398	784	M.E.C.
1952	30	29	7	282	590	M.E.C.;WCH 1952
1953	-	-	-	260	582	M.E.C.
1954	-	-	-	440	880	M.E.C.
1955	-	-	-	391	836	M.E.C.
1956	-	-	-	543	956	M.E.C.
1957	32	6	17	570	921	M.E.C.;WCH 1957
1958	-	-	-	654	1076	M.E.C.
1959	-	45	-	742	1365	IMB*
1960	-	41	-	858	1624	IMB
1961	-	36	-	955	1690	IMB
1962	56	15	44	1082	1852	IMB
1963	-	-	-	1163	2143	IMB
1964	-	-	-	1386	2448	IMB
1966	-	-	-	2011	3336	IMB
1967	65	162	35	-	3480	CGRILA 1967; WCH 1967

* Iglesia Metodista en Bolivia

Methodist growth (Figure 7) falls into four rather definite periods.

PERIOD I: 1911 - 1925

The first statistics show that the Methodist Church had 136 members in 1911, and in 1925 the figure had remained virtually the same at 116. During this time from three to six congregations were functioning, and the work was built mainly around the mestizos in La Paz and Cochabamba, undoubtedly by contacts made through the American Institutes in those cities. These churches would probably have been composed of those who could afford to keep their children in the schools, and therefore of a higher economic status. Since the membership of the Cochabamba church remained rather constantly at around 12, not many more than the school staff

LOCATIONS OF PRINCIPAL METHODIST CHURCHES

FIGURE 8

Source: Methodist Church 1966:362

could have been members.
   The most notable growth of the time took place in the
Corocoro church. As Hamilton explains (1962:53-54), these
believers were won in several small Aymara villages around
the mestizo village of Corocoro, and their names were
included on the rolls of the place where the pastor who
worked the circuit lived. During this period the membership
rose from 14 to 64, and most likely was a small people
movement. If at that point resources could have been taken
from the institutional work in the cities and shifted to the
Aymara communities north of Lake Titicaca, great growth might
have resulted.

PERIOD II: 1925 - 1939

   This period shows a total growth of 116 to 833 members, a
per decade rate of 440 percent, which is excellent. In 1924,
the merger of the La Paz and Cochabamba congregations with the
Baptists came about, and they ceased to report. Where, then
was the growth? Again, it came among the Aymara Indians, this
time not only those in the Lake Titicaca area, but also those
in the city of La Paz. In La Paz the El Redentor Aymara
church made its first report of 37 members in 1925. By 1939
it had 250 members, having hit its peak in 1930 with 414.
Aymara believers who moved into the city from the country
areas joined this church, and it flourished. Plans had been
made to construct a building for this church when the
depression cut funds in 1930.

> The missionary had to tell the enthusiastic congregation
> that funds had been curtailed. The response was immediate.
> We can build ourselves! Laymen volunteered labour and work
> began in July, 1930. The church seating 300 people was
> finished and dedicated in December of the same year
> (Hamilton 1962:55).

This is when membership was at its highest, but the church
remained the backbone of the denomination, membershipwise,
and is still the largest church.
   Whereas the drop in El Redentor membership was probably
largely due to the manpower drain of the Chaco War, the drop
in the Corocoro church was due mainly to the depression. By
1930 Corocoro had increased to 90 members. Both churches
were tied to schools, day schools for the children and night
schools for the adults. The classic pattern of church

decline when associated with institutions operated in Corocoro when "due to the depression ... Corocoro's school was closed and effective church supervision ceased" (Hamilton 1962:55). If the movement toward Christ could have been maintained in the Corocoro area such as it was in the Ancoraimes area, the total growth would have been much more than 440 percent per decade.

PERIOD III: 1939 - 1957

During this period, a decline through World War II and slow growth afterward reduced the per decade growth rate from 440 percent to 1.07 percent, virtually nothing.

The losses took place in the 1939 to 1945 period. Hamilton suggests the following reasons:

> Reversions to the world, members "lost" by transferring territory to other missions, concentration on the school and church in La Paz city, deaths in the Chaco War and severe persecutions, including martyrdom of five Christians in the Ancoraimes area in 1942 - all were contributing factors in the decrease ... The basic cause, however, was due to the reduction of personnel and funds. This precisely indicates one of the greatest weaknesses of the mission station approach which, relying primarily on foreign resources, suffers immediate reversals when these are curtailed (1962:55-56).

From 1945 on, growth increased because for one thing the La Paz and Cochabamba mestizo churches began to function once again as Methodist churches, and exceptional growth took place in the Ancoraimes Aymara region north of Lake Titicaca. Membership rose from 95 to 341 in a ten-year period, a 260 percent per decade rate.

PERIOD IV: 1957 - 1967

The "Land of Decision." In 1956 Bolivia was declared by the Methodist Church in the USA as a "Land of Decision," and a massive push in terms of resources, study, analysis, dedication and redefinition of goals was undertaken. Under the over-all leadership of Bishop Sante Uberto Barbieri from Buenos Aires, and the direct supervision of Paul McCleary, Executive Secretary of the Bolivian Annual Conference, the program has been an outstanding success from almost every point of view. The sustained growth rate over this period has been a vigorous 253 percent per decade.

Waskom Pickett's Visits. Creative thinking and courageous action on the part of the Methodist leadership is ultimately responsible for this renewed growth. One of the great pioneers of church growth theory, Bishop J. Waskom Pickett (whose *Christ's Way to India's Heart* remains a missionary classic), was sent to Bolivia for consultation in 1957 and again in 1959 (Hamilton 1962:80). Then Keith Hamilton, himself a Methodist, studied in the Institute of Church Growth, then located in Eugene, Oregon, and published his *Church Growth in the High Andes*, the first look at this vast and responsive area through church growth eyes, in 1962. Hamilton also convened a Consultation on Andean Indian Work in 1964. The cumulative effect of these studies was the increased emphasis on church planting already mentioned. For almost sixty years the Methodist Church had just been playing with church growth as almost a superficial justification for the existence of their institutions. Around 1960, however, church multiplication and growth was adopted as a supreme goal, and the statistics point up the outstanding success the Church has had.

McCleary describes this shift of emphasis in these words:

> the institutional work experienced a serious re-orientation. Now institutional work was being started, but less for the motive of evangelism and more for the purpose of providing Christian service. The large institutions continued, but new work took on the form of mobile, service agencies which needed little or no home base for operations (1965:5).

This is an important philosophy. Methodist institutions had not been successful as evangelistic tools because they were too big and too deeply rooted. Whether the "mobile" institutions will retard or stimulate church growth in the future remains to be seen.

The current Methodist policy on schools indicates that they are cutting back on this program rather radically. Three guidelines are now in effect, according to Paul McCleary:

1) Do away with the schools which the government will assume responsibility for. In 1955 the Methodist Church operated 40 grade schools on the Altiplano. Today they have only 3.

2) Where the school is no longer needed due to the

availability of government or other private schools, close the school.

3) Some institutions, like the American Institutes, are too large and represent too heavy an investment to turn over to the government. Studies are under way to discover how present structures can be modified to meet the demands of changing social conditions.

Ministerial Training. A definite effort was begun to train Bolivian ministers during this period. Instead of continuing to send candidates to the Union Seminary in Buenos Aires, a Bolivian institution named Wesley Seminary was established in Montero, north of Santa Cruz. Full scholarships were provided for students there. Funds were forthcoming from the USA to subsidize pastors' salaries, and several from other denominations were attracted to the Methodist ministry. Capable national leadership was rapidly acquired and developed. At the present time, five of the six district superintendents are nationals.

Laymen the Key. A new effort to train and involve laymen in the development of the Church was inaugurated during this period, and has given good results. The Methodist Church has now appointed one of its top men, Mortimer Arias, to the position of Director of the "Department of Lay Training." As trained laymen are brought into positions of responsibility in the Church, the work will continue to grow. Derby and Ellis cite the "dedicated efforts of laymen" as one of the reasons for growth, and go on to say, "Every organized church in Bolivia has at least one additional outpost where laymen of the church conduct regular services of worship and study" (1961:140).

Mobility and Responsiveness. Today McCleary attributes the seeking out of those who have moved geographically and thus are "ready to make changes socially, economically and religiously," as the "key to growth in Methodism" (1968:1). The Methodists are looking at Bolivia in terms of a mosaic of ethnic groups, some more responsive than others. Their strategy is to move into the responsive groups and reap the harvest. Their good growth in the 1930;s came from Aymaras who were moving into the city. Much of their growth now is among those who are moving to the lowland colonies. This fruitful area will be described in more detail in Chapter 10.

Will Methodist churches continue to grow? The several steps mentioned above will undoubtedly carry them forward. Still there are some weak spots to be considered. Hamilton in 1962 warned against using schools to enter new territories. McCleary says that institutions are no longer used for evangelism. But even though the foreign money invested in institutions is not tied directly to church growth, one wonders if the Bolivian Church would ever be able or even willing to maintain the institutions as "avenues of Christian service" if something happened to the foreign subsidies. Instead of reducing investment in institutions, the Church is asking at the present time for $437,000 more. Foreign funds are also used to pay the lion's share of the Bolivian ministers' salaries, and to pay full scholarships to the seminary. An appeal is presently out in the USA for a total of $204,600 for the purchase of properties and construction of churches and parsonages. In addition $100,000 is being requested for a revolving loan fund. This type of heavy foreign financing poses problems. If wisely used, it can help lay the base for good future church growth. On the other hand, it could make the national Church all too dependent on subsidies from the outside. The Methodist churches are now on a program of attaining self-support within the next few years. Whether this will come about will depend on the economic progress of Bolivia and the firmness with which the United States mission board cuts down its subsidies to the churches.

THE EVANGELICAL CHRISTIAN UNION
(Unión Cristiana Evangélica)

The Evangelical Christian Union, Bolivia's largest denomination after the Seventh-day Adventist Church, is the offspring of several foreign mission groups. The major mission contributing to its development was the Andes Evangelical Mission (until 1964 the Bolivian Indian Mission). The Evangelical Union of South America (American Section) brought its national churches into the organization in 1959. The Midnight Call Mission (Missionswerk Mitternachtsruf) from Zurich, has also expressed its desire for affiliation with the ECU. The present administration of the ECU is encouraging other national churches, especially those planted by faith missions, to join with them.

The office of the ECU breaks membership figures into three categories: baptized members, non-baptized members, and community (Torres 1967:1). For the purpose of comparative study the total of baptized and non-baptized members will be used, as was done in the case of the Methodist Church.

The Andes Evangelical Mission

George Allan. Roots of the Evangelical Christian Union go back to 1903, when George and Mary Allan moved from Argentina to Cochabamba. They had gone out from New Zealand in 1899 under the South American Evangelical Mission of Toronto after establishing an Australasian council for that mission at Toronto's request. In 1902 the Toronto council disbanded and merged with the Regions Beyond Missionary Union. The British council became one of the founding members of the Evangelical Union of South America. By correspondence, Allan pulled the councils in Australia and New Zealand together into a new organization he called the Australasian South American Mission, but the group was short-lived. To complete the story, Allan journeyed to England in 1907 and formed the first council of the Bolivian Indian Mission, then in 1908 reformed councils in Australia and in his native New Zealand (Goddard 1967:33,264,601; see Figure 9). The Dunedin council was virtually a continuation of the ASAM (Hudspith 1958:38).

From the beginning, Allan felt called to reach the Quechua Indians in Bolivia. Back in 1902 Will Payne wrote of Allan's desire to "engage in aggressive Gospel work among the many Quechua-speaking people of this district" (Payne and Wilson 1904). Allan made his first trip to Bolivia with Charles T. W. Wilson and Pedro Guerrero, leaving Buenos Aires on August 30, 1902. Of the trip, Wilson later wrote:

> The Roman Catholics of South America need the pure, unadulterated Gospel of Jesus Christ just as much as the heathen in China, Africa or India. Not one in a thousand has the least idea of what spiritual or eternal life is, and the dozen priests with whom I have spoken were also sadly in the dark as to these things (Payne and Wilson 1904:41).

As a result of the trip, Allan decided to move his family to the city of Cochabamba in 1903. There he studied Quechua, and with the help of Bolivians Antonio Salazar and Moisés Orruel worked on the translation of the Gospel of John into Quechua. He also visited San Pedro de Buena Vista which was one of the strategic centers of Quechua movement, and decided to make that town his headquarters after he had taken a

HISTORICAL DEVELOPMENT OF THE EVANGELICAL CHRISTIAN UNION

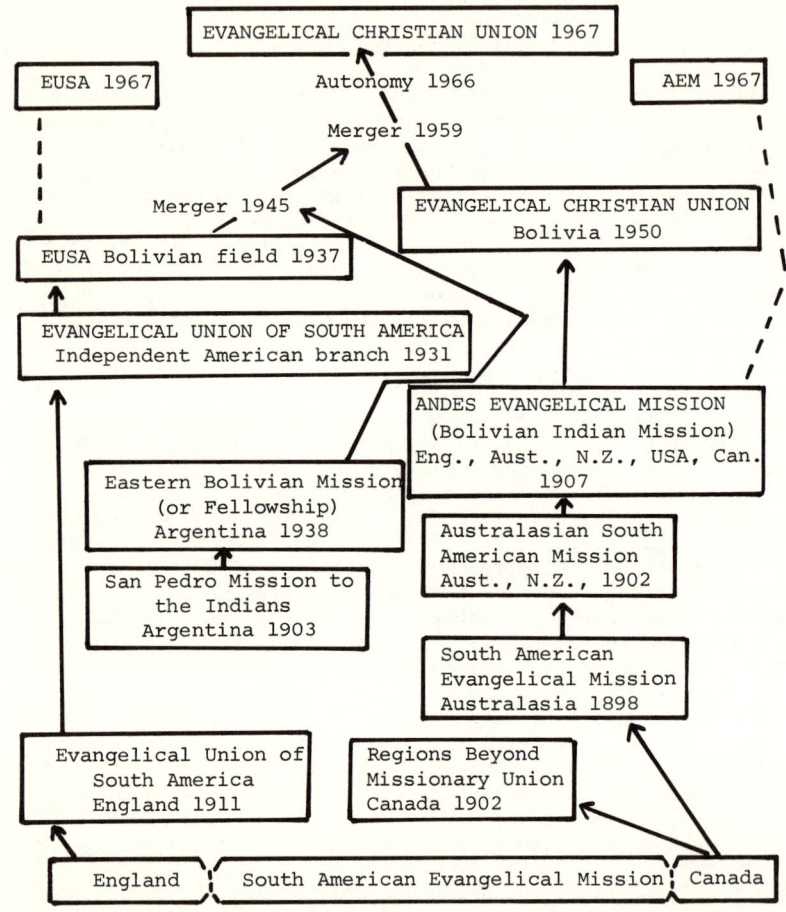

FIGURE 9

Sources: Goddard 1967:33,232,264,601; Grubb 1938:12

furlough (Hudspith 1958:33-34).

Arriving in San Pedro in 1909, Allan kept the mission headquarters there for twenty-five years until it was moved to Cochabamba in 1934. The mission at that time had no interest in ministry to other than the Indian population of Bolivia. Concerning the rural nature of the AEM, Grubb writes in 1930 that the BIM

> has studiously avoided the cities and sought to occupy the pueblos (villages) of the Indians. Some of the smaller groups are not sufficiently equipped to meet the changing outlook and thought characteristic of the larger cities, and in this respect they have realized their true genius and have taken up work in the country to the undoubted benefit of the rural inhabitants (Browning 1930:32).

The Place of Institutions. Being a faith mission, and therefore lacking the support of an affluent denomination in the homelands, the AEM did not have the funds to build expensive institutions such as the American Institutes or the Colegio Reekie. If they had the resojrces, they undoubtedly would have undertaken more extensive social work, since no difference in thinking between such men as Allan, Reekie or Beck is detected in the early records. Even in the AEM "schools and medical work were the chief means used for gaining an entrance into new places" (Hudspith 1958:43). George Allan wrote, for example, that the Indians had looms and

> as this mountainous province is better adapted for running sheep than for grain growing, we hope to try and help the Indians improve their weaving industry (1920:n.p.).

Other records show Allan from time to time desirous of receiving subsidy from the Bolivian government for schools. While they may not have realized it at the time, this poverty was probably a blessing in disguise since it kept the AEM mobile, free from the binding moral commitments that permanent institutions produce.

Partially with labor provided by local authorities, Bolivia's first Protestant church building was completed in San Pedro (Phillips n.d.:n.p.). Because it was so long and narrow, it was affectionately nicknamed "The Railway Carriage" (Hudspith 1958:70).

Slow Progress 1903-1934. 1903 to 1934 was a time of very slow and difficult growth. Missionaries were sent to towns and ranches in the valleys surrounding San Pedro but conversions were few, and those who came to the Lord did so usually against the social opinion of their own groups. Verne D. Roberts was the first to break away from the San Pedro district and go to the mestizo town of Aiquile, planting enduring churches there and in the neighboring town of Misque. Persecution was strong and both George Allan and Kenneth Powlison were imprisoned, the latter for an extended period of time (Hudspith 1958:77-79).

Study of the Indian language was stressed during this period. Horace Grocott wrote, "in working among an Indian community, the missionary must have a knowledge of Castellano as well as of the language of the particular Indians among whom he is located" (1960:30). Allan would gather his fellow workers for prayer each evening and have them all read from their Spanish and Quechua Bibles. The day that Max Rohrsetzer brought the first Quechua grammars from Buenos Aires was a red-letter occasion. "Just what we had been praying for," exclaimed Grocott (1960:31-32).

The Quechua New Testament. The translation of the Quechua New Testament was beyond doubt George Allan's major contribution to Bolivian church growth other than his founding of the AEM. Stillwell of the Canadian Baptists wrote after a visit to Bolivia,

> The one outstanding event in the history of Evangelical Missions in Bolivia is the translation of the New Testament into Quechua by the Bolivian Indian Mission (Hudspith 1958: 48).

The detailed story of this epochal work is told by Allan's daughter, Margarita Hudspith, in her history of the AEM, *Ripening Fruit* (1958:48-57). Suffice it to say here that as a result of over six years' work with Crisólogo Barrón, the work was finished in 1920, and the first shipment of Testaments, published by the American Bible Society, arrived in 1923.

From San Pedro, workers, armed with their Bibles, simple medicines and rudimentary Quechua, moved out into the Pocoata valley, Puna, Punutuma, Pancoche, Caiza, Vilacaya, the Tomoyo valley, Aicarapi, Encuyo, and other places. In spite of this effort, there were probably not more than 300 believers in

1934. The only evidence I have been able to find of an incipient people movement was in the ranch of Quesimpuco (Hudspith 1958:107). This church remains strong today, and has even sent missionaries out to reach neighboring tribes such as the Jucumani.

The Transition to the City. A shift of emphasis in the mission work began when headquarters were moved from San Pedro to Cochabamba in 1934. Analyzing the situation, Grubb gave the following reasons for the move:

> need of a better situated headquarters, the dislocation caused by the Chaco War, the desire to evangelize new territory, concentration upon work among the Indians, and the growing strength of the local church in certain places where the continual presence of a missionary is, in consequence, no longer necessary (1938:11-12).

But even after arriving in the city there was no thought of ministry to other than the rural Indian population. Cochabamba was simply a base of operations. The missionaries attended the Baptist Church on Calle Calama, and encouraged their country believers to attend there when they came into the city. The man who pioneered the break from strictly rural work to a ministry to the urban population was Verne Roberts, the same person who first pulled the work out of the immediate San Pedro area. In spite of opposition from some other missionaries, with his own funds he purchased a choice property near the central plaza in Cochabamba and constructed the Calle Bolivar Church, which has remained one of Bolivia's largest and most influential congregations.

Ministerial Training. The first formal Bible institute for Quechua believers was held on the mission property in San Pedro in 1936, led by Leslie Shedd (*Andean Outlook* 1967:6,8). In 1938, Verne Roberts held the first Spanish Bible institute on his farm outside of Cochabamba. These efforts led to the permanent establishment of the denomination's two main centers for training the ministry, the Quillacollo Bible Institute (1945) for rural pastors and the Emmaus Bible Institute (1946) for *mestizo*, urban pastors. These institutions have played a major role in providing the leadership for the development of the Evangelical Christian Union and the growth of the Church. A fruitful area for further study would be determining the cost of preparation on the part of the mission in producing each pastor. (Purely as a matter of interest, both Shedd and Roberts, each in their 47th year of missionary service, are active in Bolivia as this is being written.) Subsequently other Bible institutes have been located in Sucre, Pocoata and Guayaramerín for training rural pastors.

The Beni. Allan was not only interested in reaching the highland Indians with the Gospel, but the lowland Indians challenged him as well. In 1923 he toured the vast Beni region with Henry Webendorfer, preliminary to opening work there (Allan 1936:34-37). In 1928 the first resident missionaries moved into the area with the intention of evangelizing the jungle Indians (*Andean Outlook* 1967:5). The direction of this work changed in 1935, however, when younger missionaries, Wally Herron and Alec Clark, after an extensive survey, "recommended that the AEM concentrate its Beni program, not on the savage Indians, but on the unevangelized centers of population" (Wagner and McCullough 1966:35). These centers of population were mostly former Jesuit reductions which had their social life closely integrated with the Catholic Church and proved to be relatively resistant. Growth of churches in this area has come more from a multiplication of small groups rather than large congregations in one place. Exceptions to this have been the towns of Magdalena and Baures whose Protestant churches were planted by Wally Herron, an unusually capable worker who used his air and medical ministries to great advantage in winning the people.

Small People Movements. Around 1945 some small people movements began. Hamilton says there were three but unfortunately does not identify the areas he discusses (1962:34). Mrs. Hudspith tells the story of two of these in detail (1958: 111-117), and the outlines bear repeating. Larry and Mary Alice Maze opened the work in the mestizo town of Challapata in 1936, providing a base for reaching the highland Indian population round about. The church in the town itself has not grown, but the Gospel has spread among the peasants out on the ranches. Several missionaries were deployed in the region, maintaining a high degree of mobility, although Challapata itself became a "mission station" with a large property used for Indian gatherings. In one of the small ranches, Eldon Johnson led a Quechua, Ciprián Quispe, to Christ. His tribe, as Hamilton points out, was "tribally-speaking Aymara, i.e., in 1532 they spoke Aymara" (1962:34), although they had since switched to Quechua. In the Pajake ranch itself a small group of Christians was formed. The Johnsons spent only a year in Pajake, but after they left, the work continued to spread into neighboring ranches through the witness of Quispe and other Christians. In 1957 there were over 700 believers, representing over eighty different ranches and villages.

The Gospel spread from there to the Carangas Aymara region, located on the Altiplano southwest of Oruro. An Aymara from Andamarca in the Carangas province on the other side of Lake Poopo came to Quispe's ranch to sell salt, and stayed overnight. Quispe witnessed to him and he became a believer. He went back to Carangas a new creature in Christ and in turn witnessed to his own people.

Then in 1946 the First Indian Political Congress was held in La Paz. Mrs. Hudspith tells the story in these words:

> Thousands of Indians gathered from all corners of Bolivia. Ciprián, with two years' experience in Christ, attended this Congress. Around 150 to 200 Indians were quartered in a large room. The one in charge of the room where Ciprián was quartered had apparently heard of the Gospel. He asked if there were any evangelicals present. Three men stood up. The leader asked if one would explain the Gospel to them. Ciprián seemed to be the most qualified of the three, so he began. He preached the Gospel to them for three or four hours. Then, after taking time out to eat, he continued until evening. By this time, he was hoarse and weary. However, his hearers were not satisfied and continued to ask questions. He answered questions and continued explaining until time to retire. This continued for three days.... Later events seem to indicate that this was responsible for the awakened interest in the Gospel in the Carangas Province (1958:114).

Both the AEM and the Canadian Baptists recognized the ripe harvest field in Carangas, so they divided the territory with the Baptists to the north of Corque and the AEM to the south. A detailed study of the resulting people movement in this area would prove most fruitful for clues as to future church growth among highland Indians. The webs of family relationships along which the Gospel spread would undoubtedly reveal how the "bridges of God" are being crossed among this people.

Figure 10 shows the location of principal AEM works.

LOCATIONS OF PRINCIPAL STATIONS
OF THE ANDES EVANGELICAL MISSION

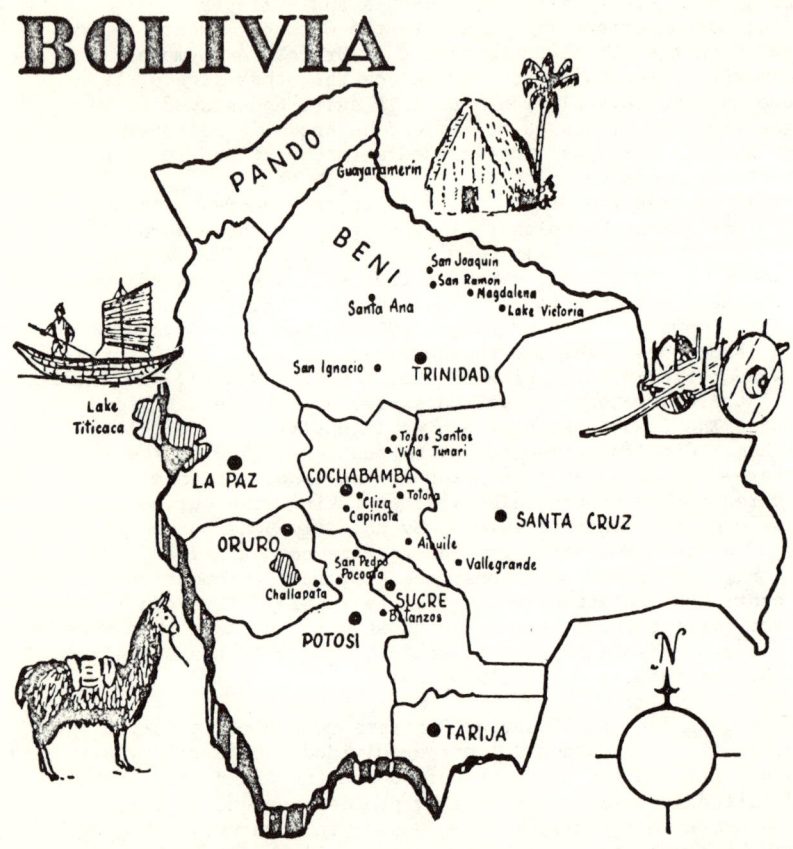

FIGURE 10

Source: AEM Prayer Calendar 1967

The Evangelical Union of South America

In 1931 the American council of the EUSA became independent of the British, and then sent its first missionaries to Bolivia in 1937. Cook, Winstanley and Bowman were the first workers (Phillips n.d.:n.p.). With the goal of evangelizing the Quechua Indians, they opened work in Aripalka in the Department of Potosí with the consent of the Brethren already in the area (Grubb 1938:12). Later they moved into the Department of Sucre and the southern tip of the Department of Santa Cruz. Their work has largely been evangelistic and church planting. Many of their churches have been started among the large population of Guaraní Indians found in the Camiri region.

A group called the San Pedro Mission to the Indians, founded in San Pedro de Jujuy, Argentina, in 1903, had been carrying on a small work in the same area. In 1938 it had become known as The Eastern Bolivian Mission (Goddard 1967: 232;see Figure 9). In 1945, this group merged its work among the Chane and Chiriguano Indians (Goddard 1967:232) at places like San Antonio de Parapetí (Crivelli 1933:409-414) with the Evangelical Union of South America.

For the training of the Bolivian ministry in the churches planted by the mission, the EUSA has established Hebron Bible Institute in Camiri. The institution operates two sections which are kept distinct, one for Spanish-speaking pastors and one for Guaraní-speaking pastors. This institution has graduated some fine workers and leaders. The missionary force for the EUSA is normally 30-35, and for the AEM 75-90.

Formation of the Evangelical Christian Union

Indigenous church principles were known by the early leaders of the AEM, and attempts were made to practice them whenever possible. They were not, however, bound by them to the extent that they were willing to allow them to retard the work, as perhaps the Brethren did. In 1928, for example, the AEM decided to cease mission support to national workers beginning January 1929. Field Council struggled with this, however, and finally decided "while recognizing that the establishing of a self-supporting and self-propagating indigenous church is their objective, the Council felt that the time was not yet ripe for the discontinuance of native evangelists supported from the homelands" (Browning 1930:140).

By 1950 some forty places of worship had been founded, some

of these churches being pastored by missionaries and some by nationals (see Table 9). The churches were located among

TABLE 9

Evangelical Christian Union 1903 - 1967
(Includes Andes Evangelical Mission and Evangelical Union of South America)

Date	Foreign Workers	National Workers	Churches	Baptized Members	Total Members	Source
1911	9	-	-	-	-	Dennis 1911:97
1916	12	2	-	4	-	Beach 1916:73
1920	-	-	-	-	25	CGRILA 1967
1925	40	2	1	1	1	Beach 1925
1930	-	-	-	-	200	CGRILA 1967
1938	53	3	1	-	-	Parker 1938:119
1940	-	-	-	-	415	CGRILA 1967
1949	64	29	40	333	538	*WCH* 1949
1950	-	-	-	-	625	CGRILA 1967
1952	94	29	40	333	538	*WCH* 1952
1957	104	36	109	885	2962	*WCH* 1957
1960	-	-	-	1537	-	CGRILA 1967
1962	81	69	152	1557	5549	*WCH* 1962
1967	98	117	213	2955	9229	Torres 1967:1

country Quechuas and Aymaras, village mestizos, city mestizos, and lowland mestizos. Some leaders had been trained in the Bible institutes, and one had studied in the Latin American Bible Seminary in San José, Costa Rica. The time seemed ripe both to missionaries and nationals to

> organize these churches into a solid entity on the foundation of Jesus Christ, with the purpose of cooperating in prayer, in defense of common interests and liberties, and above all to unite efforts to preach the Holy Gospel, making provision for pastors of the churches and financing their support (Torres 1965:1).

On April 30, 1950, representatives of the Calle Bolivar

Pioneer Church-planters 83

Church of Cochabamba, the Calle Esteban Arze Church also of Cochabamba, and the churches of Aiquile and Capinota, two mestizo towns, met and formed the ECU with the counsel of two missionaries from the AEM. The AEM agreed to provide support for recognized pastors, and the ECU agreed to attempt to raise funds for the support of its own workers as soon as possible. A representative of the AEM was included as a voting member of the ECU Board of Directors.

Dangers in a Multicultural Church. Church growth experts will at once see certain problems inherent in this organization. For one thing, despite the fact that most of the members of the newly formed denomination were full-blooded Quechuas or Aymaras, it was a group of four mestizo churches in consultation with missionaries who actually formed the structure, a structure which was then to be presided over by a Board of Directors that was foreign and mestizo. Furthermore, the promised foreign subsidy for pastors could become a drawback in the future. This is undoubtedly what precipitated Hamilton's remarks:

> growth is retarded because the BIM is no longer an "Indian Mission," but a "Mestizo-Indian-Mission-Church." Control rests not in the Mission, but in the "Church plus Mission." Effort is no longer focused exclusively on the Indian. It falls on the Mestizos fully as much as on the Indians. To attain maximum growth in Indian churches, we must ask if Mestizo pastors can reach Indians as well as their own kind can do? (1962:77).

Hamilton did his research when this was still a live question, but in spite of the danger signs to which he rightly points, the ECU has thus far shown very good growth, second only to the Seventh-day Adventists. How can this be explained?

Joseph McCullough

In 1956 a new epoch began in the AEM with the arrival of Joseph S. McCullough in Bolivia as General Director. McCullough, who had spent one term with the Quechua Indians in the Department of Potosí, and had then served as North American Home Director for many years, gave top priority to the development of the national church organization. After a careful study of the situation, he projected four important steps which were carried out within one decade.

Merger with the EUSA. The first step was a broadening of the base by encouraging the merger of the national churches born of the work of the EUSA. In 1959 they entered the ECU. The figures for 1959 are not available, but in 1965 their district had 22 national pastors and 55 churches and congregations (Torres 1965:1).

Decentralization. The second step was perhaps the most significant for future growth. Recognizing both the danger of overcentralization of ecclesiastical authority and the need for closer supervision of the churches in particular districts, a plan for decentralization of the ECU was undertaken. It must be remembered that both the AEM and the EUSA are interdenominational missions. Many missionaries, especially from the USA, participated in the faith-mission movement as a part of widespread protest against the abuse of denominational power during the fundamentalist-modernist conflicts of the twenties and thirties. The missionaries felt they had been burned by denominations and were not going to take the risk that the same thing happen in Bolivia. As a matter of fact, as late as 1964 I heard an experienced missionary tell a group of visitors that the Calle Bolivar church was "interdenominational." For many years, mission leaders refused to recognize the fact that their interdenominational missions had created a denomination in Bolivia.

This anti-denominational instinct was surely one of the considerations which impelled the leaders to decentralize. Challapata led the way by forming its own Board of Directors sometime around 1957 (Hudspith 1958:113). This was made up of Quechuas, not mestizos. Carangas then set up their Aymara Board, and Pocoata a Quechua Board. When the EUSA churches entered, they formed a Mestizo-Guaraní Board. Now the ECU has nine regional "sub-committees," which supervise the churches in their areas, pool support for some pastors, coordinate regional Bible conferences, handle local discipline problems, and relate their churches to the Cochabamba ECU office. While some of these boards operate more effectively than others, the principle of decentralization may in general be a sound church growth principle where a multicultural denomination is involved. This procedure has probably done much to avoid the dangers which Hamilton indicated.

Self-support of Pastors. The third step suggested by McCullough was the most painful. From 1950 to 1965, the ECU had come to the point where it was only providing 30 percent of its budget, with the AEM providing the other 70 (Torres 1965:1). Rather than improving, the situation appeared to be worsening. The AEM decided to give the ECU adequate notice (predictably considered inadequate by the ECU) that from September 1, 1963, each church would be expected to support its own pastor. All were in favor of withdrawal, but the question was whether it should be gradual or abrupt. It was decided that the most effective step would be abrupt withdrawal, recognizing at the same time that this is the most difficult arrangement for both parties. It did not hinder the growth rate in the slightest, however (see Figure 11). Other factors such as the social effects of the Revolution of 1952 undoubtedly influenced this growth, but the self-support of the pastors cannot be overlooked.

ECU Autonomy. The fourth step was a logical one. The ECU needed its complete autonomy from the foreign missions. The AEM counselor continued on the Board of Directors, and the AEM continued to help financially with projects which were presented by the Church, but accepted or rejected by the decision of the mission. The EUSA continued to subsidize part of the support of the pastors under its sub-committee. In 1966 the AEM and the EUSA jointly granted autonomy to the ECU. The missionary would no longer serve on the Board, and financial assistance for the administration would be given by the mission in a monthly sum granted on the faith principle, with no strings attached. The ECU would be completely responsible for its own administration and financial matters.

Restructuring. Each of these key steps spurred the ECU on to new efforts and continued growth. The next step, a result of the planning of ECU President Jaime Ríos, will be a restructuring of the Board of Directors of the ECU so as to give more of a voice to the sub-committees and to allow the foreign missions which cooperate with the ECU a voice (but not a vote) in administrative matters.

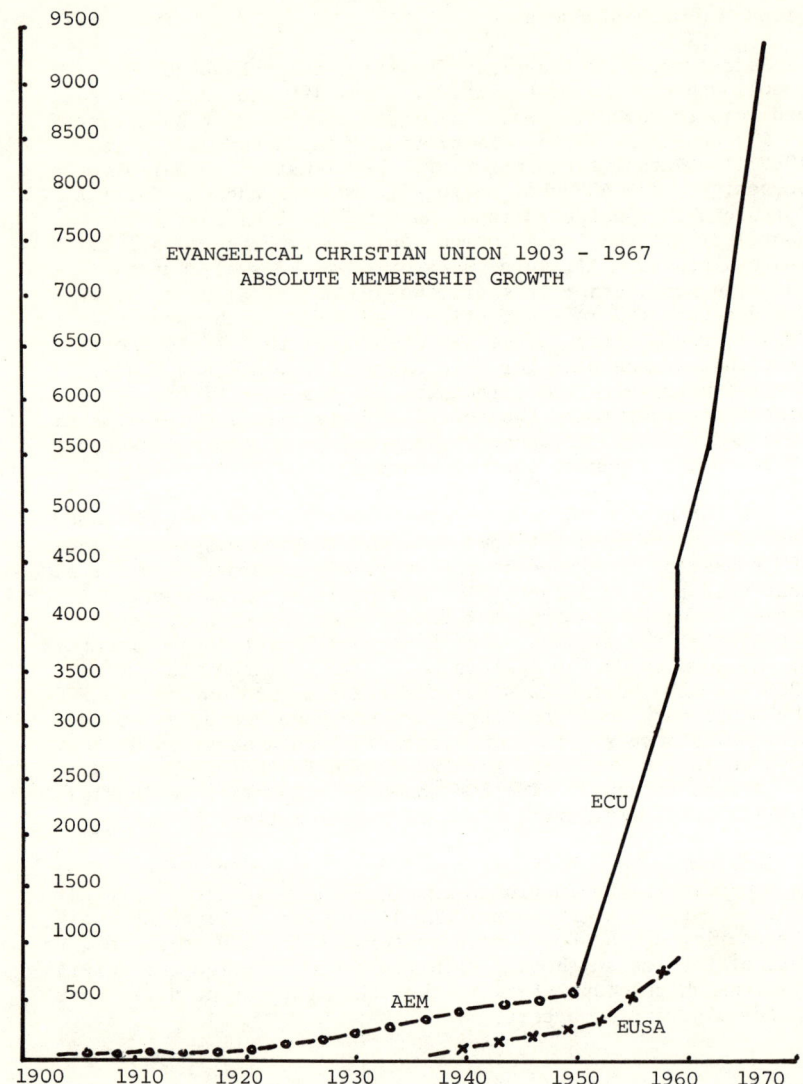

FIGURE 11

SEVENTH-DAY ADVENTISTS
(Adventistas del Séptimo Día)

The Seventh-day Adventists were the last of the five pioneer missions to establish work in Bolivia, entering in 1907. It required five years of work to celebrate the first baptism (1912), six to establish the first Sabbath School (1913), and thirteen to begin rapid growth (1920). But once it started, the Church grew more rapidly than any other in Bolivia. In September 1956, 1,137 converts were baptized in one day - a number which at that time exceeded the entire membership of all except two of the other Protestant denominations.

Position in the Protestant Community. Curiously, many of the other Protestants do not realize that the SDA Church has shown such rapid and sustained growth. This is partly due to a lack of communication between Adventists and non-Adventists. Many non-Adventists consider the insistence on Christians' keeping the law on the part of the Adventists, not as a doctrinal point upon which flexibility can be allowed, but as a heresy. This, as well as unpleasant experiences of believers from the other denominations being "converted" to the SDA Church and doctrine, have caused mainline Protestants to accuse Adventists of "sheep stealing" and to isolate them, not inviting them to participate in ministerial associations or in other joint efforts. On the other side, the Adventists themselves have not seemed particularly anxious to relate to other Protestants, but have been content to go it alone. Neely expressed the fel ing of many Protestants of the day when he wrote in 1906:

> Indeed the most the Seventh-day Adventists seem to accomplish is to give trouble to other missionary organizations by trying to disturb the minds of the converts in regard to the day on which the Sabbath should be observed (1906:70).

Disturbing the minds of others, however, cannot be a full explanation of the unusual success enjoyed by the SDAs both in Bolivia and Peru, especially among the Aymaras.

Juan Pereira. Adventists trace the beginnings of their witness in Bolivia to the visit of Juan S. Pereira in 1897. As the *Missionary Magazine* for January 1899 (p. 13) reported:

The last message has been taken to Bolivia by a colporteur named Pereira. He was a former colporteur for the Presbyterians who have a Bible Society established in Valparaiso, but he was discharged from their service for propagating Seventh-day Adventist doctrine, as was made public in the annual calendar of the society. Brother Pereira went to Bolivia at his own expense. He was arrested at the instigation of a priest for selling bad books ... However, he remained and continued his work for 18 months (SDA 1966:142).

Edward W. Thomann. Edward W. Thomann and José Luis Escobar visited La Paz, Cochabamba and Oruro in 1902 to investigate the possibilities of establishing permanent SDA work and sell literature. They decided that the time to enter was not yet propitious because of the lack of religious toleration. But as soon as the religious liberty law was passed in 1906, the Adventists began to make plans for moving in. Thomann himself was the man chosen to pioneer the work. He and his wife spent some time in Oruro in 1907, then settled in Cochabamba to reach the mestizos, the Quechuas and the Aymaras. In 1909 they left for Chile and Ferdinand A. Stahl took their place. Stahl, author of the book *In the Land of the Incas,* used medical work as a means of reaching the people. He baptized the first full convert, Rosa N. Doering, in 1912 (SDA 1966: 142-143).

Effects of the Peruvian People Movement. Very little growth was experienced until 1920. The SDA *Encyclopedia* (p. 143) blames this small growth on the inability of the missionaries to withstand the harmful effects of the high altitude. No doubt, this had much to do with it, but growth at the same altitude did begin in 1920. The change was not so much geographical as ethnic. Stahl had been sent to Peru to help Manuel Zúñiga Camacho in the exciting people movement among the Peruvian Aymaras in 1911 (Kessler 1967:231), also described by Hamilton (1962:46-48) and Stahl (1920). By 1919 the Peruvian mission had established 46 primary schools for the Aymaras, 45 of them being taught by Indians trained at Camacho's original school at Platería. Baptized membership was approaching 2000 (Kessler 1967:233,238). Stahl saw the opportunity of extending the people movement to the Bolivian Aymaras, and sent Reid Shepard to Bolivia in 1920 to undertake this work. After contacts with the proper authorities, and with their enthusiastic support, Shepard had established the first SDA school in Rosario within six months. This school produced the first "national missionaries," they reported (SDA 1966:143). This began a period of vigorous growth which reached a rate of over 400 percent per decade, sustained until the depression; the Chaco War and World War II caused a plateau and decline from 1934 to 1944 (see Figure 12).

Educational Evangelism. Today the Adventists have 226 primary schools in Bolivia carrying on "educational evangelism" (SDA 1966:145). All of the teachers in these schools are Adventists, trained in the Bolivia Training School now located at Vinto in the Cochabamba Valley. I have been informed by an Adventist leader that none of the schools is self-supporting. All are subsidized from North American funds. This is undoubtedly one factor in the growth stoppage and decline 1934-1944, and thus one of the big drawbacks of the school system: when foreign funds and personnel decline because of conditions in the homeland, church growth also shows a decline. In spite of this, the success of the Adventist work cannot be denied. The Oregon Friends also used the school approach to good advantage as we shall see. A detailed study on the use of schools in the church growth in Bolivia would be a fruitful project for future research.

While most SDA growth has taken place among the Aymaras, they also have churches in the major cities for the middle classes and work in several towns in the Beni. Whether the school approach will be as successful among the mestizos in the Jesuit-founded Beni towns is another question. Three of their four churches have schools accompanying them, and the fourth soon will have a school. When the SDA missionary enters a town, growth in the church usually climbs rapidly to about 100, then slows down or even declines. Their excellent hospital in Guayaramerín "gives them good standing in town," but church membership declined in the past year. An SDA missionary estimates that some 10 percent of the school children in the Beni become Adventists (Frampton 1968:1).

Stewardship. The high level of giving among the Adventists in Bolivia should be mentioned as a basis of comparison to other denominations which constantly face the problem of not being able to raise money from the Bolivian churches. SDA theology stresses tithing very strongly, and the teaching seems to have significant results. The *Statistical Report for 1965* shows that in one year a total of over $80,000 (U.S.) was raised through tithes, church offerings and Sabbath school

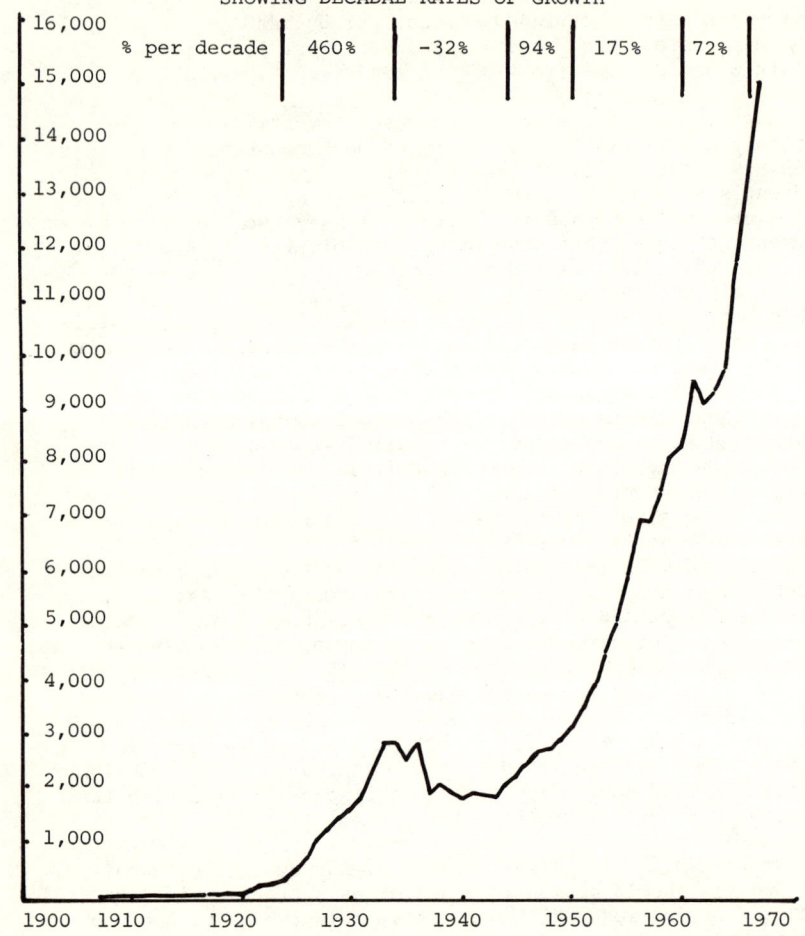

FIGURE 12

offerings. This is quite remarkable especially in view of the fact that the denomination is not generally made up of the wealthier class of persons. How this would compare to giving in other denominations should be a subject for future study.

A glance at Table 10 and Figure 12 shows that the SDA Church has been growing well since the 1934-1944 decline. D. J. Sandstrom, President of the Inca Union of the SDA, attributes this growth to "God's blessings on the preaching of His word," the medical work, and the schools, then makes the following helpful observation:

> In the fifties the districts in Bolivia were reorganized and each pastor was responsible for the work within his district territory, using the laymen and school teachers to help in the evangelization of his area. We have regular meetings with our workers in the Bolivia Mission where instruction and inspiration is presented and goals are set for each man to strive for during that particular year (1968:2).

As we have already observed, where a multicultural Church is involved the division into districts is of utmost importance, and probably one important secret of growth.

TABLE 10

Seventh-day Adventists 1907 - 1967

Date	Membership	Laborers*
1910	8	8
1917	10	4
1918	12	9
1919	15	7
1920	25	6
1921	174	12
1922	234	9
1923	271	10
1924	373	9
1925	523	16
1926	789	29
1927	1,083	11
1928	1,325	37
1929	1,469	40

TABLE 10, cont.

Date	Membership	Laborers*
1930	1,634	44
1931	1,905	23
1932	2,378	20
1933	2,815	26
1934	2,815	22
1935	2,558	11
1936	2,801	16
1937	1,905	27
1938	2,026	28
1939	1,913	38
1940	1,865	26
1941	1,940	19
1943	1,884	41
1944	2,088	29
1945	2,213	36
1946	2,437	33
1947	2,703	55
1948	2,789	38
1949	2,952	39
1950	3,192	141
1951	3,532	151
1952	3,964	162
1953	4,518	178
1954	5,020	128
1955	5,918	243
1956	6,974	238
1957	6,977	221
1958	7,456	276
1959	8,082	239
1960	8,324	246
1961	9,504	367
1962	9,046	352
1963	9,227	350
1964	9,619	188
1965	11,603	456
1966	13,243	184
1967	14,955	-

*Total foreign and national.
Source: General Conference SDA, Statistical Department, *Annual Statistical Reports* 1910 - 1967.

4

Second Sowing of Missions

No other missions entered Bolivia after the Seventh-day Adventists established their work in 1907, until after World War I. In the realm of international missions, great meetings were held at Edinburgh in 1910 and at Panama in 1916. At the Edinburgh conference, Latin American territory was not considered a legitimate mission field but delegates to Panama, almost all from the Americas, were unanimous in their opinion that the Protestant Church had a responsibility to preach Christ to the millions of pagans or pseudo-Christians in Latin America. This gave a new impetus to missionary activity, and seven missions entered Bolivia before the Chaco War (1932-1935) brought about another pause.

UNION BIBLE SEMINARY AND BOLIVIAN FRIENDS HOLINESS MISSION
   (Seminario Bíblico) and (Iglesia Evangélica Los Amigos)

These small Friends groups should not be confused with the Oregon Friends whose national Church is the Iglesia Nacional Evangélica Los Amigos, INELA. They will be discussed in a later section.
The Bolivian history of the Union Bible Seminary and the Bolivian Friends Holiness Mission, an arm of the Central Yearly meeting of Friends, is somewhat intertwined (Figure 13), and they will be discussed together here. Unfortunately neither of these groups has answered correspondence and data is rather

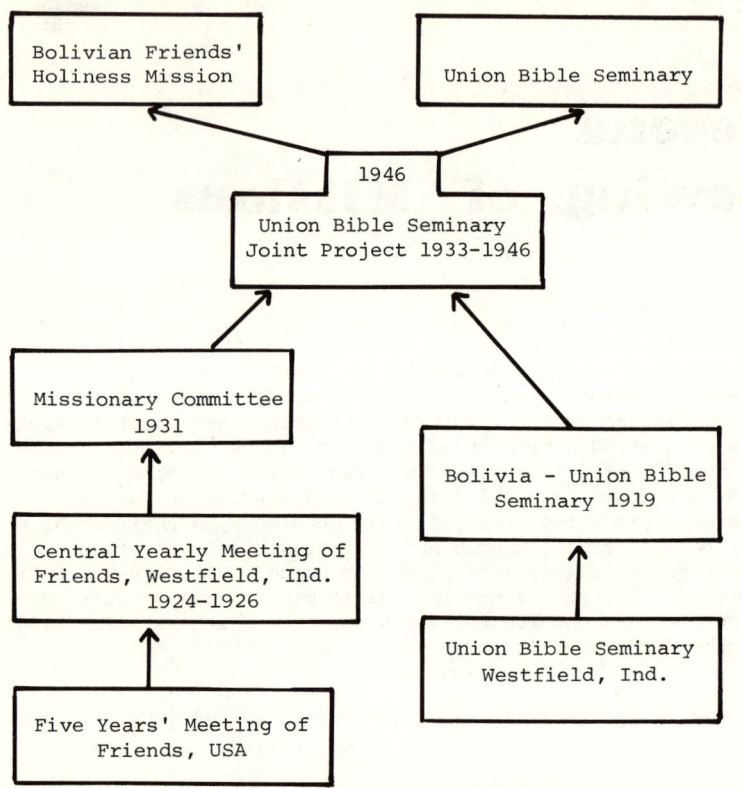

FIGURE 13

Sources: Goddard 1967:91-92,124,647;Crivelli 1933:169-172.

sparse.

The pioneer missionaries of this group were two single ladies who had graduated from the Friends-sponsored Union Bible Seminary in Westfield, Indiana, Emma Morrow Langston and Mattie Blout Marca. Soon after they arrived in 1919, they were joined by Alva and Mabel Hinshaw, and they set up headquarters in Sorata. The Hinshaws soon moved to Riberalta in the Beni and set up pioneer work there (Goddard 1967:124). At this time the work apparently was associated with, although not sponsored by, the Five Years Meeting of Friends.

TABLE 11

Union Bible Seminary and Bolivian Friends' Holiness Mission 1919 - 1967

Date	Foreign Workers	National Workers	Churches	Full Members	Total Members	Source
		Joint Project 1933-1946				
1930	-	-	-	-	27	CGRILA 1967
1938	12	1	-	-	127	Parker 1938:119
1940	-	-	-	-	178	CGRILA 1967
		Bolivian Friends' Holiness Mission*				
1949	4	3	5	30	605	WCH 1949
1952	4	3	5	30	605	WCH 1952
1957	4	3	5	30	605	WCH 1957
1962	-	8	6	30	605	WCH 1962
1967	4	3	5	30	605	WCH 1967
		Union Bible Seminary*				
1949	17	3	12	200	300	WCH 1949
1952	17	8	18	400	800	WCH 1952
1957	17	8	18	400	800	WCH 1957
1962	25	23	17	248	868	WCH 1962

*
The World Christian Handbook for 1949, 1952, and 1957 lists separate entries for Bolivian Friends' Holiness Mission and Central Yearly Meeting of Friends. In 1962 they list Bolivian Friends' Holiness Mission and Union Bible Seminary. I take it that the earlier statistics for Central Yearly Meeting are really those of Union Bible Seminary.

In 1924 a group split from the Five Years Meeting and the Discipline of the Central Yearly Meeting was adopted in 1928 (Crivelli 1933:169-172). Their Missionary Committee was set up in 1931. Prior to that, the Central Yearly Meeting worked through the Board of the Union Bible Seminary. In 1933 the two organizations began to work jointly, and this arrangement continued thirteen years until in 1946 they went their separate ways. The Bolivian Friends Holiness Mission is the name under which the Central Yearly Meeting works in Bolivia today. They have churches in such places as Riberalta, Rurrenabaque, Reyes, Achacachi, La Paz, Irupana, and Lanza. In 1965 the mission reported 8 missionaries and 15 national pastors in Bolivia (Goddard 1967:91-92).

The Union Bible Seminary owns "the largest Protestant church in La Paz," and twenty-two other churches on the Altiplano, all pastored by nationals (Goddard 1967:647). Perhaps the best-known missionary with this group was Samuel E. Smith.

Hamilton points out that although the total membership of the Bible Seminary Mission is relatively small, the potential is great (1962).

Available statistics for these two groups are found on Table 11.

SWEDISH FREE MISSION
(Svenska Fria Missionen, Pentecostales Suecos)

Phillips mentions a Pentecostal missionary, George Burnan, who was working in Sucre in 1911 (n.d.:n.p.). This is the first Pentecostal I have found in any of the available sources, but he is not identified further than that. The first mission of a Pentecostal nature to establish permanent work in Bolivia was the Swedish Pentecostal mission, entering in 1920 (Beach 1925).

Undoubtedly due to the fact that there is no mission board which coordinates the work of this movement, statistics are very difficult to discover. Ake Boberg, writing in 1967 says,

> It is a common statement in the Pentecostal movement in Sweden that each assembly should be independent. There is no central organization with control over the assemblies.

Even in its missionary work the same principles are
observed. The individual assemblies appoint their
missionaries and send them to the mission fields. If any
local assembly is too small to be responsible for a
missionary by itself, it makes an agreement with one or
more other assemblies to sponsor the missionary jointly.
The rapid growth of missionary endeavor has been due in no
small measure to the intimate relationship between
missionary and assembly. Missions is considered the
business of each member of each assembly (Goddard 1967:625)

Apparently the Bolivian field of this group has not been
one of the areas experiencing "rapid growth." The article in
Goddard's encyclopedia makes scant mention of Bolivia. It does
admit that from 1926 to 1939 "The work in Bolivia faced major
difficulties and grew slowly" (1967:627).

Available statistics show that the Swedish Pentecostals had
a membership of 12 in 1930 (Browning 1930:171), 100 in 1960
(CGRILA 1967), 250 in 1962 (*WCH* 1962:128), and 343 in 1967
(CGRILA 1967). Fourteen workers are listed for Bolivia
(Goddard 1967:629). Work centers in the Department of Cochabamba.

SALVATION ARMY
(Ejército de Salvación)

The work of the Salvation Army in Bolivia, which began in
1920, has not been outstanding in regard to growth in church
membership. They are, of course, not concentrating solely on
church planting. In 1930 Browning listed fourteen communicants
(1930:170), but no other reference to them or their statistics
is found in the literature available. The *World Christian
Handbook* includes Chile and Peru in the statistics, so is
useless for our purposes (1962:128). They have not answered
correspondence. Perhaps future field research will be able to
discover more facts concerning their work.

OREGON YEARLY MEETING OF FRIENDS CHURCH
(Iglesia Nacional Evangélica Los Amigos INELA)

In some respects, the missionary work of the Oregon Yearly
Meeting of Friends has been the most outstanding of all
Protestant efforts in Bolivia. With a minimal missionary

staff, "never more than five couples, usually less" (Willcuts 1965:23), they have developed Bolivia's largest Aymara Church and the third-largest denomination.

Juan Ayllón. William Able, an American Indian, went from Los Angeles to La Paz in 1920 as a Quaker missionary. He died in less than a year, but left behind an Aymara convert, Juan Ayllón (Goddard 1967:515). Deciding to prepare himself for the ministry, Ayllón went to Chiquimula, Guatemala, where the California Friends had recently established a Bible Institute. He married a girl named Tomasa there and the Guatemalan churches decided to support the Ayllóns as their missionaries to Bolivia. In December, 1924, they began work in La Paz (Haines 1955:7).

California to Oregon. In 1930 the La Paz work was offered by the California Yearly Meeting to the Oregon Yearly Meeting "believing in the integrity of Oregon Yearly Meeting as to soundness in Quaker faith and the doctrine of Holiness" (Haines 1955:8). The offer was accepted, and the following year, 1931, Carrol and Doris Tamplin, who had served for four years in Central America, became the first missionaries.

A Monocultural Church. A very important church growth factor to be kept in mind is that the INELA from the beginning has been a fully Aymara Church, founded by a Spirit-filled Aymara Christian worker. The INELA has thus avoided some of the difficulties resulting from the multicultural situation we find in many of the other Bolivian Churches.

1924 - 1948

In order to observe the profile of the INELA growth to the best advantage, we will divide the history into five historical periods. This first period from 1924 to 1948 was one of very gradual growth, as characterized most of the other denominations in Bolivia (Figure 14). Under Ayllón, the La Paz church had 75 members by 1929 (Haines 1955:8), as is shown by Table 12, and by 1948 membership in all the churches was approaching 500. Compared to some other denominations, this was not bad growth, but compared to the later INELA growth, it was small. Missionaries worked largely in visitation, leading field conferences, and teaching, but the work was "all entirely under the domination of missionary leadership" (Willcuts 1968b:1). Willcuts, who served for some years in Bolivia and now is

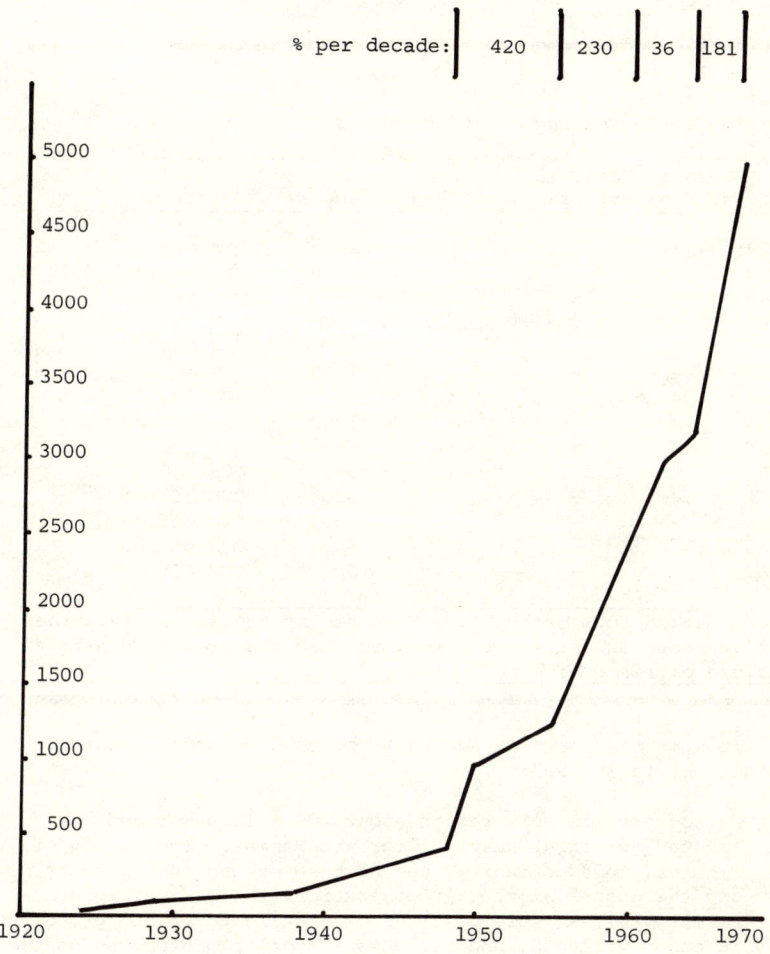

FIGURE 14

General Superintendent of the Oregon Yearly Meeting, feels that this "colonization approach" was the chief retarding factor. He, as all others, recognizes that it also was a time of "planting and seed-sowing" (1968b:2)

TABLE 12

Oregon Yearly Meeting of Friends Church (INELA)

Date	Foreign Workers	National Workers	Churches	Members	Sources
1929	-	-	-	75	OYM office*
1938	4	2	2	120	Parker 1938:119
1948	-	-	-	450	OYM office
1949	4	5	5	700	OYM office, WCH 1949
1950	-	-	-	1000	OYM office
1952	4	5	5	-	WCH 1952
1955	-	-	-	1300	OYM office
1957	4	5	5	-	WCH 1957
1962	19	35	82	3000	WCH 1962
1964	-	-	-	3200	OYM office
1965	-	-	-	3800	OYM office
1966	-	-	-	4400	OYM office
1967	-	-	-	5000	OYM office

*Data marked "OYM office" was received by the author from the headquarters in different forms, refined and presented here as a close estimate of membership.

In some places there seemed to be good response. Carrol Tamplin wrote in 1932:

> We now have in this region about 200 believers, and have located our first pastor, Cipriano Mamani. The Canton of Tiquina, this community, has been so opened to believers and the Gospel since the persecutions there, that upon a recent visit we were besieged with calls to go and preach in other villages, and the Roman Catholic church was opened to us by the Indian head man. We entered and preached the Gospel, with the idols at our backs, a heap of human skulls under the altar, and 100 hungry souls seated on the floor

Second Sowing of Missions 101

before us. When the altar call was given, the 100 with one
accord moved forward, and the walls of the old idolatrous
Roman Catholic church re-echoed with prayers of repentance
and cries of victory (Haines 1955:10).

On wonders what happened to these hundred souls interested in
serving Christ. The possibility of a people movement
developing from such a good beginning is obvious, but for some
reason this does not seem to have happened.

The congregation in La Paz remained strong. Under the
oversight of Tamplin, the members built their own chapel which
seated 300 and was more than filled at the time of the yearly
meeting (Haines 1955:13). A highlight of this period was the
publication in 1942 of the Gospels and Acts in Aymara. Both
Tamplin and Ayllón were chosen by the American Bible Society
to serve on the translation committee (Haines 1955:15).

Toward the end of this period the Tamplins transferred to
the World Gospel Mission and the Ayllóns went independent.
God raised up others such as Jack Willcuts and Ralph Chapman to
take their places (Haines 1955:17).

1948 - 1952

In 1947 a large hacienda of some 3000 acres had been purchased for $30,000 as a site for a Bible Institute. There were
good buildings, water, farmland, livestock and 146 serfs.
Bible Institute classes opened at the farm, called Copajira, in
1947 with seventeen students (Haines 1955:19-20). When the
first graduates began coming out of Copajira in 1951, they
became an important factor in accelerated growth.

Nationalism. The growth in this particular period, however, was not so much on the Altiplano as in the city of La
Paz. From 1942 the La Paz church had been pastored by
missionaries but in 1948 Jack Willcuts, then pastor, stepped
down and turned the church over to his Aymara assistant.
Within two years the believers started seven branch churches in
the surrounding parts of the city, all of which are still
continuing (Willcuts 1968b:1). The Amacari church was also
nationalized, and in 1951 the INELA was established.

Walter P. Lee, President of the Mission Board in Oregon,
visited the field in 1951, and with the missionaries and
nationals there worked out plans for a national Church. Marie
Haines describes the event in these words:

The plan was presented to the nationals during the sessions of the annual meeting at La Paz. It was accepted with some misgivings on the part of the nationals. They agreed to try the plan for one year. The plan was, that at the end of the first year, the older churches were to assume the entire obligation of the salaries of their pastors. An Executive Committee of six nationals and one missionary was set up to work out the details of the actual functioning of the work under national leadership, to evangelize and to teach tithing. The mission was to continue mainly in the field of education, counselling, and in helping develop new groups and work (1955:24)

Decentralization. During this period of nationalization the per decade rate of growth was a healthy 420 percent. The type of decentralization which is a part of traditional Quaker structure helped further in producing this growth. In 1951 the Quarterly Meetings were organized, representing regional government of the churches in a given area. This is similar to the arrangement already described in relation to the Evangelical Christian Union. It might not be apparent that regional administrative units would be as needful in a monocultural Church as the Friends, than in a multicultural Church as the ECU. But, as Hamilton points out, the Aymaras themselves are not a completely homogeneous unit even though they speak the same language. They are made up of several subtribes which are to varying degrees ethnocentric.

1953 - 1959

The rate of growth went sharply upward during this period. This was due to churches being planted outside of La Paz, as well as continued good growth in La Paz. Table 13 shows the growth by regions.

TABLE 13

INELA Regional Church Growth

Region	1950	1955	1960
La Paz city churches	450	245	606
Altiplano rural churches	118	893	936
Yungas churches	–	50	570
SOURCE: Hamilton 1962:82			

Second Sowing of Missions

The most important new factor during this period was the evangelization of the Aymaras in the Yungas. It will be remembered that the Yungas is the region of tropical valleys formed when the Andes mountains break off sharply into the Amazon basin. Roscoe Knight was one of the missionaries influential in discipling the Aymaras in the Yungas, using a gospel-tent-meeting approach. Several people movements were started, in some cases practically the whole community coming to Christ at the same time (Willcuts 1968b:2). Willcuts says, "Interestingly enough, many of these conversions are genuine, and a church could be in existence one week with it never even having been evangelized the week before" (1968b:2).

1960 - 1963

Undoubtedly the Bolivian National Revolution of 1952 had much to do with the growth of the INELA during the previous period, as it did in the Protestant Church in general. The effect of the Revolution on the Friends work, however, was more important in the area of the Bible Institute and missionary-national relationships. The slowing down of growth between 1960 and 1964 reflects the tensions created. The per decade growth rate dropped to 36 percent, compared to 230 percent for the preceding period (1955-1960) and 181 percent for the succeeding period (1964-1967).

Communist influence in Bolivia was especially strong at this time as Paz Estenssoro's power was coming to an end. This produced, especially among the Aymaras, a strong nationalism which was detrimental to missionary-national relationships. The first outward manifestation of this came when the Copajira hacienda was lost to the neighboring peasants who took it by force in 1960. As Willcuts says,

> just preceding this, there was a great deal of tension over the management of the farm, a feeling on the part of the nationals that missionaries were making money rather than ministering, and there was some jealousy which arose (1968b:2).

Before the school was closed it had successfully trained more than 150 Aymara men, most of whom were in Christian service (Goddard 1967:515). Nevertheless, the closing of the school was a severe blow, and a long and serious break in the ministerial training in the denomination. Only in 1966 did the theological education program pick up again.

The INELA "Revolt." One of the reasons for the delay in the new start was the unique development between the INELA and the Mission. In 1963 the INELA put pressures on the Oregon Friends Mission for material concessions, which according to Ralph Chapman, "would have meant a complete reversal in our mission-national church relationships and a loss of all ground which we felt we were making toward the establishment of a national or indigenous church." The mission, therefore, saw no other path open but to withdraw the mission presence from Bolivia. Clare Willcuts, president of the Mission Board, and Dean Gregory, General Superintendent of the OYM, both traveled to Bolivia from Oregon and were on hand when the decision was made. In a letter to the Yearly Meeting at home they wrote:

> This came as no great surprise to the mission staff ... A number of years ago it was determined by our workers and the Board that the indigenous plan for missionary ministry is the most practical and effective. Consequently steps were taken from time to time to place more of the responsibility for the church organization and leadership upon the national brethren. Material aid, such as the support for pastors, teachers, school supervision, church aid, construction, etc., were gradually withdrawn. This did not always meet with the approval of the brethren ...
> Perhaps the time will never come when the missionaries and the National Church will be in complete agreement that NOW is the time for National Church independence ...
> We cannot help but feel that there is a strong possibility that after the organization of the National Church in January that they may extend to us an opportunity to further service among them (1963:1).

The Browns, the Nordykes, the Roberts, and the Comforts left Bolivia, with the Chapmans and Pucketts remaining to care for legal matters. The wisdom of this decision was evident as subsequent events developed.

The meeting for the reorganization of INELA was held January 17-19, 1964. This was the first time missionaries were not present in an INELA meeting, and the Aymara leaders began to realize what a help they had been, although the new freedom was undoubtedly exhilarating to many of them. The master plan for reorganization was drawn up by Carmelo Aspi, one of Bolivia's top Aymara leaders, and was accepted virtually as written. Then a resolution to write a conciliatory letter to the OYM Mission was taken and a letter signed by the INELA

Board was sent January 19. Ralph Chapman analyzed the situation as follows:

> we now see in the October meeting and in the subsequent withdrawal of missionaries from direct work in the churches for this period of time, a method used of the Lord to awaken the brethren here as no other thing could have done. It has been a period of soul searching for them. It has helped them to realize that we still love them though we adopted a drastic method ...
>
> Confusion and bickering ... was without doubt avoided by the complete, well studied-out plans which Carmelo Aspi worked out by the time of the meeting ...
>
> The INELA is now a national church. A new stature is unquestionably noticable. There is a feeling of fellowship and a desire on their part to have the missionaries present with them ... but INELA has come into its own and must be respected as such (1964b:1-2).

In spite of the predictable decline in church growth as a result of these developments, the groundwork was laid for a national Church which would subsequently grow with or without missionary aid. The Church had become indigenous.

1964 - 1967

When the transition to an autonomous national Church had successfully been made, the believers could once again direct their efforts to winning other Aymaras to Christ, and the 181 percent per decade rate of growth, at which the INELA is presently increasing, testifies of their success and to the blessing of the Lord.

At present INELA has 122 churches all pastored and supported by nationals. Over two-thirds of the church leaders are products of the Copajira Bible Institute. Carmelo Aspi was the director of the new Patmos Bible Institute. INELA recently completed its fiscal year not only in the black, but with a balance on hand (Willcuts 1968a:1).

Church Growth Factors

In conclusion, several growth factors, outlined by Willcuts (1968b:2-4) should be listed. They are most important principles and have brought good results in the case of the Friends.

1. *The Effort to Maintain a Monocultural Church.* The Friends have not attempted to reach cultures other than the Aymara.

> We do feel work is needed among the Spanish, of course, and the Cholos and hope that more can be done for them, but we have discovered that whenever a Cholo or a Spanish convert comes, he immediately is a leader in the church whether he is spiritually prepared or not, and this is resented by the Aymaras, and as a result we have discouraged this type of thing (Willcuts 1968b:2).

2. *The Successful Use of Christian Fiestas.* It is well known that the social life of the highland peasants is centered on the recurring fiestas. While for the world these represent drunkenness and immorality, the INELA has seen no reason why they cannot be won for Christ. The drinking, dancing and excessive expenses of renting costumes has been eliminated. But for the Christians these fiestas, especially at the time of the yearly denominational meeting is "a time for dressing up in their best clothes, which the ladies love to do, of course, for football playing and big meals" (Willcuts 1968b:3).

3. *The School Approach as an Instrument for Church Growth.* While we have seen that in some cases the school approach has retarded church growth, the Friends feel that it has helped their Church to grow. The Friends school approach, however, is a very special kind, different from both the Methodists and Seventh-day Adventists. The Friends have avoided the large capital investment in buildings that the Methodists have, and the need for a large annual subsidy from the USA for the running expenses such as the SDA's have. Jack Willcuts describes their particular school approach:

> Almost from the beginning we have had a day school in conjunction with the church. I might add that we had these *only* in connection with the church. We have never started schools apart from the church being planted previously ... At the beginning the missionaries taught the schools, but quickly trained national teachers to take over the first and second grade classes ...
> In the beginning the teachers were trained personally by the missionaries, then there was a great emphasis on teaching in the Copajira Bible School with normal classes, then some of our men went to the government schools for

their training to return to the mission ... We have not had missionary teachers at all since 1948.

In the beginning the mission supported the teachers, and then we gradually shifted to half support, and since 1952 we have not supported the teachers at all, but what support we have given has been given into the treasury of the National Church and allocated by National Church administrators. Then in 1963 we discontinued aid of any kind whatsoever in a financial way, and of course the schools have been self-supporting since then ...

The teacher receives his support by living with a family for room and board and the tuition of the students is his salary. Frequently now in the better established churches, there is a teacher's parsonage too. Frequently the pastors did combine teaching with pastoral work, but on the whole the teachers are full time and the pastors are also full time.

The mission did help with building of schools at first, but we no longer do this ... The children of the school are largely from the believers in the community. We have permitted others to attend, and this has been a means of evangelism on occasion, but when they do attend, they follow the rules (Willcuts 1968b:2-3).

This rather lengthy quotation should be pondered carefully by those who care to evaluate the school approach in a receptive population.

4. *The Discriminating Use of Foreign Funds*. A former President of INELA once said to Roscoe Knight: "As long as the mission continues to send money to us, our people will never tithe nor support their own work. You should stop sending this money" (Knight 1966:5). As we have seen, the OYM no longer supports pastors or teachers, and in this respect is not only preparing the INELA well for the day when the foreign mission may no longer be welcome in Bolivia, but also is taking the pathway to improved missionary-national relationships. In the 1964 arrangements with INELA, the OYM offered to help with medical insurance for pastors and workers, hymnals, records and record players, literature, accordions, Bible classes, tent campaigns, and missionary personnel (Chapman 1964a). Much care has been taken to avoid a spirit of "professionalism" that has damaged pastors from other denominations. The mission is also careful not to exercise indirect control over the INELA through economic pressures. As Knight argues,

indirect control of the mission church is often established through finances. The mission provides money for some phase of the work on the field. This may be handled by a national organization or a national treasurer, but both missionary and national know that if things do not go just right the funds can be cut. Thus the national remains subservient, though resentful, and sometimes rebellious (Knight 1966:4-5).

SOUTH AMERICA INDIAN MISSION AND NEW TESTAMENT MISSIONARY UNION
(Misión Neotestamentaria)

These two small groups which work in the Chaco area of Eastern Bolivia have a common history (Figure 15). Their founders entered Bolivia in 1926 and 1927.

Samuel Decker and George Haight. Samuel and Mary Decker, he an American and she a Canadian, began evangelistic work in 1926 in Puerto Suárez, just across the frontier from Corumbá, Brazil. George Haight, a Canadian, joined them in 1927; his fiancée, Helen, arrived in 1929 and they were married. The Haights moved to Santiago de Chiquitos, opening the second station of what was then the Inland South American Missionary Union. In 1932 the Bolivian work split, the Deckers going with the newly formed New Testament Missionary Union and the Haights and others staying with what would soon be known as the South America Indian Mission.

The work of the South America Indian Mission has centered on the Chiquitano-mestizos of the villages in the provinces of Chiquitos, Velasco, and Ñuflo de Chávez as well as the jungle tribe of Ayorés.

The School Approach. The Haights used the school approach in their evangelization of the Santiago village and surrounding area, in 1932 establishing a school of great prestige in the region, now including both primary and secondary divisions, and with boarding facilities. This work withdrew from the SAIM in 1957, and subsequently was taken over by the Canadian Baptists.

Due to the generous cooperation of the Haights in this research project, we have more data for the Santiago school available than for other schools in the country. In its thirty-six years, the primary section has graduated 270 students, and the high school 34 in nine years. About 50 percent

HISTORICAL DEVELOPMENT OF
THE SOUTH AMERICA INDIAN MISSION AND
THE NEW TESTAMENT MISSIONARY UNION

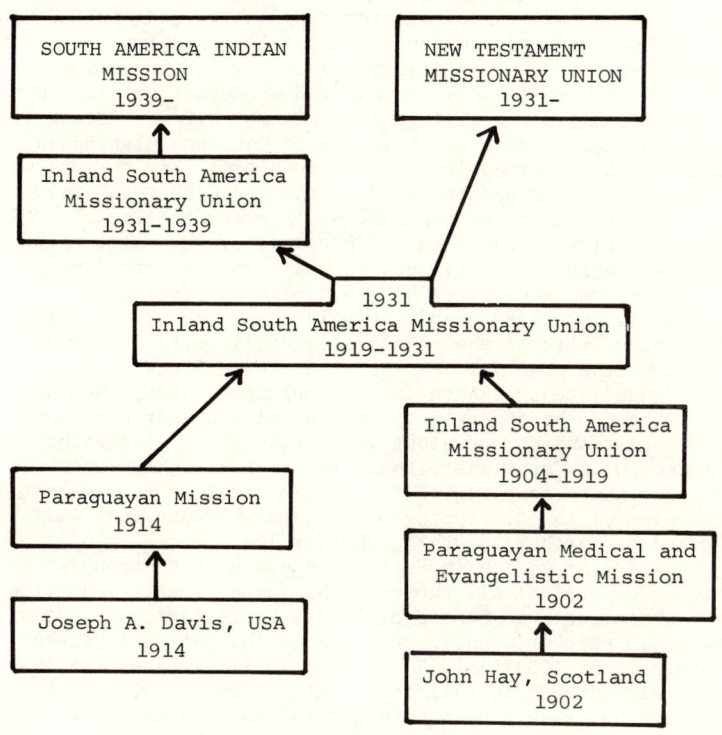

FIGURE 15

Source: Goddard 1967:478,600.

of the primary school graduates are known to be active evangelicals, but the percentage rises to about 85 for the secondary. The school, naturally, has been influential in training many who today are outstanding Protestant leaders.

Jesuit Reductions. In the meantime the village work had spread through the mission-station approach to Concepción, San Ignacio, San José and San Javier, all villages which, like Santiago, were originally Jesuit reductions (towns composed of Indians which were founded and managed by Jesuit priests in the 1600s and 1700s). The village work has met with resistant populations and notably small success. Churches planted in the villages usually were able to win twenty or thirty persons who for various reasons had become disenchanted with the Catholic Church, but the churches remained at this level. Their vitality usually depended on the presence of the missionary. When missionaries left villages such as San José and Concepción, the church would decline, then pick up after other missionaries came. So deeply ingrained was the Catholic Church in the social life of the people originally settled in the villages by the powerful Jesuits, that the effects have remained until today. When conversions take place, they are usually the one-by-one-against-the-social-tide variety. Sometimes conversions spread along webs of kinship relationships, but I know of no case where these relationships have been the bridge for the discipling of the entire extended family unit. The problem of the discipling of the Jesuit reductions will be discussed at further length in Chapter 10.

Probably the church in Santiago has been the strongest through the years of all those in the former Jesuit reductions. Of 500 inhabitants in Santiago, 50 are Protestants, making a total of 10 percent, considerably above the national percentage of 1.05 percent (CGRILA 1967). There is little question that the school approach in this resistant segment of Bolivia's population has resulted in more growth than in the Jesuit reductions where it was not used, at least in the Department of Santa Cruz.

The evangelization of the Ayoré tribe, which I have described in detail in *Defeat of the Bird God* (Wagner 1967), was an outstanding example of heroic missionary endeavor on the part of the SAIM. Exact church statistics are not available, but a solid Church has been planted among this people. Unfortunately, however, no people movement resulted from the contact with the Ayorés. The tribe, now semi-civilized, is divided between Christians and non-Christians.

Second Sowing of Missions 111

The NTMU has extended along the railroad line from Puerto Suárez to Roboré, including such villages as El Carmen in between. While the church in Puerto Suárez has never shown much growth, the church in Roboré is more vigorous than other churches in Eastern Bolivia, especially those planted in the former Jesuit reductions. One reason for this is probably the fact that Roboré is a new town, having been created south of Santiago as a railroad center since building the railroad through the Santiago hills would have been impractical. George Haight made an effort to plant a church in Roboré in 1930-1931, but found little response and "shook the dust from his feet." Others also tried, but no congregation was formed until the New Tribes Mission entered in 1943. The railroad work had begun, and Roboré was growing. Several families of believers from Santiago had moved there and formed the nucleus of the congregation, then other Santiago families transferred membership in subsequent years. A group of Latvian Baptists immigrated to Roboré from Brazil and joined the church. Then a good deal of growth came from conversions in the town itself. The NTMU took over the work subsequently. Their approach to church planting is virtually identical to that of the Brethren, described in an earlier section.

Annual conferences bringing together the believers from all these churches for Bible study and fellowship have been a means of advancing the work. These were started by Haight in Santiago, and later held in Roboré and San José. Bolivian leadership for the Church has not been forthcoming to any extent, with missionaries dominating the scene in almost all the larger churches. The SAIM sponsored the Eastern Bible Institute first in Santiago, then in San José from 1953 to 1961, but only two graduates are in full-time Christian service at this time, and one of them has moved out of the area.

Statistics available on the SAIM and the NTMU are shown on Table 14.

TABLE 14

South America Indian Mission and New Testament Missionary Union

Date	Foreign Workers	National Workers	Churches	Baptized Members	Total Members	Source
		South America Indian Mission				
1938	7	-	-	-	-	Parker 1938:119
1949	14	3	4	220	-	WCH 1949
1952	19	3	5	220	-	WCH 1952
1957	28	8	12	350	-	WCH 1957
1962	21	8	13	200	-	WCH 1962
1967	17	13	13	225	-	WCH 1967; CGRILA 1967
		New Testament Missionary Union				
1938	2	-	-	40	-	Parker 1938:119
1949	1	1	2	50	-	WCH 1949
1952	4	-	2	50	-	WCH 1952
1957	3	3	6	200	-	WCH 1957
1962	3	3	6	200	-	WCH 1962
1967	-	-	-	200	-	CGRILA 1967

INTERNATIONAL CHURCH OF THE FOURSQUARE GOSPEL
(Iglesia Cuadrangular)

In 1920 Thomas and Fannie Anderson made a visit to Cochabamba as they considered Bolivia a possibility for beginning a Foursquare Mission. They returned in 1929 and took up residence in the city of Trinidad, capital of the Beni Department. The Foursquare work has thus far consisted of a church in Trinidad among mestizos, and a camp at Ebiato, fifty miles into the country, where a group of some 300 Sirionó Indians has been encouraged to settle down. Thomas Anderson died in 1949, and his wife in 1966. Their son, Jack, and his wife, Darlene, however, have taken over the work from their parents. Official statistics for 1967 provided by the Los Angeles Foursquare office, set the membership of the churches at 100.

OTHER GROUPS

Two smaller groups worked in Bolivia during the pre-Chaco War period, and they will be mentioned here purely as points of historical interest.

South American Missionary Society. The first is the Anglican South American Missionary Society (SAMS). We find SAMS mentioned in connection with Bolivia in the person of Barbrooke Grubb whom they sent to penetrate the Chaco in 1888. Although it was mentioned that the Chaco "borders the three republics of Paraguay, Bolivia, and Argentina" it is not known whether Grubb ever set foot on what is now Bolivian soil (Goddard 1967:601).

In 1926 SAMS had a mission in Charagua among the Chriguano Indians. By 1930 they had also occupied Izozog and Aguaraigua with some four missionaries including a medical doctor (Crivelli 1933:87). Browning reports that their missionaries had learned the language of the Izoceño Indians and held school for them (1930:131). They closed work at the opening of the Chaco War and did not return (Grubb 1938:12). The stations they occupied are now under the Evangelical Christian Union in the territory first worked by the EUSA.

German Lutherans. The second group to be mentioned is the German Evangelical Lutheran Church. Crivelli says that in 1933 they had 800 members in their congregation (1933:18). I would suppose that this refers to a group of immigrants in La Paz where a German pastor resides and ministers to the German-speaking community there today.

5

Chaco War
and Post·war Influences

Bolivian author Charles W. Arnade has said that the Chaco War was "a crucial event, if not *the* most crucial in Bolivian history" (Zook 1960:13).

BOLIVIA'S DEFEAT

The Chaco War was a painful and humiliating experience for Bolivia, but subsequent history has shown that it was a turning point for good, since "the Chaco War made the Revolution of 1952 inevitable" (Alexander 1958:22). A process of rapid social change was begun after the Chaco War that did not occur in either of the other Andean countries, Peru and Ecuador, and as a result the peasants of Bolivia not only enjoy more liberty than their neighbors, but they are more receptive to the Gospel.

The boundary between Bolivia and Paraguay had never been carefully marked, but the brown, sandy expanses of scrub brush and salt flats held little interest for either party until rumors began to fly that there were vast reserves of petroleum lying beneath the surface for the taker. In 1932 the two countries decided that the oil would go to the strongest, and the war broke out. Some claim that Bolivia was pushed into the war by USA oil interests and Paraguay by Anglo-Argentine interests, although no proof for this accusation has yet come to light. Indeed, there was not even enough proof that the oil under the Chaco was worth fighting over.

Bolivia should have won the war by all odds. She was a larger nation, she had more wealth at her disposal at the time, she was more advanced as far as developing nations go, and her army was trained by the German expert, General Kundt, and regarded with awe by many. But Paraguay had one important element on her side that won her the war - nature. The Paraguayans were fighting on familiar soil. They knew how to withstand the heat, they were immune from the insect bites, could stand long periods of thirst, and were able to live off the forest. The highland Indians, on the other hand, were in another world. Paraguayan bullets could not have defeated them. If the war had been fought on the 12,000 foot high Altiplano, the Paraguayans would not have had a chance. But insects, disease and thirst took their toll and the Bolivian army suffered a sad defeat after three years of difficult combat in which 60,000 Bolivians were lost. Fighting stopped in 1935, and the peace treaty was signed in 1938.

Paraguay won the war, but her victory had no measurable lasting effects. She is still the most backward land in South America, under the absolute control of Alfredo Stroessner, a classical caudillo. The furious sweep of twentieth-century progress is leaving Paraguay almost completely behind.

A TIDE OF PROGRESS

On the other hand in Bolivia the tide of progress rose from the rubble of the war. As Edmundo Flores says:

> Though a fiasco the war effort galvanized the country into action and broke, or at least cracked, the prevailing rigid caste system. Afterwards, it was impossible to restore the structure that had prevailed in the past. The stony immobility of the Indian could not be maintained once he left the lands that had been his only horizon. He began to be attracted to the city, where he became a cholo and climbed several steps up the social ladder, or to the mines where he lost his ties with the community and ceased psychologically to be an Indian (Alexander 1958:25).

The movement caused by the war broke the shell of isolation that surrounded many of the highland Indian communities. "The Indian had been awakened and would soon be heard from" (Fagg 1963:882). The very disillusion in the hearts of the veterans

of the war caused them to take objective stock of their
situation and demand a better government which would afford
them social justice. Furthermore the war "discredited the
traditional ruling class" (Wells 1966:7) and marked the
beginning of the fall of the elite class from exclusive control
of the republic.

In their analysis of the rise of nationalism in Latin
America, Whitaker and Jordan pinpoint the Chaco War as the
starting point of modern Bolivian nationalism. It "had shocked
the Bolivian Indians into a more general awareness of their
exploitation than the Indians in any other Andean country ...
Revolutionary nationalists blossomed everywhere" (1966:146,142).
The process begun in the Chaco War "reached its high point on
April 9, 1952" (Alexander 1958:22), the date of the revolution
which put the MNR in power (Chapter 6).

THE WAR AND THE CHURCHES

The immediate influence of the war on the churches was
negative, but the long-term effect was positive.

Losses During the War. During the war almost every one of
the thirteen Protestant denominations working in the country
experienced a slump. One, SAMS, left the country and did not
return. The decline was most pronounced in the denominations
such as Seventh-day Adventists and Methodists which were tied
to foreign funds by their institutions. Of course the
depression in the USA also contributed simultaneously to this
decline.

Carrol Tamplin of the Oregon Friends gives us a particularly graphic firsthand description of some of the difficulties
in his churches in 1934:

> If workers were few in the past years, they are now almost
> non-existent ... Of 18 men, 12 of whom were preparing
> definitely for the work of the Gospel, not one remains.
> Some have entered the service as soldiers, some could not
> stand the persecution and bloodshed and have deserted the
> army. Others have gone into hiding because they will not
> fight. Our last and only interpreter has been called to
> the colors (Haines 1955:11).

Two missionaries in particular were notable for their
direct involvement in the war. Dr. Frank Beck of the

Methodists gave of himself unstintingly to relieve pain and suffering on the battlefields. Peter Horne of the Brethren also spent much time on the front lines ministering to the spiritual needs of the soldiers. Several who came to know the Lord through Horne's testimony returned from the war as faithful Christians and faithful church members.

Post-war Gains. While church membership generally declined between 1932 and 1935, the gains after the war more than compensated for the losses. The uprooting, social dislocation, and increased mobility of the people caused by the war opened thousands for new ideas. Nationalism, revolution, agrarian reform, education, economic progress, labor unions, social justice, and profit sharing in the mines gripped the receptive minds and hearts of many. The claims of Jesus Christ gripped others. Many more, especially those peasants moving into the cities and to the mining centers, would also have been responsive to the message of the Gospel if the Church had been more sensitive to her opportunities.

However, the trend toward a greater receptiveness to the Gospel as a result of the war would not gain enough momentum to produce dramatic growth for at least another decade. At the end of the Chaco War in 1935, there were eleven missionary agencies working in Bolivia. The immediate effects of the war upon them and upon their Bolivian churches were negative although not devastating. Then the Great Depression in the USA, with its worldwide effects, reduced the resources available in the sending countries and thus discouraged new works from starting and old works from expanding operations.

NEW MISSIONS ENTER BOLIVIA

When the effects of the depression began to wear off, three new missions entered Bolivia between the years of 1936 and 1938, the first since the Oregon Friends took over the work of the California Friends in 1931. If the Oregon Friends are made an exception, since their work was already under way when they took over, the early history of the entrance of Protestant missions into Bolivia breaks down into three distinct periods: 1895-1907 The five pioneer groups; 1919-1926 Five additional missions; 1936-1938 Three new missions. Then, 1943-to date, One mission a year.

The later history in which nearly a mission a year has entered the country carries us to the present. This breakdown omits only the Foursquare Church (1929), confined virtually to a one-family effort, and the Eastern Bolivia Fellowship (1938) which became a part of the EUSA work. Undoubtedly more missions would have chosen Bolivia as a field of ministry, were it not for the deterioration of the international situation and World War II.

One of the missions which entered in this period, the Evangelical Union of South America, has been discussed under the Evangelical Christian Union. Since the split between the British Council and the American Council of the mission left the Americans with only a section in Northeast Brazil, the occupation of a new field was quite urgent if the scope of ministry was to match the name of the mission. Bolivia was the field chosen and was entered in 1937.

United World Mission
(Misión Unida Mundial)

In 1936, Walter Ackerle and his wife moved into La Paz, later settling down in the city of Santa Cruz for evangelistic ministry. Their work resulted in the Templo Evangélico Cristiano (Evangelical Christian Temple), which has been one of the city's most vigorous Protestant churches through the years. Sunday School attendance at the Templo is presently over 200, and a branch church has been established in Portachuelo. CGRILA (1967) estimates their membership at 300.

In 1946 Sidney Correll organized the United World Mission (Goddard 1967:675) in order to serve America's independent churches and evangelicals in the historic churches who were not pleased with their own denominational mission program. Walter Ackerle brought his work in Santa Cruz under the UWM, where it has remained.

The UWM has not established a denominational type of national church organization as other faith missions have done. They have founded no Bible Institute nor Seminary. The churches have been under the direct or indirect control of missionaries. Church members are mestizos, typical of the lowland regions of Bolivia.

A good radio ministry has been maintained throughout the years, using purchased time on the commercial stations of the city. Results of the radio preaching are not known, but the UWM has made more of an effort in this field than many of the other groups.

Perhaps the major service the UWM has been to Protestants in general in the Santa Cruz area has been through its first-class Christian bookstore, Vida Nueva, founded and managed by Carl Walter.

World Mission Prayer League
(Iglesia Evangélica Luterana Boliviana)

In 1932 a group of students at the Lutheran Bible Institute in Minneapolis began to pray earnestly for the evangelization of Latin America. In 1937 they formed themselves into an independent mission board (WMPL 1965:3). The World Mission Prayer League "is not officially affiliated with any Lutheran Church body but functions as a free movement within the Lutheran family of churches. It accepts missionary candidates from any Lutheran church" (Goddard 1967:702).

In 1937 Ernest Weinhardt and John Carlson were chosen to become the first World Mission Prayer League missionaries, and sent to South America "to look for a field." While still in the USA they contacted a Señor Guzmán who gave them a Macedonian call to his native land, Bolivia.

> These missionaries went forth without any guaranteed financial support, just trusting that the Lord would supply, which He did, although they were tested (WMPL 1965:3).

After studying the language, Weinhardt and Carlson opened the first Lutheran mission station in the village of Mocomoco in 1939 (WMPL 1965:3).

The mission purchased a farm at Coaba, which was first an orphanage, but later developed into a Bible Institute, a grade school and a high school. Several Bolivian leaders have been trained there. In 1957 the Iglesia Evangélica Luterana Boliviana was founded with a Board of Directors composed of twelve Bolivian Christians and a missionary as "coordinator" (WMPL 1965:1).

The mission bookstore, Librería Emanuel, has been of great service to the entire Protestant community in the La Paz area, and through extensive mail service to other parts of Bolivia.

A large and modern church building has recently been constructed in one of the residential sections of the city of La Paz. This will be a middle-class mestizo congregation, as is their second church in La Paz. The majority of the other IELB churches, however, are among Aymaras of one particular tribe on the Altiplano, and there is also one that is Quechua-speaking (Hamilton 1962:71-72). In the past two years, five

120 THE PROTESTANT MOVEMENT IN BOLIVIA

Aymara congregations have been established in the suburbs of La Paz. Possibly future denominational leadership will become dominated by the La Paz congregations. This is the multi-cultural situation which the Oregon Friends have studiously attempted to avoid. How it has affected the growth of the Lutheran Church should be the subject of a detailed study.

The figures recorded on Table 15 were supplied by memory by Pastor Arthur Gustafson, and the growth is plotted on Figure 16.

TABLE 15

World Mission Prayer League 1937 - 1967

Date	Foreign Workers	National Workers	Churches	Baptized Members	Community	Source
1949	30	-	2	-	75	WCH 1949
1952	38	1	10	50	250	WCH 1952
1957	36	4	9	60	115	WCH 1957
1962	36	12	13	800	2400	Gustafson
1967	24	21	21	2000	6000	Gustafson

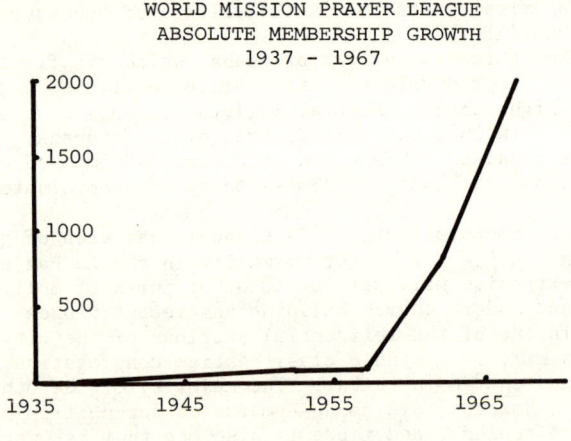

WORLD MISSION PRAYER LEAGUE
ABSOLUTE MEMBERSHIP GROWTH
1937 - 1967

FIGURE 16

6

National Revolution 1952

The republics of Bolivia and Peru are so closely related geographically and ethnically that Bolivia was once known as "Upper Peru." For 219 years they were united in the Viceroyalty of Lima. Bolivia's first native-born President, Andrés de Santa Cruz, dreamed of reuniting the old Inca empire, Tawantinsuyu, and was successful in forming a short-lived Confederation of Peru (Patch 1967:100).

Church Growth in Bolivia and Peru. In spite of this close relationship, the Protestant Church is currently growing twice as fast in Bolivia as in Peru, 112 percent as compared to 55 percent for the years 1960-1967, according to the CGRILA estimates (1967). Why this great difference? Perhaps a more detailed analysis would bring out several other factors, but one sure to be toward the top of the list is the fact that Bolivia had her social revolution in 1952 and Peru still awaits hers.

The Feudal System. Before 1952 the Bolivian Indians, who constituted over two-thirds of the nation's population, were almost as far removed from national life as if they had been on another continent. While it is true that some of the Indians owned their own land or held it communally, they were the small minority. Most of them were so bound to the land they lived on that they were bought and sold along with the real estate. We have already seen how both the Canadian Baptists and Oregon

Friends bought farms whose value was partially determined by how many Indian families lived on the property. In 1950, 4.5 percent of the rural landholders owned 70 percent of the private agricultural property. Of 3,500,000 Bolivians, only about 500,000 had entered the market economy. The rest handled no money; they bartered (Alexander 1958:58). The absentee landowner, whose concern for the human well-being of his serfs was nil, could exploit them almost at will. The men would work from three to six days per week with no recompense but a daily ration of coca leaves, the women would be required to perform domestic service, and the children were sent out in the fields to tend the sheep and llamas. Back in 1904 Will Payne wrote:

> I have again and again had the offer from men in Oruro to bring Indians from other farms, at a small charge per head, and establish them on any farm we wished, payment to be made after the Indian had built his house and commenced to plough (1904:89).

With no education, no health facilities, no contact with the outside world, no hope for advancement, no economic power, nor even a vote in national affairs, little wonder that the Indian became a passive, almost fatalistic, introvert, living from fiesta to fiesta.

Although these feudal Indians usually passed through the Catholic rites of baptism, confirmation and extreme unction, they had little heart commitment to the religion of the oppressors. Pachamama, Mother Earth, was their most immediate God. None would take a drink of chicha without first pouring out a bit on her dusty breast. Those who had heard of the Protestant religion showed little interest. They were too suspicious to accept new ideas, especially when advocated by the very whites and mestizos who had enslaved them. This vast piece of ethnic mosaic of the Bolivian population would likely not have become receptive to the Gospel until the bonds of serfdom were broken and they attained some sort of more significant social freedom.

The Revolution of 1952 broke those bonds. Bolivia was the second Latin American country to pass through a true social revolution, Mexico (1910-1917) being the first. Cuba followed in 1959, but went Communist.

THE RISE OF THE MNR

We have already mentioned that the Chaco War was the turning point in Bolivian history. New ideas and a broadened world view made indelible changes in the Indians. The white ruling class was discredited by the defeat, and the day of the Indian was just around the corner. The Indians went back to their farms and would not be heard from for another decade. But the young army officers took advantage of the loss of prestige on the part of the older officers, joined with a group of profressive intellectuals, and formed the MNR party (Movimiento Nacionalista Revolucionario), which took on its organizational form in 1940. Gualberto Villarroel led the pro-Fascist military sector of the MNR, while Victor Paz Estenssoro, an economist, led the civilian and intellectual wing. This pro-Nazi group took control of the government in 1943. Villarroel became President and Paz Estenssoro Finance Minister. But the defeat of the Nazis in World War II brought discredit to the movement, and contributed to the fall of the MNR in 1946. Villarroel was hanged from a lamp post in the central plaza of La Paz. Paz Estenssoro was fortunate enough to flee the country successfully.

Paz, still in exile, ran for President in the 1951 election and received the largest number of votes. But since he fell short of an absolute majority, constitutionally he could not assume office: the congress had to determine the outcome of the election. A military junta took over but the MNR was successful in arming a militia and in gaining the support of the military police (carabineros). On April 9, 1952, they made their play for power, and won it three days later after a bloody battle in La Paz. Paz Estenssoro returned as President and the revolution was under way.

The Revolution of 1952 must be seen as the vindication of Bolivian nationalism (Patch 1967:109). One of the important elements of the new program was the integration of the Indian into the national life which gave him identity as a Bolivian citizen rather than leaving him to his animal-like fate. How was this accomplished?

Nationalization of the Mines. The nationalization of the mines was the first step. Simon Patiño had become perhaps the wealthiest man in the world through the cold exploitation of his nation's mineral resources and his fellow countrymen, the Indians. He and two other "tin barons," Aramayo and Hochschild had virtually monopolized Bolivia's exports and controlled the economy of the country. Their combined income was larger than the national budget (Patch 1967:109). The MNR expropriated the mines and put them under the administration of a government mining corporation, COMIBOL. While this predictably began an economic chain reaction that brought the country to the brink of financial disaster, it was a necessary step to break up the old oligarchy which had so long run the country.

Army Dissolved. The most far-reaching result of the Revolution, the agrarian reform, was precipitated, not by the MNR leaders, as commonly supposed, but by the peasants themselves who had been gaining power ever since the Chaco War. After the war, the veterans were able to organize themselves into the Confederation of Chaco War Veterans (Confederación de Ex-Combatientes del Chaco), and into several so-called "agrarian syndicates," or farmers' unions. The most powerful of these was located in Ucureña in the Cochabamba valley. As Patch points out, these syndicates grew in power throughout the 1940's.

> They took no direct part in the 1952 revolution, but with the breakdown of army and police authority in the provinces after April 1952 the organizations spread widely and rapidly among the Quechua speakers, mainly in the heavily Indian department of Cochabamba ... Finally the syndicates were strong enough to challenge the landowners ... When the challenge broke into open battle, the major landowners were driven into the cities or into exile. The Indians carried out their own land distribution (1967:111).

The MNR's agrarian reform bill was hurriedly passed as a result of the de facto breakdown of the feudal system. Paz signed the bill on August 2, 1953 at Ucureña, where reportedly some 500,000 Indians gathered for the occasion. At that time the word "Indian" (indio) was stricken from Bolivian vocabulary, and the word "peasant" (campesino) substituted for it. Today, no one sensitive to Bolivian feelings would call one of them an Indian.

In an eloquent passage of his book, *Resultados de la Reforma Agraria en Bolivia,* Luis Antezana describes the effect of land ownership on the peasants:

> A profound psychological transformation was produced in the peasants when the announcement of the reform was made; they

began to walk on their own land and to feel free, as if
they were standing on the top of a mountain. They learned
to speak in a loud voice, with pride and without fear ...
The worker of the countryside had been dignified by being
given land and liberty in all of its aspects. "Indian," a
feudal concept, was the serf of an epoch which had
disappeared. Today the peasant is the equal of anyone ...
a human being capable of receiving instruction, of reaching
the University (Alexander 1958:75-76).

Writing from a Catholic point of view, Houtart and Pin
criticize the agrarian reform by stating that "it must be noted
that the Indian masses were plunged into a state of normlessness
and social and economic disintegration" (1965:98). This is
understandable since the Catholic Church has had a vested
interest in the ruling class of the traditional feudalistic
Latin America along with the military and the oligarchy. On the
other hand, Protestants see in the freedom of the Bolivian
serfs a new openness to fresh ideas and a responsiveness to the
Gospel message that could not have existed previously.

Universal Suffrage. A fourth reform introduced by the MNR
was to give the peasants a vote. Previous to 1952, property
and literacy requirements effectively froze out the landless
and illiterate peasant. These requirements were abolished, and
for the first time the vote was also extended to women.
Whereas only 120,000 votes were cast in the 1951 election,
917,000 were cast in the following election of 1956 (Wells 1966:
32). The problem of illiteracy was partially overcome by
printing the ticket for each party on a distinctively colored
slip, and allowing the voters to cast their ballot by color.

Education. The educational reform was a fifth step taken
by the MNR to assure the continuity of revolution. This, of
course, could not be accomplished as quickly as a redistribution of land, but the groundwork was laid for a steadily
progressing government school system designed to furnish the
benefits of a good education to peasant as well as patrician.

Economic Progress. Economic stability and progress were
the most difficult, but one of the most important goals of the
MNR. Development of commerce, transportation, communications,
agriculture, industry, and public utilities were necessary for
the country. In spite of the leftist tendencies of the Paz
government, the USA decided to provide large-scale economic aid

to the MNR, and this aid has been one of the major factors in allowing the policies established in 1952 to continue. It has also been a major factor in averting the possibility that the revolution would swing, as did Castro's, into the Communist orbit. How this has indirectly helped church growth will be examined toward the end of this chapter.

In the economic realm, the MNR ran into some very serious problems. The mining corporation, COMIBOL, began to lose money because of a fall in the world price of tin and also because of featherbedding and inefficient mine operation. Tin exports no longer brought income into the government; they cost the government money. An inflationary process began that dragged the boliviano from 190 to the U.S. dollar in 1952 to 16,000 in 1957 (Carter 1964:12). The stabilization of the currency at 12,000 was one of the major contributions of the successor of Paz, Hernán Siles Zuazo (1956-1960), with the help of the International Monetary Fund. Until the stabilization, however, foreign exchange was pegged at an artificial "official" rate of exchange, which enriched some but caused insuperable problems for most merchants and industrialists. New labor laws, designed to give utmost benefits to the workers, also contributed to the slowing down of industry. Agricultural production fell when the large latifundios were broken into tiny minifundios which were no longer farmed for the market, but rather for the individual family which owned it.

In spite of these problems, the MNR did make progress in other phases of economic development. One of the most significant was the completion of the asphalt highway linking Santa Cruz with Cochabamba. Not only did this provide a market for the produce of the agriculturally rich Santa Cruz area, but it also opened the way for the migration of highland Indians to the tropical zone. One of its most obvious effects has been the unification of the country with the gradual reduction of the barrier of regional and racial prejudice which separated the "cambas" of the lowlands from the "collas" of the highlands. Although more will be said about the migrations and colonization projects in Chapter 10, their significance for church growth can perhaps be anticipated by Richard Patch's observation:

> they all find themselves changing habits of dress, of speech, of food, of hygiene and also changing in their relations with their fellows. The almost religiously traditional diet of potatoes is abandoned for yucca and rice. The ancient invocations to the Pachamama lose

National Revolution 1952

meaning as abundant crops, no longer threatened by drought and hail, yield more than the colonist can eat or sell ... the rewards which one can achieve by one's own initiative in the new lands attack the roots of the pervasive fatalism of the high altitudes (Patch 1962:13).

Part of the fruits of this planned migration has been the attainment of national self-sufficiency in sugar and rice. Petroleum production has also increased with the encouragement of foreign capital, and now Gulf Oil is exporting crude oil through a pipe line running to the port of Arica, Chile.

RENÉ BARRIENTOS O.

During Paz Estenssoro's final term (1960-1964), the problems began to outweigh the successes, especially the increasing losses in the mines. "Widespread corruption, police brutality against political opponents, and extreme dependence on U.S. aid for economic survival, further discredited the government" (Wells 1966:9). Also the MNR militia was getting too strong, and Paz had decided to counterbalance it by reconstituting the army. The army's strength grew fast, and in 1964 General René Barrientos Ortuño, backed by General Alfredo Ovando Candia, were able to oust Paz Estenssoro and take control of the government. During his four years in office, Barrientos has led his country forward and has become one of Bolivia's most popular Presidents.

Barrientos' largest grass-roots support comes from the peasants. Most of them have had firsthand contact with their President who spends much of his time piloting his helicopter or his Air Force DC-3 to virtually every town and village in the country. Probably few, if any, of the presidents of any nation have made such a determined effort to know their people personally. The net effect of these visits is not only to gain votes, which it effectively does, but to draw the peasants into the mainstream of national life and create a bolivianidad or national pride (Llosa 1966). While Barrientos' background is the military, he represents a new type of military leader in Latin America, a progressive approach which has the good of the lower classes in focus and does not cater exclusively to the oligarchy. Barrientos is not counter-revolutionary. He is, in fact, a fulfillment of the revolutionary aspirations of the MNR, although he left the Paz Estenssoro-controlled MNR in 1964. In the 1966 general election he won more popular votes than any presidential candidate in history.

Several developments in Bolivia under the Barrientos government have something to say concerning the potential for Protestant church growth. Barrientos, of course, does not deserve exclusive credit for these. The foundation was laid with the MNR beginning in 1952. Then Barrientos' close colleague, Alfredo Ovando Candia, and several others have advised the President well. It is said that Paz was a good man, but his advisors ruined him. On the other hand, Barrientos, a good man, has been made even better by his advisors.

International Relationships. Barrientos has been successful in walking Latin America's most difficult political tightrope: he has projected an image of strong nationalism in hiw own country while keeping a close friendship with the USA. Patch concludes a chapter on Bolivian nationalism by saying,

> Bolivia has accomplished a greater social revolution than Mexico in a fifth of the time. Yet it has done so under a nationalism that, unlike Cuba's, has preserved the forms of democracy. In a way the nationalism is pure - unaffected by anti-colonialism, anti-imperialism, anti-communism, communism, or recent independence. It is a nationalism concerned with the social, economic, and political integration of the people with the national problems which this integration raises (1967:126).

Communism. Communism is not appealing to the Bolivian people at this juncture of history. Perhaps Fidel Castro's greatest disappointment came when his close friend and foremost guerrilla leader, Ernesto "Che" Guevara was apprehended in 1967 by the Bolivian army after trying to promote insurrection against the Barrientos government, and shot as a foreign invader. One of the imponderables of this historic episode was how a man of Guevara's intelligence could have dreamed that his guerrilla tactics could have worked in present-day Bolivia. Perhaps he was so impressed by the low per capita income figures that he neglected to take into account (1) the psychology of a people who have had their social revolution, (2) the popularity of a President whom his people know personally, and (3) the thought patterns of the semi-literate Andean peasant. The one thing he could have offered that would have appealed to every Bolivian would have been a seaport on the Pacific coast.

It seems that the present freedom for foreign missionary work will continue. Of course the possibility that some missionary work is hindering rather than helping church growth is a live one, but it does seem that there is a general trend toward wiser missionary-national relationships and toward the kind of use of resources which will aid the growing Bolivian Church.

At the same time, therefore, the drastic slow-down in church growth which has come to other countries of the world where Communism has taken over seems very remote for Bolivia. While the Communist threat to the Church cannot be ignored, at the present time this does not need to play an important part in planning church growth strategy.

Renewal of Cultural Pride. Even on national radio hookups, Barrientos at times addresses the nation in the Quechua language. When he speaks to peasant groups, he uses their native tongue. Quechua is taught in the universities, and is highly respected especially in Cochabamba and Sucre. Even after a downtown church service, conducted entirely in Spanish, one can hear the church members gather afterwards and unconsciously switch to Quechua.

The significance of this can best be seen by contrasting the attitude toward Quechua in Peru. There "an Indian who has acquired Spanish will often pretend to be ignorant of Quechua" (Patch 1967:119).

> In Cochabamba most Spanish speakers also speak Quechua. This is not remarkable; it is also the case in the Peruvian sierra. But in Cochabamba the Spanish speakers are truly bilingual. Their Quechua is not a halting and rudimentary version learned from servants in the nursery, but a fluent and eloquent Quechua in which they take pride and which they use as much in singing and telling stories as in directing servants (Patch 1967:120).

When one recalls that some 55 percent of all Bolivians know Quechua as a first language, the significance for future church growth is evident. The Aymara language, although spoken by fewer people, is just as important since the Aymara people are presently the most responsive to the Gospel in the country. Any ministry to these people which does not intend to use the autochthonous languages will suffer proportionately.

Social Mobility in the Cities. The urban social structure of Bolivia preceding the 1952 revolution might be diagrammed as seen in Figure 17.

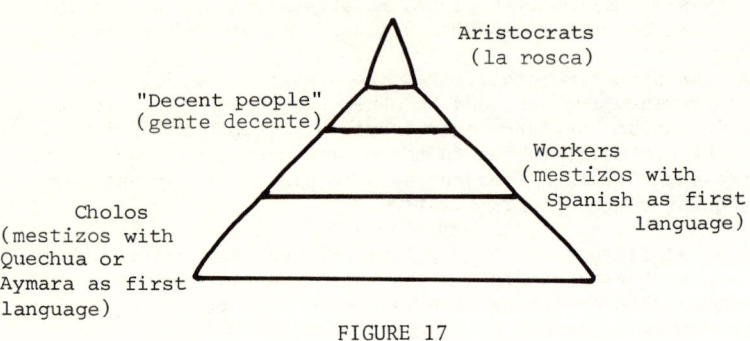

FIGURE 17

Patch (1967:121-122) describes the aristocracy as those who owned the land and came from high class families; the decent people as the professionals such as doctors, lawyers, teachers, businessmen; the workers as those who used their hands in their occupations; and the cholos as those who presumably had come to the city from the country and who were employed as household servants or who sold their wares in the market. The class line between the decent people and the workers was the most rigid.

The aristocracy were wiped out by the revolution. Their land was first taken, then all but their international savings disappeared in the subsequent inflation. The cholos gained status, and the line separating them from the workers became very dim. With the new political power and integration into national life of the lower classes, largely gained through labor unions, the decent people have not been able to maintain such a rigid distinction from those lower in the social scale than they. As a result, the picture now looks more like that seen in Figure 18.

The decent people, the professional classes, have not yet become receptive to the Gospel. On the other hand, the worker and cholo class has responded well, and urban churches which are growing are doing so in this social class.

NEW SOCIAL STRUCTURE

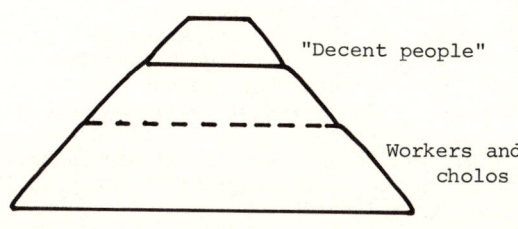

FIGURE 18

Geographic Mobility. The fact that Bolivians are able to move for the first time is causing some profound changes and some new opportunities for church planting. Whether by truck, bus, train, or airplane, many Bolivians are moving around the countryside, some just to visit and see what the rest of the world is like, others to seek out new lands and a new way of life. It is well known that people who move are usually receptive to innovations. Wise mission administrators, such as Paul McCleary (see pp. 70-71) will be sensitive to this open door and enter it whenever possible.

Undoubtedly the government-encouraged colonization projects are the most significant phase of the new geographical mobility. They will be examined more closely in Chapter 10.

Economic Progress. When Barrientos took office, the major problem facing him was that of the mines. The government corporation, COMIBOL, had shown a 40 percent decrease in yield over its first ten years, while the working force rose from 18,000 to 26,000. In 1962 the mines showed a $16,200,000 deficit. By 1965 COMIBOL earned $2,000,000. The accomplishment of this objective was the most severe test of Barrientos' political strength he has faced. The miners, organized by Marxist Juan Lechín, still had the arms that Paz Estenssoro had given them, and constituted a formidable militia. But Barrientos knew that many of the guns and their users were rusty, that the much stronger peasant militia was solidly behind him, and that the army had regained much of its pre-1952 power. On this basis he took the calculated risk of laying off two thousand featherbedded mine workers. The reaction came from the miners, but they did not have the strength to impose their will on the country. This move was an absolute prerequisite for any economic progress.

In the past three years export sales have gone up 30 percent to $150,400,000. Petroleum production has doubled. New sections of the country have opened up to migration and commerce because 20,000 miles of new roads have been constructed. Then in December of 1967, Barrientos left little doubt about his willingness to participate in Bolivia's austerity when he requested Congress to cut his $13,000 salary by 25 percent (*Time* 1968:25).

As economic prosperity increases, the Bolivian Church will more and more be able to pay its own bills. The less it must depend on foreign subsidy for its own programs, the stronger it will become. While the withdrawal of foreign funds is never justified for its own sake, the step should be taken when this seems likely to aid the Church in future growth.

In summary, the revolution of 1952 produced a new Bolivia. For the first time in history, all human beings who were born into the nation geographically can now in some measure participate in her national life. The resulting social, economic, and political ferments have been favorable to the growth of the Protestant Church. As the revolution progresses, the promise for future growth should be even greater.

7

Third Sowing of Missions

World War II mainly interrupted the entrance of new missionary groups into Bolivia. Only the New Tribes Mission and the World Gospel Mission entered during the war itself. Since the war, ten additional missions have entered Bolivia with enough strength to have made a noticeable contribution to church growth. Fourteen smaller groups have also come in, and they will be mentioned in order to complete the picture.

NEW TRIBES MISSION
(Misión Nuevas Tribus)

The first field chosen by the New Tribes Mission for their work was Bolivia. The mission was organized in the USA in 1942 for the purpose of tribal evangelism and the establishment of New Testament indigenous churches. In 1942 the first party of missionaries arrived in Bolivia under the leadership of Cecil Dye, one of the mission's founders. They settled in Roboré, east of Santa Cruz, and from there attempted to reach the savage Ayoré tribe. Five of the men were murdered by the Ayorés in November, 1943. The story of their martyrdom, and the subsequent evangelization of the Ayorés has been told in the books, *God Planted Five Seeds* (Johnson 1967) and *Defeat of the Bird God* (Wagner 1967). In establishing the base of operations in Roboré, the missionaries were successful in planting a congregation in Roboré, which today, under the NTMU is the largest in Eastern Bolivia. Several smaller churches were planted in San Juan, Entre Ríos, Portón, El Chochís, and San José (now under the SAIM).

Today the bulk of the NTM work is carried out in the Beni Department where it works with the Chama, Chimane, Yura and Trinitario tribes, as well as more recent contact with the Toromono (Araona) and Yuqui (Goddard 1967:479). Eighteen churches have been planted (Wyma 1965), some under the leadership of graduates of the short-lived Bible institute held in Arboleda north of Santa Cruz in the late fifties. No attempt has been made to join these churches into a denomination.

Statistics of church membership have not been kept, although Field Chairman, Richard Wyma, admits that "we should have been more concerned about just how work is progressing, and to keep some statistics on these works we have been in for several years" (Wyma 1968:1). The 1967 CGRILA estimate of membership was 200.

Comparison of Bolivia to Paraguay. A thorough study on the responsiveness of the jungle tribes of inland South America would be a fruitful area for church growth study. As NTM General Secretary, Jack Knutson says, "for some reason or other, our Bolivian field has not been as fruitful as most of our other fields in converts or churches planted" (1968a). This is perplexing since good church growth has been experienced among tribes just across the border in Paraguay among the Chamacocos and Lenguas. One hint given by Knutson is that the latter two tribes "had much previous contact with civilization" (1968b). Another curious fact is that the breakthrough with the Chamacocos came through a ministry in Spanish, but with the Lenguas it resulted from a ministry in their own tongue, both after an almost identical period of preliminary work with them. Knutson observes:

> We have found that some tribes are ready for a change and if missionaries move in at the right time and learn the language, that this change comes about rather quickly. On the other hand, there are tribes that are not ready for change and we have worked with them for fifteen years or more and have seen relatively little fruit (1968b).

If further church growth research, perhaps by the Wycliffe Bible Translators along with the NTM, could uncover the precise reasons for this difference in receptivity and establish criteria upon which reasonable predictions as to responsiveness of the tribal Indians could be made, this would be a great service to those missions dedicated to the evangelization of this small, but needy, segment of the population-

WORLD GOSPEL MISSION
(Iglesia Evangélica Mundial)

Personnelwise, the work of the World Gospel Mission was a continuation of that of the Oregon Friends. Carrol Tamplin of the Oregon Friends felt called to evangelize the jungle tribes, but his mission board was not prepared to undertake this type of work (Trachsel 1961:91). Tamplin therefore in 1944 transferred to what was then known as the National Holiness Missionary Society, now the World Gospel Mission. At first, both the Tamplins and their co-workers, the Marshal Cavits, worked along with the Oregon Friends in the La Paz area. The first WGM mission station was established at Guanay with the intention of using it as a base to reach jungle Indians. The stations in Asención de Guarayos and Santa María were established for similar purposes. However the mestizo residents of the villages were not neglected and a strong congregation was planted, for example, in Asención. In 1952 the work in the city of Santa Cruz was established by Garnett Townsend, who also founded the Berea Bible Institute. In 1960 the national church organization, Iglesia Evangélica Mundial, was established. The statistics for the World Gospel Mission are recorded on Table 16.

TABLE 16

World Gospel Mission 1944 - 1967

Date	Foreign Workers	National Workers	Churches	Full Members	Source
1952	10	-	3	-	*WCH* 1952
1957	22	3	18	-	*WCH* 1957
1962	27	23	17	248	*WCH* 1962
1967	20	20	45	950	*WCH* 1967; CGRILA 1967

CHURCH OF THE NAZARENE
(Iglesia del Nazareno)

TABLE 17

Church of the Nazarene 1944 - 1967

Date	Foreign Workers	National Workers	Churches	Full Members	Total Members*	Source
1946	2	12	6	225	315	Ch. of Nazarene
1947	2	16	8	300	400	Ch. of Nazarene
1948	2	11	9	349	551	Ch. of Nazarene
1949	2	13	10	412	610	Ch. of Nazarene
1950	4	14	10	397	494	Ch. of Nazarene
1951	4	17	10	377	453	Ch. of Nazarene
1952	4	21	14	—	700	*WCH* 1952; Conrad 1967
1953	—	—	—	—	580	Conrad 1967
1954	—	—	—	—	775	Conrad 1967
1955	—	—	—	—	745	Conrad 1967
1956	—	—	—	—	1150	Conrad 1967
1957	6	37	18	—	850	*WCH* 1957; Conrad 1967
1958	—	—	—	—	870	Conrad 1967
1959	—	—	—	—	880	Conrad 1967
1960	—	—	—	—	900	Conrad 1967
1961	—	—	—	—	1100	Conrad 1967
1962	10	35	22	—	1200	*WCH* 1962; Conrad 1967
1963	—	—	—	—	1100	Conrad 1967
1964	—	—	—	—	1250	Conrad 1967
1965	—	—	—	—	1400	Conrad 1967
1966	12	59	41	—	1398	Ch. of Nazarene

*Full members plus probationers

Nazarene statistics are given on Table 17 and plotted on Figure 19.

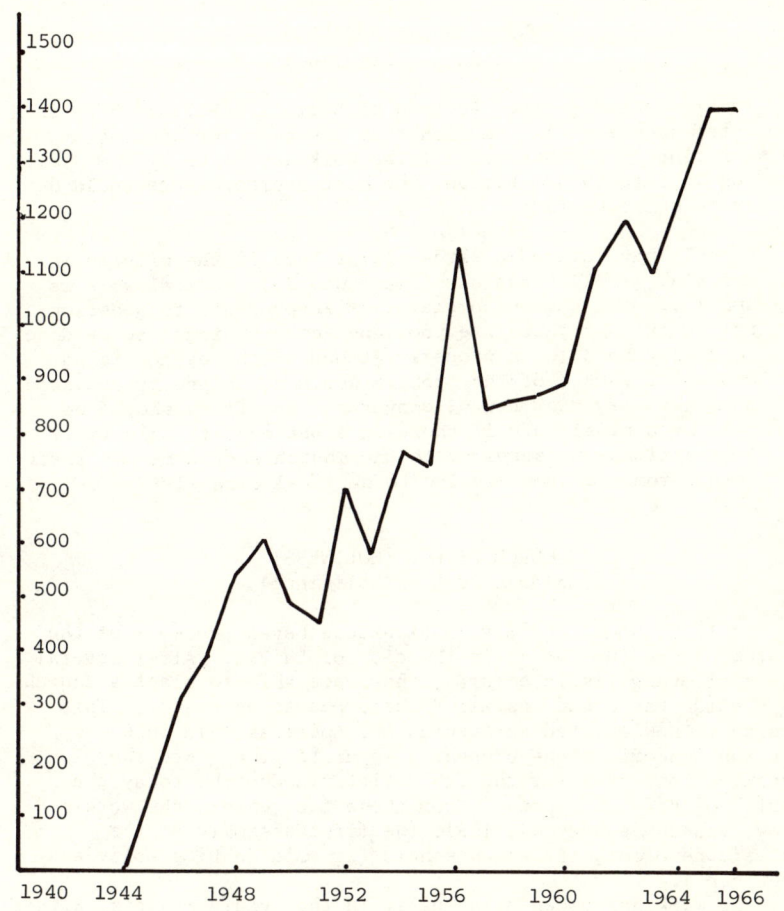

CHURCH OF THE NAZARENE 1944 - 1967
ABSOLUTE MEMBERSHIP GROWTH

FIGURE 19

CHURCH OF THE NAZARENE
(Iglesia del Nazareno)

Howard Conrad's brief section on Bolivia (1967:369-371) is the chief source of information that has been forthcoming at this writing. He mentions that the work was begun by the N.J. Brailes in late 1944. Perhaps the best approach here would be simply to quote Conrad:

> Schools have played a rather large role in the mission in Bolivia. In 1965 the enrollment was 29. Medical work is small ... the common complaint of respondents to questionnaires is that there are too many "other things" to be done to really be able to properly attend to the evangelizing mission ... Much of the problem would be solved by a change in missionary distrust of converts. No office should be held by a missionary if there is a national to hold it ... Institutions and services to the Church should be the first things removed from mission to national care (1967:370-371).

CHURCH OF GOD (HOLINESS)
(Iglesia de Dios Boliviana)

In 1946, Homer and Elvira Firestone began the work of the Church of God (Holiness) in the city of La Paz. After several years of evangelistic efforts, they were able to plant a church on Avenida Pando and install Marcelo Duarte as pastor. This church is now located on Avenida Las Américas. In 1950 Luciano Condori Ticona brought a separate group into the denomination, creating the Villa Victoria Church, today the Church of Bajo Munaypata. From these two centers the work grew, and on January 24, 1951, the first assembly of the Iglesia de Dios Boliviana was held (Iglesia de Dios Boliviana 1968:n.p.).

The work has grown principally in the Aymara regions, with little success among the mestizos and Quechuas. The two mestizo churches in the city of Cochabamba, for example, have never moved well, in spite of the placement of capable missionaries in the work. One of the church buildings is up for sale at this writing. Why have not these churches grown? Undoubtedly the fact that the Church of God (Holiness) in Bolivia is known as an Aymara denomination, has much to do with

it. Their Bible school in La Paz trains Aymara pastors. They
are building a tabernacle in the Aymara center of Alto La Paz
which will seat 2500. The Bolivian denominational leaders are
Aymaras. Therefore, it would seem that the reason is basically
ethnic. Cochabamba mestizo Christians would prefer to join a
church composed on the national scale of "their own people"
rather than join an Aymara church.

Figure 20 shows a marked increase of growth beginning in
1962. According to missionary Philip Urquiola, most of this
growth is taking place in the Aymara regions close to the city
of La Paz. The denomination would undoubtedly do well to
devote itself, like the Oregon Friends, entirely to Aymara
work. The sale of the Cochabamba building is a good move from
the church growth point of view. Investment of resources in
the Cochabamba area will probably not prove to be good
stewardship for this particular denomination, since an equal
investment in the Aymara region is certain to produce much
greater results in terms of church membership. Cochabamba
mestizos are winnable, but denominations which have a mestizo
or multicultural image will be the ones which will probably win
them.

Table 18 and Figure 20 give the present statistics, furnished by Philip Urquiola. Membership in the Church of God
(Holiness) churches is by conversion experience. Water baptism
is not required for membership, although it is practiced.

TABLE 18

Church of God (Holiness) 1945 - 1967

Date	Foreign Workers	National Workers	Churches	Full Members	Total Members	Source
1952	5	5	5	200	-	F. Urquiola
1957	5	5	5	1025	-	F. Urquiola
1962	6	20	19	1270	-	F. Urquiola
1967	7	29	28	2100	-	F. Urquiola

140   THE PROTESTANT MOVEMENT IN BOLIVIA

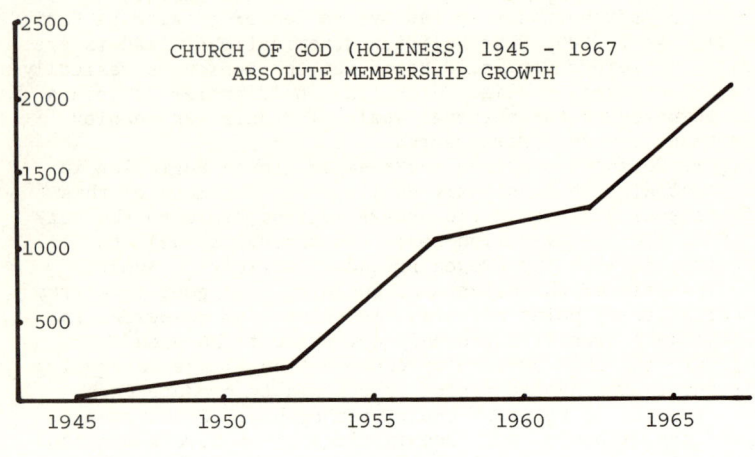

FIGURE 20

BRAZILIAN BAPTISTS
(Convención Bautista Boliviana)

The Brazilian Baptists, founded in Brazil by the Southern Baptists from the USA, have long shown a desire to fulfill the Great Commission. Their Foreign Missions Commission was organized in 1907, and the first missionaries sent to Chile in 1908. Bolivia became a mission field for them in 1946 when Waldomiro Mota and his wife were sent to Sant Cruz to pioneer the work (Salles 1966:1).

Up to 1966, twelve churches had been organized in eastern Bolivia, with a membership of 400-500. A school called Instituto Bautista Boliviano functions in attractive buildings in Santa Cruz with 250 students. On the same property the Baptist Theological Seminary of Eastern Bolivia has some 25 students studying for the ministry (Salles 1966:2).

The missionary spirit of the Brazilians carried over to Bolivia in that the first commission to be formed under the Bolivian Baptist Convention was that of Home Missions. Their desire was to extend their Church as rapidly as possible throughout the eastern part of Bolivia (Salles 1966:5).

ASSEMBLIES OF GOD
(Asambleas de Dios)

Although missionaries of the Assemblies of God are listed in Browning's work (1930:130) as having a mission in Todos Santos, the present Assemblies of God trace their work back only to Waldo Nicodemus and his wife who moved to Cochabamba in 1946. Within a year a La Paz station was opened by Earl Wilkie and a Santa Cruz station by Everett Hale (AG 1960:6).

Excellent statistics supplied by missionary Monroe Grams enable us to study this denomination on a regional basis. No comparable statistics are available from other multicultural denominations, although it will become quite evident that the most meaningful type of study in terms of church growth absolutely requires such a breakdown into the growth figures for each sub-population. Notice how the upper line of Figure 21, which is the total growth curve of the Assemblies of God, tells us very little. The lower curves and Figure 22, however, break down the growth into regions and tell us that in some places the Church is growing greatly while in other places it is declining. Figure 23 introduces another type of comparison. By plotting the same data as shown on Figure 21 on a three-cycle semi-logarithmic paper, the relative rates of growth can be seen somewhat more clearly. The parallel between the curve is striking, especially during the years 1961-1967. The fluctuations in the rates of growth of the four mestizo churches almost cancel each other out. Only by breaking down the statistics according to regions could this interesting fact be discovered. Whereas this type of data is essential in understanding the true picture of a multicultural Church, it is also very helpful in understanding the growth within a given culture. For example, the INELA (Oregon Friends) Church could profitably be studied by a careful membership accounting in each sub-tribe of the Aymaras in which they work. Future church growth studies in Bolivia should undertake to do this very thing. The preliminary nature of the present study precludes such a process.

Aymara Growth. Nevertheless, it will readily be seen that the bulk of the growth in the Assemblies of God Church has come among the Aymaras. Aymaras compose almost 60 percent of the current membership. The churches in La Paz city, Cochabamba, Oruro, Santa Cruz and Tarija are basically mestizo. They have not all shown outstanding growth, although since 1965 the Santa

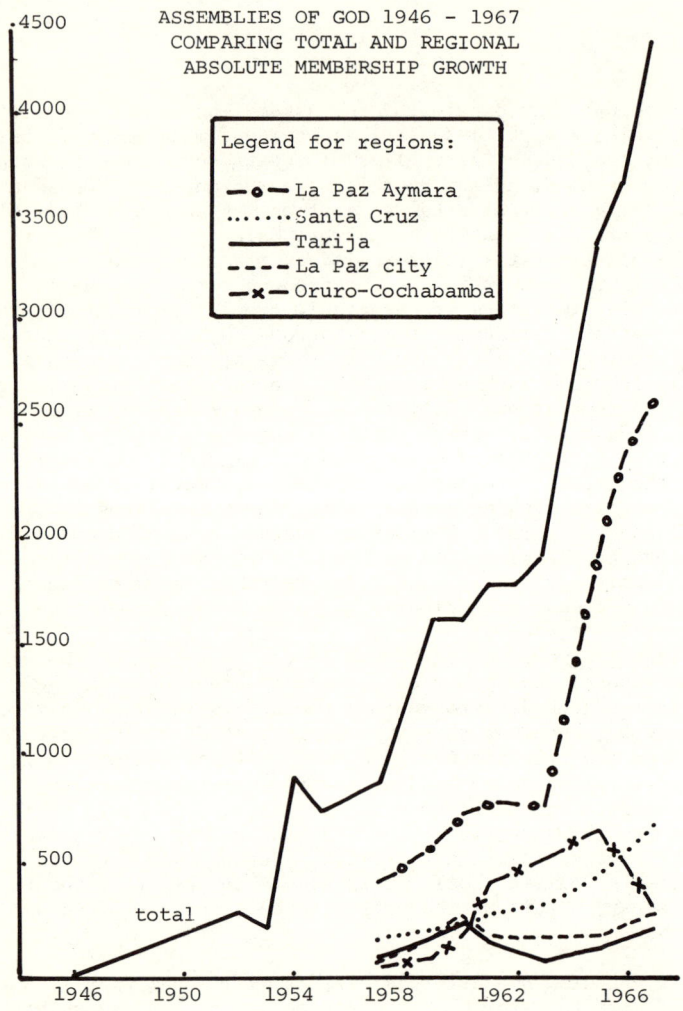

FIGURE 21

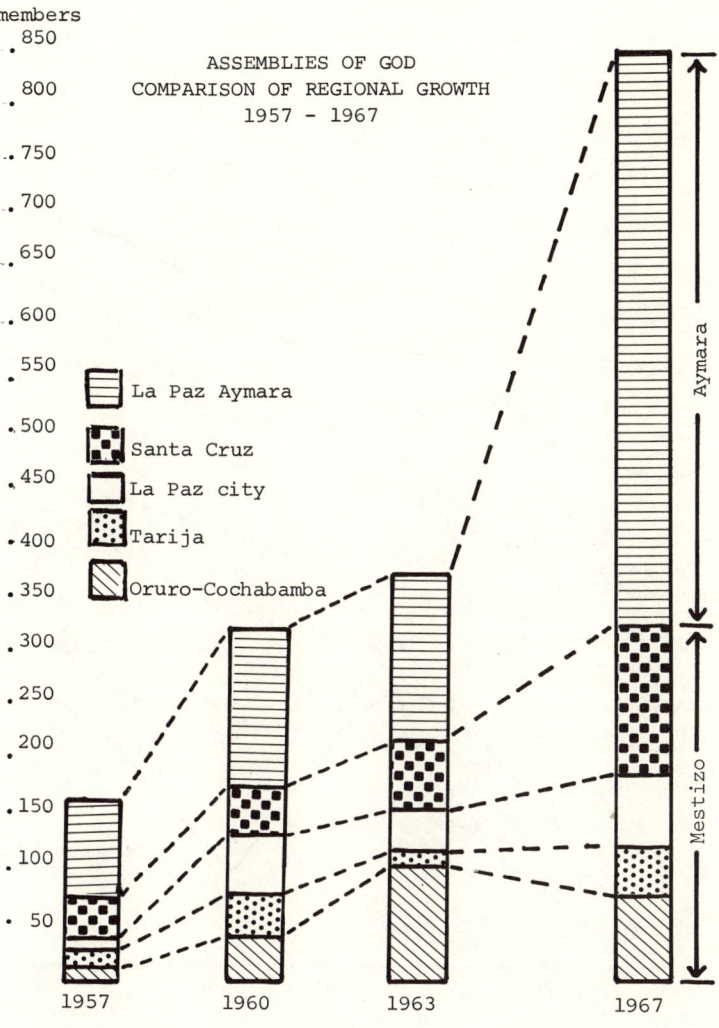

FIGURE 22

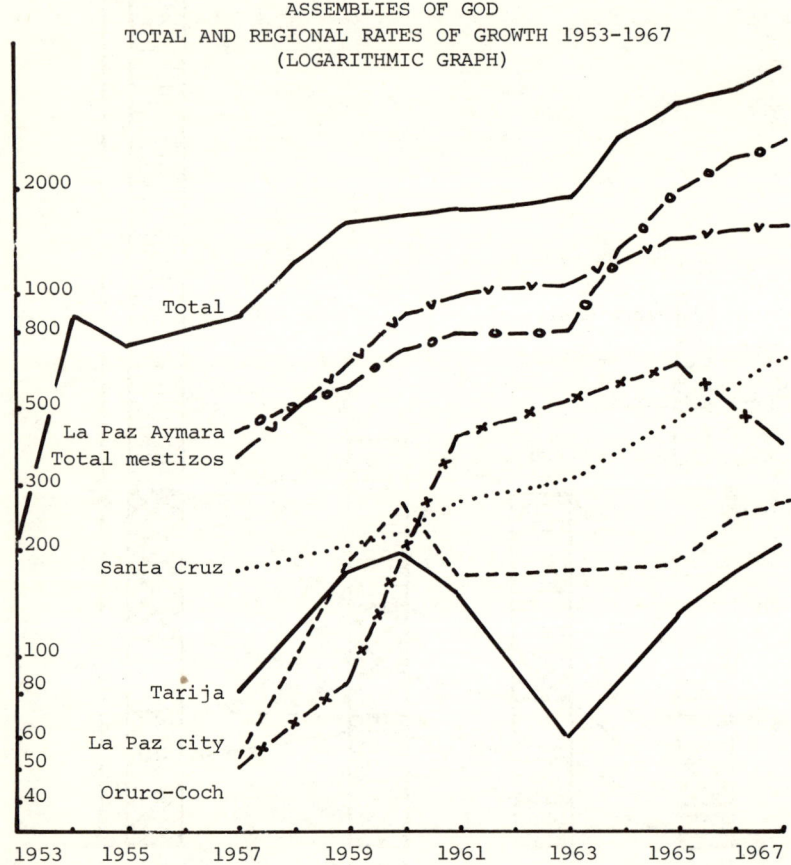

FIGURE 23

Cruz, La Paz city, and Tarija churches have grown faster than the Aymaras as Figure 23 shows. The Cochabamba and Oruro rate has declined. In the city of Cochabamba, for example, the Assembly of God church has an excellent downtown location and one of the most attractive church buildings in the city; still after twenty years of labor in the city it has only 10 members. In contrast, the Brazilian Pentecostal church, located in an unimposing church building near the outskirts of the same city on an unpaved street, reportedly has a higher membership.

A Multicultural Denomination. Why this is true is not completely clear at the moment. It would seem, however, that the multicultural aspect of the denomination is a hindrance to growth. The denominational leaders recognize the problem, and wrote in 1960: "The Assemblies of God of Bolivia has been organized on a regional rather than a national basis due to the geographical and ethnic divisions of the country" (AG 1960:6). However, they have not been able to put this sound policy into practice. The entire denomination is under one Superintendent and one Board of Directors, elected in an annual convention of representatives of all the churches. I clearly recall that after a recent convention, a mestizo leader in the denomination who was not elected to any post on the Board of Directors in spite of the fact that he undoubtedly has more formal education than any other Bolivian on it, expressed with some irritation that the Aymaras had carried the voting.

Perils of Integration. The principle of integration in the Church can be a good testimony as to God's love for all men and brotherhood within the Christian family. At the same time, if not properly handled, it can be a deterrent to church growth. If the original principle of organizing the denomination on a regional instead of a national base had been carried out, it is quite possible that the Aymaras would have grown at an equal or greater rate, but that the mestizos would have shown much better growth over the years. If the ratio were reversed, with 60 percent mestizos and 40 percent Aymaras, although that would not be an ideal arrangement either, probably the mestizos would be more attracted to the denomination. But when joining the church means to a mestizo that he must be outvoted by Aymaras, he may think twice before committing himself into membership, or remaining in the denomination if he is already a member.

These rudimentary observations, of course, do not provide the whole answer. Much more study needs to be done. The churches in Santa Cruz are showing steady growth, although not

at the good rate of those in La Paz. Perhaps some of this
growth could be accounted for by Aymaras who have migrated to
the Santa Cruz area. The multicultural problem mentioned above
would in any case affect the city churches in closest proximity
to country Aymaras, since status rivalry often diminishes with
geographical distance. The city churches in La Paz and Oruro
could thus be most affected, with Cochabamba a close third.
Tarija and Santa Cruz might not feel it as much, if at all.

As to the growth in the Aymara sector of the work, Grams
again has supplied a thoughtful analysis. When he and his wife
Betty Jane, arrived in La Paz in 1952, the work had fallen back
perhaps due to an extended period with no resident missionary.
The laymen were not yet well enough prepared to carry the work
forward. The renewed activities in La Paz, especially with the
Aymaras, account for the upsurge shown on Figure 21 in 1953.
The Grams' furlough fell in 1956, and again there was a
leveling off of the growth. When they returned there was good
growth until the time of a serious split in the work in 1961,
when 260 baptized members were taken off (Grams 1968a:2). This
split-off, under the leadership of Fernando Monrroy, has
diminished over subsequent years (Grams 1968b:1). The split,
however, produced a spiritual cleansing, and a new surge was
felt. Around 1965 the administration of the Aymara work was
taken over by Aymara graduates of the Bible training center in
General Pando, south of La Paz (1968a:2).

Statistics of membership for the Assemblies of God may be
seen on Tables 19 and 20.

TABLE 19

*Regional Statistics of Assemblies of God 1957 - 1967**

Region	Race	1957	1959	1960	1961	1963	1964	1965	1966	1967
La Paz	Aymara	429	537	718	784	788	1314	1908	2355	2611
La Paz City	Mestizos	53	188	270	170	175	180	182	240	270
Oruro-Cochbba	Quechua, Mestizos	50	88	196	418	515	-	653	-	387
St.Cruz	Mestizos	176	206	223	273	316	-	460	-	681
Tarija	Mestizos	81	175	197	150	63	-	135	-	206

*Provided for the author by Monroe Grams, 1968.

TABLE 20

Assemblies of God 1946 - 1967

Date	Foreign Workers	National Workers	Churches	Full Members	Total Members	Source
1949	3	1	4	-	-	*WCH* 1949
1951	-	3	-	128	249	Assemblies of God*
1952	11	11	11	118	261	Assemblies of God
1953	12	5	12	163	240	Assemblies of God
1954	13	20	20	460	900	Assemblies of God
1955	15	22	17	490	744	Assemblies of God
1956	14	30	10	544	801	Assemblies of God
1957	13	27	15	562	883	Assemblies of God
1958	16	29	17	639	1230	Assemblies of God
1959	17	33	18	796	1609	Assemblies of God
1960	16	33	18	796	1609	Assemblies of God
1961	13	36	20	824	1793	Assemblies of God
1962	14	36	20	824	1795	Assemblies of God
1963	14	45	27	934	1857	Assemblies of God
1964	12	65	29	1120	2728	Assemblies of God
1965	14	65	39	1411	3338	Assemblies of God
1966	12	23	49	1759	3641	Grams 1968
1967	-	-	-	1932	4255	Grams 1968

*These statistics are from the annual Overseas Statistical Reports, sent to the author on Xerox copies by the Foreign Missions Department.

BOLIVIAN HOLINESS MISSION OR THE HOLINESS METHODIST CHURCH
(Iglesia Boliviana de Santidad)

The mission was founded in 1948, and led by Raimundo and Matte Marca, he a Bolivian and she a North American (Goddard 1967:318). The missionary staff has always been small, and four are presently on the field. Due to the generous efforts of missionary Mark Frink, this denomination is the only one which responded 100 percent to the research questionnaire.

This allows some basis for analysis that other denominations do not have. Of the 34 churches and congregations of the Iglesia Boliviana de Santidad, 32 are Aymara and 2 Quechua.

TABLE 21

Comparative Statistics of Thirty-Four Bolivian Holiness Churches 1955 - 1968

Church Name	Province	Building?	Membership			
			1955	1960	1965	1968
Department of La Paz (Aymaras)						
Ricardo Bustamante	Murillo	no	20	25	35	40
Villa Victoria	Murillo	no	30	40	60	80
Munaypata	Murillo	no	-	-	10	50
Alto Lima	Murillo	yes	3	25	60	90
12 de Octubre	Murillo	yes	-	-	-	25
Villa Fatima	Murillo	yes	10	15	15	25
Tahapalca	Murillo	yes	-	-	4	15
Cebullullu	Murillo	no	-	-	-	6
Millucato	Murillo	no	-	-	-	4
Hilata Arriba	Ingavi	yes	20	40	45	30
Hirpa Chico	Ingavi	yes	15	20	28	40
Choquinaira	Ingavi	yes	-	-	9	20
Viacha	Ingavi	yes	30	35	50	65
Chacoma	Ingavi	no	-	-	8	15
Cachuma	Ingavi	yes	-	-	12	20
Collahua	Ingavi	no	-	-	-	8
Pillapi	Ingavi	yes	-	-	-	55
Chusñupa	Ingavi	yes	-	15	24	30
Coniri	Ingavi	yes	-	15	19	12
Hilata Centro	Ingavi	yes	15	20	25	30
Tiahuanacu	Ingavi	yes	7	10	25	50
Taraco	Ingavi	no	6	6	6	15
Ancoraimes	Omasuyos	yes	15	20	35	45
Sapahaqui	Loayza	yes	-	-	8	40
Caluyo	Aroma	yes	-	-	-	40
Colquencha	Aroma	yes	-	-	-	40
Canton Machacamarca	Aroma	yes	20	25	30	15
Ventilla	Aroma	yes	-	-	20	25
Alto Beni	Nor Yungas	no	-	-	-	1
Villa San José	Nor Yungas	yes	-	-	-	18
Incahuara	Nor Yungas	no	-	-	-	8
Oro Verde	Nor Yungas	no	-	-	-	20

Third Sowing of Missions 149

TABLE 21, cont.

Church Name	Province	Building?	Membership 1955	1960	1965	1968
Department of Oruro (Quechuas)						
Machacamarca	Cercado	no	15	20	25	22
Oruro	Cercado	yes	15	20	20	7
	Totals by Province:					
	Murillo		63	105	184	335
	Ingavi		93	161	251	390
	Omasuyos		15	20	35	45
	Loayza		-	-	8	40
	Aroma		20	25	50	120
	Nor Yungas		-	-	-	47
	Cercado		30	40	45	29
	Membership Totals:		221	351	573	1006
	Number of Churches:		14	16	23	34
	Average Membership:		15.7	21.9	24.9	29.5

SOURCE: Research questionnaires by author.

A glance at Table 21 will allow us to draw the following conclusions regarding the growth of this church:

1. *Aymara Growth*. Virtually all growth has taken place among the Aymaras. The two Quechua churches have declined since 1965. The lack of response among the Quechuas may be the reason that some twenty new churches have been planted among the Aymaras since 1955, and none among the Quechuas. Finding the ripe harvest field and concentrating on it is a sound church growth principle.

2. *Multiplying Congregations*. Whereas the average church membership has increased about two times since 1955, the total membership has increased almost five times. This means that growth has not come so much from building up large churches (exceptions would be the city congregations of Villa Victoria and Alto Lima) as multiplying smaller congregations in many centers of population. This has been especially true in the 1965-1968 period. In all probability, good growth in the

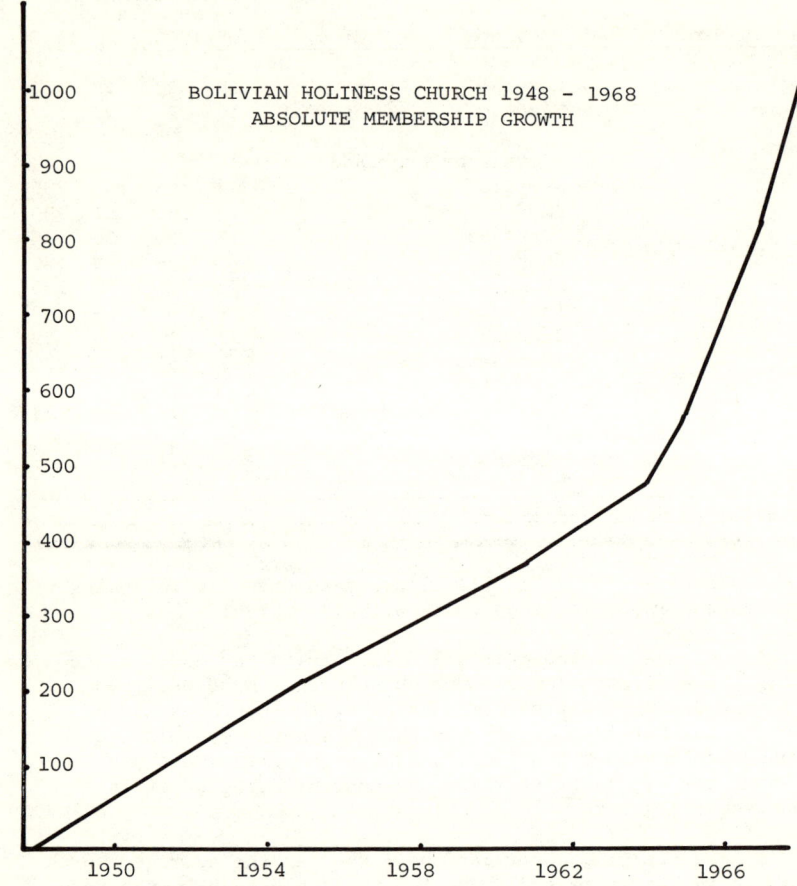

FIGURE 24

Third Sowing of Missions

future will be proportionate to the number of new churches planted.

3. The twenty-three churches which have buildings average 33.0 members while the eleven without buildings average 22.5 members. But in the period 1965-1968 the per decade rate of growth for churches with or without buildings was identical, at 127 percent (see Figure 24). This would seem to show that possessing a church building is not a prerequisite for growth among the Aymaras.

Lay Leadership. Of the thirty-four churches, six are cared for by pastors and twenty-eight by laymen. None of the pastors are fully supported by their churches; they all earn some of their income through their own work, consequently. The churches with pastors have grown at a rate of 134 percent per decade in the 1965-1968 period, slightly under the overall average for the period of 151 percent per decade. The conclusion is that laymen are very active, and are successful in spreading the Gospel. Undoubtedly many of these soul-winning laymen are being trained by faithful pastors.

TABLE 22

Bolivian Holiness Church Annual Membership 1948 - 1968

Year	Churches	Membership
1955	14	221
1960	16	351
1964	22	481
1965	23	573
1966	30	704
1967	34	837
1968	34	1006

SOURCE: Research questionnaires by author.

BETHESDA MISSIONS
(Iglesia Nacional Bethesda)
and
Iglesia Evangélica Nacional

The first missionaries under Bethesda Missions were assigned to Bolivia, arriving in Cochabamba in 1950 (Goddard 1967:80). They soon shifted their acticities to the Santa Cruz area, where they started an orphanage, planted churches and established a Bible Institute. In 1957 a group under Harold Stansbury split from Bethesda and founded the Iglesia Evangélica Nacional.

The CGRILA estimates put the membership of the Bethesda Church at 300, and the Iglesia Evangélica Nacional at 60.

MIDNIGHT CALL MISSION
(Misión Llamamiento de Medianoche)

This evangelical mission was founded in 1955 in Zurich, Switzerland as Missionswerk Mitternachtsruf, and entered Bolivia in 1960. Evangelistic work is carried on in the departments of Beni and Pando, based in the town of Riberalta. No statistics of this group are available other than a CGRILA estimate of 1967 of 100 members. Some preliminary talks have been held concerning the incorporation of these national Churches into the Evangelical Christian Union.

MARANATHA BAPTISTS
(Bautistas Maranata)

Beginning in 1962, this group, pioneered by John Gunther, has been working to plant churches in the town of Samaipata on the Santa Cruz-Cochabamba highway, as well as in some towns in the Cochabamba valley. No statistics are available for the work, although CGRILA (1967) estimates their membership at 60. Two of their Bolivian evangelists were formerly members of the Christ Redeemer Mission, founded by the ex-priest, José María Rico, who was associated at that time with the Andes Evangelical Mission. The Christ Redeemer Mission was established to evangelize priests and help them make the transition out of the Catholic Church. In 1963, Rico joined the Assemblies of God and the Christ Redeemer Mission disintegrated. The two ex-priests working with the Maranatha Baptists are Benigno Zúñiga and Angel Carreón.

OTHER SMALLER GROUPS

The Directory of Protestant Churches and Missions in Bolivia, found in the Appendix of this book, lists a few more groups not yet mentioned here. These missions have not played a significant part in Bolivian church growth, or if they have, their activities are unknown to the author. Some have entered Bolivia for specialized purposes and have not intended to plant churches. These would include the Summer Institute of Linguistics, which reduces primitive languages to writing and translates Scriptures; the Bolivian Faith Mission, which operates a printing press; and the Mennonite Central Committee, which works in social service projects.

Others are churches which minister to foreign colonies, such as the Latvian Baptists in Rincón del Tigre and the Mennonite colony near Santa Cruz which is German-speaking. Some, like the Church of the Open Door and the Seattle Bible Union have planted only a single congregation. Several Pentecostal groups are somewhat isolated from other evangelicals and have not yet met with much success such as the Brazilian Pentecostals, the Chilean Pentecostals, the Norwegian Pentecostals, and the Church of God (Cleveland). Others, such as the International Baptist Mission, are too new to have made a significant contribution as yet.

8

Protestant Cooperation

During the early days of Bolivian Protestant missions the nature of the situation brought the missionaries together in a high degree of cooperation. In the midst of Catholic persecution and with only a small missionary force, workers were naturally drawn together. Joint colportage and evangelistic trips were frequent. George Allan, founder of the AEM, attended a Baptist church in Cochabamba, and even took charge of it for some time when a Baptist personnel crisis arose. When the AEM moved its headquarters to Cochabamba in 1934, all its missionaries attended and worked with the Baptist church while they were in the city. Methodists and Baptists worked together on the Guatajata project, and for some time the Methodists met together with the Baptists in a joint congregation in La Paz.

REGIONAL CONFERENCE FOR BOLIVIA

The first formal meeting to plan cooperation was held on December 11, 1916, as a direct result of the Panama Congress on Christian Work in Latin America held earlier that same year. Of the five missions in the country, only two attended: the Canadian Baptists and the Methodists. The Adventists, of course, would not have been invited because of the general Protestant feeling at that time that they were a false cult. It is probable that the Brethren would not have had much interest in such a gathering. They have not yet been involved in any of the nation's cooperative projects. Why the AEM was not present is unknown.

This "Regional Conference for Bolivia" met in La Paz, where A. G. Baker was elected President and A. Haddow Secretary, both missionaries of the Canadian Baptists. Decisions included the plan to establish a Protestant paper for Bolivia, the substitution of the word evangélico in Spanish in place of the word protestante, the fixing of salaries for Bolivian workers in the range of Bs. 100-150 per month plus rent, and the formation of territorial divisions or comity agreements (CBFMB 1917:16-17). David Phillips reports the comity agreements as follows:

1. Works and congregations already begun in the main cities of Bolivia will continue as they are.
2. The Methodists will be permitted to occupy the territory east of the railroad to Arica and northeast to Chulumani. They will also control Punata, Totora, Vallegrande, Santa Cruz and all the territory on the road from Cochabamba to Santa Cruz.
3. The Canadian Baptists have the region to the north of Guaqui including Sorata, and the region extending from Oruro to Potosí to Sucre to the southern border with Argentina. They also have Quillacollo, Tarata, Cliza, Sacaba and the towns around Cochabamba.
4. Since the AEM was not present, it was decided to suggest that they take the responsibility of all the area round about San Pedro de Buena Vista north, southeast, and west, not neglecting any of the villages (Phillips n.d.:n.p.).

In November, 1917, the second annual meeting of the Regional Conference for Bolivia was held in Cochabamba. Apparently the same two missions were represented. Items on the agenda included a study of the conclusions of the Panama Conference, the establishment of a literature department in La Paz, the decision to agitate for civil registration of vital statistics in the nation, and again the publishing of a Protestant paper for all Bolivia (CBFMB 1918).

COMITY AGREEMENTS

Comity agreements were recognized, although not fully respected. The AEM, for example, wrote the Baptists in 1917 asking their permission to occupy Capinota. The Baptists replied by stating that permission would be given on a temporary basis because according to the agreement of 1916, Capinota was theirs (Phillips n.d.:n.p.). By 1921 the agreements were being violated by many parties, and Bishop Oldham of the Methodist Church informed New York headquarters that he was not in agreement with the 1916 division of territory. The Bolivian Friends Holiness Mission was occupying the Baptist territory of Sorata. The Brethren and the AEM were moving into Baptist territory toward the Argentine border. Furthermore, Methodists were planning to enter Baptist territory in Tiquina (Lake Titicaca). The Baptists said they would agree to a redistribution of territory, but the "Peninsula of Tinquina and of Copacabana, the islands of Titicaca and Coati, the port of Santiago de Guata and the town of Achacachi are not debatable, but are reserved for the Baptists" (Phillips n.d.:n.p.). For the following decade no further formal consultation took place.

CONFERENCE OF NATIONAL EVANGELICAL WORKERS

The next known effort at forming a national council was the calling of a "Conference of National Evangelical Workers" in La Paz in 1935. The invitation was signed by the Baptists, Methodists, Friends and Salvation Army. Meetings were held in the Baptist church, but no further details of this movement are available at the present time (CBFMB 1935:2).

In 1941 another attempt was made to form an "Evangelical Council of Bolivia," inspired by Dr. John R. Mott. It was expected that all the denominations of the country, except the Seventh-day Adventists and Pentecostals, would join. It is not clear whether this exception was simply because the latter two groups were not invited or whether it was for some other reason. The purpose of this council was to be "the advisor and counsellor of all evangelicals in matters of mission comity, boundaries, and unoccupied areas, and it will lead in all cooperative enterprises" (CBFMA 1941:2). Records of what became of this council are not available at this writing.

The records of another meeting held in La Paz, April 5, 1948, are on hand, however. Missionaries of the Lutherans, Methodists, Baptists, Nazarenes, Assemblies of God, National Holiness Missionary Society, Christian Missions in Many Lands, Church of God (Holiness), Friends Missions, Salvation Army and Bolivian Faith Mission met and organized an association. On November 15, the name "Bolivian Evangelical Christian Union" was selected. Samuel E. Smith was elected President and Harold W. Yoder, Secretary (Yoder 1948:1). The image of this organization never outgrew the idea that it was simply a meeting of La Paz missionaries, and it never fulfilled the vision of becoming a truly national organization.

TASK-ORIENTED VERSUS CONCILIAR COOPERATION

Before describing some of the more recent efforts at Protestant cooperation in Bolivia, it will be helpful to define terms and analyze some of the types of cooperation. Historically the most common type of Protestant organization has been the Church, originally a state Church in Europe where citizens are born into the Church much like they are born into a nation, but becoming a series of denominations in the USA and other newer countries.

Ralph Winter (1968:n.p.) has suggested the phrase "municipal structure" for this type of organization, because its governmental character in many ways parallels that of a secular civil government. At the same time, as individuals, both Protestants and Catholics have also banded together within their own traditions in another kind of structure which cuts horizontally across the more traditional churchly lines. The Pietistic movement, which stressed a particular way of living the Christian life, did this. The Bible Societies, which translate, publish and distribute Scriptures, are a more formal example of Protestants banding together in a task-oriented effort. The London Missionary Society and the American Board of Commissioners for Foreign Missions were earlier expressions of this tendency to collaborate horizontally around the specific task of missionary work. The Catholic orders and societies also are this type of structure. Within Catholicism the orders have been willingly recognized as entirely legitimate structures and, partially due to that recognition, they accomplished the great bulk of missionary effort prior to William Carey.

Within Protestantism, due to the existence of separate denominations, a task-oriented movement may in time become a churchly structure, against the original purposes of the founders. The Christian and Missionary Alliance began as a service to already existing churches but eventually became a Church or denomination. The Pentecostal movement originally was envisioned as providing a healthy new influence in all denominations. However, when the churchly people rejected it, it became churchly itself and formed into denominations such as the Assemblies of God. Now, under the label "charismatic movement," Pentecostalism is fulfilling a part of its original intention, to work within existing denominations. Perhaps the outstanding symbol of this modern trend is Oral Roberts' switch in 1968 from one of the newer Churches, the Pentecostal Holiness, to one of the historic churches, the Methodist. The Methodist Church itself began peacefully within a churchly structure and only a generation later became a separate "Church" - literally over the dead body of its founder.

Church denominational leaders have tended to look askance at task-oriented interdenominational structures which sometimes have pulled people out to form separate denominations. Just so denominational people, who have happily cooperated as individuals in the interdenominational task-oriented structures, have tended to look askance at official cooperation between whole denominations. They remember that such cooperation has tended to lead to or stem from councils of churches, and that those councils in themselves have tended to lead to mergers or super-churches. This tension is parallel to the tension between private enterprises and municipal governmental structures in secular society.

Several interdenominational missionary groups were formed in the USA and other countries with a particular aversion to the liberal theology and inclusivistic ecclesiology commonly associated by them with the World Council of Churches and her predecessors. The aversion grew partially as a result of the modernist-fundamentalist controversy, and partially as an expression of the Protestant tendency to group together for a "private enterprise" type of operation. Several independent churches and newer denominations were formed for similar reasons.

Especially since the formal inauguration of the WCC in 1948, the identification in Bolivia of those favorable and unfavorable to the conciliar ecumenical movement became simpler. Many field missionaries reasoned that any conciliar association on the field with other denominations would have to take into account the pro or con position of these denominations in regard to the inclusivistic theology and ecclesiology of the World Council of Churches. On the other hand, the easiest positive way to identify the North American evangelicals was their membership in the Interdenominational Foreign Missions Association (IFMA) or the Evangelical Foreign Missions Association (EFMA).

Bolivian nationals usually followed the position of their

parent missionary organization, although there have been some outstanding exceptions. Understandably, nationals did not feel as strongly about the issues as the missionaries, since they did not have firsthand contact with the type of theology that evangelicals had reacted against so strongly. When Iglesia y Sociedad en América Latina (ISAL), Comisión Provisional Pro-Unidad Evangélica Latinoamericana (UNELAM), and other WCC-related organizations were planted in Latin America, the differences became more obvious to Latin Americans in general.

In Bolivia, the problem of affiliation of one denomination with other denominations in a conciliar structure caused many agonizing problems. Possibly the underlying difficulty was fuzzy thinking concerning the differences between the conciliar and the task-oriented types of cooperation. Some missionaries, for example, could not articulate reasons for their opposition to becoming members of a local or national council of churches while, at the same time, they wholeheartedly supported the United Bible Societies (affiliated with the WCC). The answer may be that the Bible Societies is a task-oriented structure, and cooperation with it does not carry conciliar implications considered by these missionaries to be so dangerous.

In addition, the distinction between a foreign organization which offers a specific service to the Bolivian churches, and a national organization which springs from the Bolivian context itself, is important. The Bible Societies would represent the foreign service organization, while COMBASE, the social service committee, would represent the national service organization.

LOCAL UNITED CHURCHES

In modern times the efforts toward Protestant cooperation became centered on local unions of churches (Iglesias Unidas) in the major cities. These correspond most nearly to a USA ministerial association, although laymen as well as ministers participate in them. The United Churches of La Paz, Cochabamba and Santa Cruz are the most revealing as to different structures and degrees of success. It should be mentioned that similar organizations have also been formed in Oruro (1957), Trinidad (1964), and Tarija (1965).

The United Churches of La Paz (Iglesias Evangélicas Unidas de La Paz) was formed in 1955. This was a loose organization, designed to bring together in fellowship all the La Paz Protestant churches. A doctrinal statement was purposely omitted from the structure, undoubtedly with the fear on the part of some that doctrine would cause disunity. The question soon arose as to whether a doctrinal statement should be included, and several denominations continually agitated for a doctrinal statement. In our terms, the battle really was over a clarification as to whether the United Churches was a task-oriented or a conciliar structure. Some who did not see the difference at that time, however, assumed that all ecclesiastical cooperation was conciliar in nature, and that therefore a doctrinal statement was necessary so as to avoid overly intimate association with the WCC-type of theological liberalism and ecclesiastical inclusivism. A crisis built up in 1963 when the matter of incorporating a doctrinal statement was voted down. The more evangelical delegates accused the liberals of packing the ballot box. Hard feelings continued, and the final split came in 1965 when the "National Association of Evangelicals" (ANE) was formed. ANE was clearly a conciliar structure with a doctrinal statement, designed to unite evangelicals while excluding liberals who were not considered by the leaders as true members of the universal Church.

The United Churches of Cochabamba (Iglesias Evangélicas Unidas de Cochabamba) was formed in 1960. Modeled somewhat after La Paz, those who founded it purposely avoided even writing a constitution, much less a doctrinal statement. The very looseness of the organization gave it a task-oriented, rather than a conciliar flavor (although these terms had not been articulated at this time), and it enjoyed wide participation by the Cochabamba churches, even churches of some of the same denominations which had insisted on a doctrinal statement and formed ANE in La Paz. It served as a focal point of fellowship, a sponsoring agent of united evangelistic campaigns, coordinator of the Easter sunrise service, etc. The organization continues today with good harmony.

The Evangelical Association of Santa Cruz (Asociación Cristiana Evangélica) was formed in 1963. From the outset this was designed as basically what we have attempted to define as a conciliar structure. The group of evangelicals who organized it desired to avoid association with the Methodists whom they accused of modernism, and whose seminary in Montero, near Santa Cruz, had gained the image of teaching liberal doctrine. A detailed constitution was drawn up including a doctrinal statement and a clause which stated that the ACE was affiliated with the World Evangelical Fellowship, the evangelical world alternative to the WCC.

THE FORMATION OF ANDEB

In a sense, the local united church organizations were precursors to the Asociación Nacional de Evangélicos de Bolivia (ANDEB), formed in 1966. Four previous events led up to its organization.
1. In November, 1958, Joseph McCullough of the AEM called a "Conference of Faith Missions" to meet in Cochabamba. It is significant that this first meeting was composed of only task-oriented missionary societies: Andes Evangelical Mission, Evangelical Union of South America, New Testament Missionary Union, Child Evangelism Fellowship, United World Mission, Summer Institute of Linguistics, and United Bible Societies. The purposes of the conference were stated as follows:

1. To look at the over-all picture of evangelical work in Bolivia and then see how far we are willing to go in cooperation with each other.
2. The second purpose is to see how far we are willing to go in regard to bringing the various groups of national believers together (Author's lecture notes).

This conference involved only missionaries and was held in English. The conclusions were task-oriented for the most part, including possible conferences, radio ministry, linguistic effort, etc. No proposal for a church council was recorded. The one most tangible result of this meeting was the merger of the EUSA churches with the ECU, already described in Chapter 3.
2. J. O. Percy, General Secretary of the IFMA, visited Bolivia in January of 1959, when another conference of faith missions was held in Cochabamba under McCullough's leadership. McCullough was named to reconvene a similar meeting whenever the time was right.
3. The subsequent meeting was called by McCullough for Cochabamba in 1962. The missions which met in 1958 were included as well as the Assemblies of God, Bolivian Faith Mission, Canadian Baptists, Church of the Open Door, Church of God (Holiness), Methodists, Nazarenes, New Tribes Mission, Oregon Friends, South America Indian Mission, Union Bible Seminary, World Gospel Mission, and World Mission Prayer League (Lutheran). This was the largest and most comprehensive gathering of its kind held in Bolivia. Delegates were still all missionaries, and the language used was English. The heterogeneity of the group did not permit any conclusions, but

full and open debates and discussions were held on such topics as Communism, Roman Catholicism, evangelical representation before government, nationalism, evangelism, Christian education, and, significantly, an evangelical fellowship. Again McCullough was named to convene the next meeting.

4. McCullough's intention was to postpone any further meetings of this nature until well after the year-long campaign of Evangelism-in-Depth, scheduled for 1965, had passed. One reason for this was that a large group of evangelicals desired the formation of a conciliar-type structure which would unite Bolivian evangelicals around a doctrinal statement and constitution similar to the one used by the Santa Cruz Association. The 1962 conference, however, had shown that many of the issues which would inevitably come up for debate were potentially explosive. By 1962 McCullough had already entered in correspondence with R. Kenneth Strachan of the Latin America Mission concerning the possibility of holding an Evangelism-in-Depth campaign in Bolivia. To allow the ferment which would accompany the formation of a conciliar structure to jeopardize the cooperation necessary for the smooth operation of EID, a task-oriented structure, would be very unwise. The council could wait. It would come, but prudence and good timing were necessary.

Unfortunately, the group in La Paz which had been attempting to introduce a doctrinal statement in the United Churches, did not agree with McCullough's timing, or possibly did not know about it. None of the leaders had attended the 1962 conference in Cochabamba for one reason or another, although none of them would have been intentionally excluded. The La Paz situation deteriorated until the break came early in the year and the ANE was set up, as has been mentioned. Predictably, this caused a disruption of the EID office in La Paz and turned many Bolivian leaders against ANE because of the failure on the part of its leaders to have continued to live up to what was considered the spirit of EID. It might have been better for those leaders to have continued to enjoy the task-oriented unity in EID throughout the entire campaign and for a prudently extended period afterward, than to have precipitated the conciliar structure prematurely. In the Protestant Church there has always been room for both, but wisdom is necessary in the arranging of such delicate matters.

This background will better enable us to evaluate the recent critical statement made by Dayton Roberts of the Latin America Mission:

In Bolivia, on the day following the conclusion of the formal Evangelism-in-Depth program, a letter was sent out inviting churches to form a new Evangelical Fellowship which excluded some of the major denominations with whom the signers of the letter had been working harmoniously during the Evangelism-in-Depth effort. This type of division is deplored by Latin America Mission leaders and causes them great concern (Roberts 1967:80).

Here again, Roberts fails to distinguish between the Evangelical Fellowship (a conciliar structure) and Evangelism-in-Depth (a task-oriented structure). He implies that unity in one necessarily leads to unity in the other. Roberts does acknowledge that "In Bolivia the tension was longstanding, and was simply held off to insure the fulfillment of Evangelism-in-Depth's program" (1967:80).

The letter in question was sent by McCullough, who deeply regretted the formation of ANE and who felt that he needed to take action to fulfill his mandate from the 1962 conference. Most evangelical leaders who were in favor of an eventual conciliar structure in Bolivia were not pleased with the turn of events, but at the same time were not fully able to control them. A group of evangelicals who wished to exclude both the Methodists and Canadian Baptists from the preliminary proceedings was successful in carrying its point of view, and these were not invited. The meeting was held early in 1966, and an ad hoc committee set up to enlist members for the Asociación Nacional de Evangélicos de Bolivia (ANDEB), secure official legal recognition of the organization from the Bolivian government, and call the first assembly. Bruno Frigoli of the Assemblies of God was elected President of the ad hoc committee.

During the subsequent year, severe opposition came not only from the Methodists and BBU, who understandably resented their exclusion, but also from the national leaders of some of the denominations which had been invited, but who had been deeply offended by the formation of ANE in La Paz, the timing of the formation of ANDEB so close on the heels of Evangelism-in-Depth, the proposal that ANDEB join the World Evangelical Fellowship, the evident overbalance of missionary as opposed to national influence in ANDEB, and the public affront to the Baptists and Methodists.

When the first ANDEB assembly was held in 1967, membership was open to all who would submit an application and signify their agreement with the constitution. Almost every Bolivian

denomination was represented, including the Baptists and
Methodists. The constitution was also open for revision, and
several changes were proposed and carried. A large majority of
the Churches then submitted their application papers and paid
their fees, including the Baptists. The Methodists, who could
also have joined as a charter member at that time, did not
submit an application. This meant that if they desired future
membership, their application would have to be approved by a
vote of a subsequent assembly. A motion to extend the period
for free enrollment of charter members by three months was
defeated. Pablo Zurita of the Bolivian Baptist Union was
elected as the first President of ANDEB. In the 1968 assembly,
the presidency was passed on to Jaime Ríos of the ECU.

EVANGELISM-IN-DEPTH

Moving from the conciliar to the task-oriented type of
cooperation, one of Bolivia's outstanding examples was the 1965
Evangelism-in-Depth campaign. A church growth study of Bolivia
could hardly pass over the opportunity to evaluate the EID
program in terms of church growth principles. This could
profitably be done for each country in which an EID campaign
has been held, and the results pooled. A body of such information would permit a creative reevaluation of techniques in the
field of evangelism in general.

As a church historian, I would mark 1965 as perhaps *the*
red-letter year in the history of Bolivian Protestantism. The
impact made upon the entire Protestant community, on non-parti-
cipating as well as participating denominations, was indelible.

The story of the origin and methods of EID has been told
both in *Revolution in Evangelism* (Roberts 1967) and *Who Shall
Ascend* (Elliot 1968). There is no need of repeating the
material here. Rather, some more general observations as to
areas of success and failure, the validity of the so-called
"Strachan theorem," and side effects might be in order.

The Latin America Mission's official history of the EID
movement concludes with a chapter on the Bolivian campaign
entitled "Right Side Up - Evangelism-in-Depth Program" (Roberts
1967:111-123). Considered by many EID leaders one of the most
outstanding of the nine campaigns now completed, Bolivia will
serve well as a laboratory specimen for analysis.

Evaluation of the Bolivian EID. Was the 1965 effort in
Bolivia successful? Roberts judges that it was. The success,

he says, "is evidenced in the marked growth of the 750 cooperating churches during the year, in the nearly 20,000 professions of faith in Christ" (1967:112). Table 23 and Figure 25 show the growth rates for the seven denominations cooperating with EID for which we have reasonably dependable statistics, and for one denomination (SDA) which did not cooperate.

TABLE 23

Church Growth in Eight Bolivian Denominations Before, During, and After Evangelism-in-Depth 1960 - 1967*

Church	1960	1961	1962	1963	1964	1965	1966	1967
Cooperating Churches								
BBU	1303	1546	1800	2100	2500	2800	3100	3435
Methodist	1624	1690	1852	2143	2448	2800	3336	3480
ECU	4800	5100	5549	6200	6900	7200	8400	9229
INELA	2800	2900	3000	3100	3200	3800	4400	5000
Nazarene	900	1100	1200	1100	1250	1400	1398	1441
AG	1609	1793	1795	1857	2728	3338	3641	4255
Holiness	351	360	400	420	481	573	704	837
Totals	13,387	14,507	15,596	16,920	19,507	21,911	24,979	27,676
Non-cooperating Church								
SDA	8324	9504	9046	9227	9619	11,603	13,243	14,955

Percentage Growth of Cooperating Denominations		
Year	Members Added	Percent Annual Growth
1963-1964	2587	15.31%
1964-1965 (EID)	2404	12.33%
1965-1966	3068	14.01%
1966-1967	2697	10.79%

*These are the only denominations for which reasonably accurate statistics are available. For some years the data had to be estimated from the preceding and following points on the graph for which hard data is available.

It is not expected that the 20,000 who made professions of faith will become communicant members in one or even two years. Statistically, they would indicate community rather than communicants, so it would be expected that some one-third, or

RATES OF CHURCH GROWTH IN RELATION TO
EVANGELISM-IN-DEPTH 1960-1967 IN BOLIVIA
(Logarithmic graph)

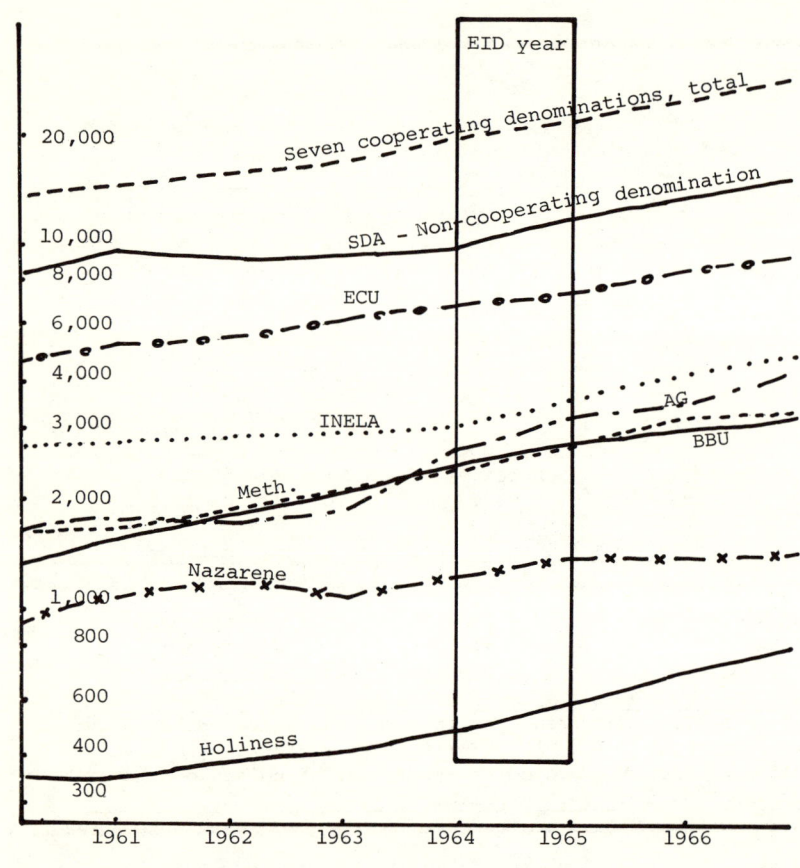

FIGURE 25

perhaps 6,000 persons, would join the churches. Even spread out over a three-year period, it could be expected that some 2,000 new members would be added to the Church each year as a result of the EID effort. During the "year of consolidation" of 1965-1966, over 3,000 were added just to the seven cooperating denominations, an increase of some 500 over the year previous to EID, 1963-1964. It is rather striking, however, that the percent of annual increase was greater (15.31 percent) during the year preceding EID than in any of the following three years. Therefore, while it is no doubt true that many of the 750 churches grew during the year, the question could be asked as to whether they might not have grown equally well if EID had not come to Bolivia.

The pragmatic aspect of EID is heavily stressed by its sponsors. An LAM brochure states, "perhaps the most important thing is that [EID] works!" (Division of Evangelism n.d.:10). LAM evangelist, Juan Isais, echoes this with his graphic comment, "[EID] is a mess, but it works" (1968:2). EID apparently has "worked" in at least eight of the nine countries that have tried it. I would be the last to leave the impression that it failed to work in Bolivia. It had tremendously significant effects. But it might well be that Bolivia, together with most of the other Latin American countries where EID has operated, presents a very special set of conditions favorable to the operation of EID in terms of church growth. Not that church growth is the only benefit of EID. Numerical increase is only one of many blessings. Roberts mentions at least eight other effects such as new zeal and enthusiasm, new leadership on every level, candidates for the ministry, Christian stewardship, opportunities for partnership between missions and national churches, new methods and techniques (1967:86-87). All these are valuable and important, and all were evident in Bolivia to the eternal benefit of the Bolivian Church. These functions in themselves may prove in the long run to be the most valuable contribution of the effort to the Bolivian Church.

But since this study is concerned primarily with church growth, it would be well to record some personal observations concerning EID's effect on that particular aspect. Although these are generalizations, they are based on firsthand experience in an EID campaign, followed by over two years of reflection and evaluation. As hypotheses, I propose that: (1) EID possesses a mystique which allows it to enjoy success particularly in Latin America; (2) EID is basically a revivalistic rather than an evangelistic technique; and (3) the success of EID has depended on the existence of certain preconditions.

　　1. The Evangelism-in-Depth Mystique. The first element of the unusual and intangible aura of spiritual power which surrounds the very term "Evangelism-in-Depth" is the image of the Latin America Mission which is extremely favorable in Latin America. The continent-wide evangelistic campaigns of Harry Strachan during the first half of this century made the mission known and respected far and wide. The enviable ability of his son and successor as General Director of the LAM, Ken Strachan, to win the friendship and esteem of the evangelicals on one side and the liberals on the other, assured a sympathetic audience for any new idea he might propose. The Bible Seminary in San José, the leadership provided for continent-wide literature organizations (LEAL) and radio-television (DIA), and the favorable impression caused by LAM personnel on every hand combined to heighten the prestige of the mission in the eyes of virtually all who were working in Latin America. It is almost certain that any other missionary organization which might have proposed identical EID principles would not have been able to promote them as widely or as successfully as Ken Strachan and his group.

　　The second element in this mystique has been building ever since the first EID campaign in Nicaragua in 1960. It is the image of EID itself. In the first place EID projects the image of evangelical doctrine. Few question the theological base upon which the program is built or the message which will be preached. In Bolivia a doctrinal statement was introduced for the first time. It was proposed and carried in one of the earlier national EID assemblies by a group which had not yet learned to distinguish between what we have called task-oriented and conciliar-type structures. To them, all Christian cooperation carried similar implications, so they introduced a doctrinal statement as a protection against association with undesirable elements. Happily, the total effect was good, since the doctrinal statement pulled some hesitant denominations into the effort while it drove no one away. The objection that EID "compromises with modernists" is adequately answered when church leaders become confident that the evangelical doctrinal position of the LAM undergirds it. If "modernists" choose to cooperate, the compromise becomes theirs, not that of the evangelicals. Then again, the image of EID is success. One feels as if he is joining a winning team. It appeals to a pragmatic mentality. In Latin America, criticisms of Evangelism-in-Depth are as rare as criticisms of "mother." Even an academic discussion such as this may be considered by some to border on sacrilege.

The third element contributing to EID's mystique is that of the impact and catalytic effect of an outside movement coming into the country involved. The importance of this should not be overlooked. In the opinion of some observers it was the major factor contributing to the disappointment of the Costa Rican campaign of 1961. Undoubtedly the reasons given by Roberts (1967:54-55) for little success in Costa Rica: lack of adequate time, shortage of personnel, and political trouble are valid. Probably, however, even their cumulative effect was not as important as the failure of the EID mystique to operate in the LAM's own back yard. In other countries, the entrance of new personnel, mostly well-trained Latins, who rent homes, buy cars, set up offices, take pictures, travel all over the country, fly out to international meetings, speak in the churches and make new friends, contributes heavily to the buildup of excitement as a part of the mystique. The spirit becomes contagious. Soon nationals are also traveling, speaking, printing propaganda, tacking up signs saying "we pray for EID" on their front doors. The mystique is in operation, and the momentum rather easily carries through the entire year.

While mystique probably did not operate in Costa Rica because it was too close to home, it should be noticed that other countries might be too far away. Whether EID will enjoy success in countries which know nothing of Harry or Kenneth Strachan remains to be seen. The Nigerian "New Life For All" campaign has reportedly given good results. EID leaders will do well to concentrate on providing a workable substitute for this mystique when they take their ideas outside of Latin America.

2. *Evangelism-in-Depth as Programmed Revivalism*. Perhaps the major departure which EID represents from the more traditional methods of evangelism is that the bulk of EID's energy is directed toward revivalism in the churches as a prerequisite for the end product of evangelism.

In Bolivia, the meetings of local committees, the national assemblies, the pastors' conference, the prayer cells, and the specialized congresses for youth, women and ethnic groups were all basically directed toward the Christians. The intensive training course in personal evangelism was designed to mobilize every believer and teach him his evangelistic responsibility. The periodical, *En Marcha*, and the daily radio program, *Llamada a la Oración*, were edited for church members. The parades through the plazas of the towns and cities gave the believers several opportunities to display their allegiance to Christ publicly. The theme song, "We shall win our homeland for Jesus," expresses the thought of Christians challenging fellow believers to unity and evangelism.

As the Bolivian churches became revived through such techniques, believers moved out to win souls in house-to-house visitation, in personal contacts, and in the large mass evangelistic campaigns. Twenty thousand decisions were recorded that year because the Church had been revived, or "mobilized" as the EID leaders prefer.

3. *Preconditions for Success of Evangelism-in-Depth.* The classic statement of EID theory is now called the "Strachan theorem." Kenneth Strachan said:

> The growth of any movement is in direct proportion to the ability of that movement to mobilize its total membership in the constant propagation of its beliefs (Elliot 1968: 109).

The success of EID during its eight-year history in several Latin American republics has been cited as the proof of the validity of this theorem. From the perspective of general church growth principles, however, its universal validity may not turn out to be a necessary deduction from success in a particular section of the world.

Latin America today possesses a certain set of characteristics which have been influential to one degree or another to EID's success. This does not necessarily mean that EID will not work in parts of the world where some or all of these factors are absent. God may use a different combination of factors to prepare other peoples. But these have been such a common denominator in the Latin American scene that they should be observed, and regarded as possible preconditions for optimum results from the classic EID approach to evangelism. Perhaps they are best expressed as a series of questions:

a. Can EID succeed where the factors contributing to the mystique are absent or weak? As EID moves out worldwide, churchmen will be most interested to see how the principles apply, especially where the movement is not directly associated with the LAM as it is in Latin America.

b. Can the Strachan theorem be applied to a church which is small, stagnant or seriously declining? If the church is too small, especially if it is a sealed-off people movement or a church which has grown in the midst of serious social opposition, the principle probably will not operate. For example, if in a town of 1,000 the church of 25 members represents only one extended family and that family is regarded as more or less an outcast by the rest who are unresponsive to the Gospel, EID could mobilize all 25 believers, 100 percent of the church, and still see no resulting growth of the movement. This condition, of course, has not been observed generally in Latin America since the Church as a whole is vigorous and growing. A leader from Eastern Bolivia, however, told me that in spite of sincere efforts to apply the principles of EID in the towns which were former Jesuit reductions, and where Protestant churches were not already growing, few or no results were experienced. On the other hand, good results were reported in the previously growing Aymara churches.

c. Can the Strachan theorem operate in a society where Protestantism is at odds with cultural values and socially unacceptable? The beginning of EID in Latin America coincided with the opening of the Second Vatican Council. This was, humanly speaking, the great turning point in the attitude of Latin American society to Protestantism. Vatican II made Protestantism socially respectable there for the first time in history. Whether the Strachan theorem, if conceived twenty years ago, would have been even to a small degree as successful in Bolivia as it was, would be a doubtful assumption, even if the same proportion of the churches were mobilized then as were mobilized in 1965.

Richard Shaull (1968:86), in a chapter unfriendly to the whole church growth school of thought, ironically articulates a good church growth principle when he says parodying the Strachan theorem:

> on the other hand, the growth of some groups seems to be in almost direct proportion to the degree of acculturation which they represent.

This "acculturation" naturally disturbs Shaull and other radical theologians who talk more of saving society than of saving souls. But even though he disapproves of what he calls "acculturation," what he says about the necessity of acculturation for good church growth is true. The point here is that in a situation where the preaching of the Gospel has not been adapted to the thought patterns and values of a particular culture, but is considered something foreign, neither the Strachan theorem nor any other evangelistic principle is likely to operate successfully.

d. Can the Strachan theorem operate in a population which is not nominally Christian? EID has enjoyed success among people who at least nominally believe in God, in the Bible, in Christ, in miracles, in heaven and hell, and in the Church. Whether it will succeed where this precondition is not present is another question. Perhaps among animists, who under pressure of twentieth-century civilization are going to change their religion to something, anyway, it will be successful. But populations solidly committed to Islam, Buddhism, Hinduism or Sokka Gakkai might well present a different set of conditions.

e. Can EID operate where the Protestant Church is disunited? Burnis Bushong of the World Gospel Mission, who has worked closely with several EID campaigns, pointed out to the author that the unity of Protestantism which has been so helpful in Latin America, came about as a result of decades of existence as a persecuted minority. In spite of denominational differences, Protestants were accustomed to sticking together. Whereas Juan Isais describes EID as a "centrifugal movement" (1968:2), this previously existing centripetal force was very important.

f. Does EID work best in a revolutionary situation? Latin America is a continent in ferment. Rapid social change is the order of the day. Revolutions are common, and where revolutions are in progress, people are generally receptive to new ideas and will listen to the Gospel if presented in relevant terms. Interestingly enough, in seven of the first eight republics where EID campaigns were held, political revolutions took place just before or during the effort. The exception was Costa Rica, where the EID campaign was least successful.

g. Does EID require a friendly attitude towards the USA? EID has tended to employ the flamboyancy and pragmatism of North American salesmanship. This is well received in Latin America, a continent rapidly adopting many North American cultural norms. But a leader of one of Japan's fastest growing denominations, for example, recently repudiated the North American type of mass evangelism in favor of a strict following up of family lines. The EID method naturally appeals to North American missionaries. When they are in a dominant position, EID is assured of a good reception. This is not to say that the opposite is true. It simply has not been tested.

h. Can EID succeed in an area less than the geographical boundaries of a given nation? The nationwide aspect of EID in Bolivia contributed powerfully to its mystique. The theme song, "We shall win Bolivia for Jesus," would have been less effective if we had sung, "We shall win Eastern Bolivia," or "We shall win the Aymaras." Modern nationalism is an important emotional factor, particularly in the developing nations. Only where a similar emotional allegiance to a particular region or a particular ethnic group exists, coujld EID's mystique develop the potency that it does in an entire nation where it reinforces already existing nationalism.

i. Can a church be growing too fast for EID to be helpful? We have already mentioned that a declining church seems less propitious for EID than a growing church, but a church which is showing very rapid growth, such as the Chilean Pentecostal Church, is already successfully employing evangelistic techniques, some of which coincide with those of EID. The Strachan theorem is already in operation. It is hardly necessary to point out that when this active and effective type of evangelism has been developed indigenously, the need for a foreign movement to help that church is not as urgent as otherwise.

Side Effects of Evangelism-in-Depth. The experience in Bolivia proved that EID produces many helpful side effects. The revival in the churches which came about as a result of the effort will influence this entire generation of Protestants for the good. As Roberts says,

> the advisers and the coordinators helped the evangelical church in Bolivia develop from a centripetal attitude ("come to every meeting") to a centrifugal one ("go witness for Jesus Christ"). They helped the church to move from a pastor-centered program of exhortation to a people-centered program of participation. They shifted the focus from pulpit to pew (1967:122).

EID helped Bolivian Protestants to emerge from the ghetto to which they had been driven by persecution. Especially the public parades in small towns and regional capitals, as well as in La Paz itself, gave them a feeling of identity and a recognition of corporate power which they had not previously possessed. The newspaper coverage of many of the aspects of the campaign had also added to the positive impact.

The economic benefits of the campaign to the churches were not immediately evident, since some even suffered financially because of heavy giving to EID. But EID uncovered a reservoir or economic resources that surprised almost all concerned.

When the effort was over, the economic potentiality was known and many churches channeled it into other aspects of their own programs.

A further side effect in Bolivia was that of exhaustion. It is difficult for one who has not lived through an all-out EID effort to imagine the tremendous amount of energy it demands. Many other church and mission programs have to be curtailed during the year to allow for the smooth operation of EID. Most Christians become so interested in evangelism that they let other interests slide. Then the national campaign is a true climax like the final stretch in a mile race. Tired as they are, believers muster up their last spurt of energy for the presidential banquet, the public parade and the two-week campaign in the capital city. When that ended in Bolivia, most people were so tired that no large-scale evangelistic efforts were attempted for over a year. But then, when Paul Finkenbinder was invited to hold campaigns in the major cities, the techniques learned during the EID year were put into operation, and many have commented that the Finkenbinder campaign in early 1967 was the most outstanding public campaign ever held in Bolivia. In a true sense, it was a fruit of EID.

Evangelism-in-Depth in Bolivia also produced a denominational self-consciousness that had not existed previously to as great an extent. For the first time, representatives of all the nation's denominations gathered together regularly for the national assemblies. Votes on certain issues were taken. In order to vote intelligently, many of the delegates for the first time asked themselves, "Who are we?" They became aware of what their own denomination stood for and that some other denominations were in agreement with them, while others were not.

The task-oriented unity of EID produced the desire on the part of many to move into a conciliar-type of unity. But this carried risks as well as blessings. For the first time the distinction between the two types of unity was becoming clear to many leaders. It was realized that the agreement to cooperate for one year in a program whose general characteristics were already established facts was one thing, but to enter into a permanent type of relationship on a council, where new policies would have to be forged through mutual give-and-take was something different. The effect of this development on conciliar unity in Bolivia has already been discussed.

Suggestions for EID in the Future. If any suggestions could be made for future EID efforts on the basis of the

Bolivian experience and from the point of view of church growth, I would make two. First, more careful planning and emphasis should be given to the ethnic mosaic which comprises a given country. In Bolivia, for example, this was practiced to a point, in the naming of Aymara and Quechua coordinators. But whereas the Aymara campaign was highly successful, the Quechua counterpart was not. Yet almost half of the Bolivian people are Quechua. There are many factors involved in this of course. One of them is that the Aymaras were enjoying the type of growth momentum, which has already been suggested as a precondition for the success of the Strachan theorem, for some years before EID came to Bolivia. On the other hand, the same precondition did not exist in the Quechua segment to such a great extent.

Secondly, I would suggest that EID include a statistician with church growth orientation on its team wherever the effort goes. Only then can the success of the movement be accurately evaluated. One of the LAM's publicity organs recently stated that during the 1967 EID campaign in Peru, the evangelical community "doubled." Just what this means in terms of hard core statistics is difficult to say. Perhaps this could mean that the number of reported decisions during the year was equal to the estimated communicant membership of the churches before the campaign. It is doubtful that it would mean that numerical church membership increased 100 percent throughout the country during that one year. A church growth statistician could tell us for sure.

COOPERATION IN THEOLOGICAL EDUCATION

Some twenty seminaries and Bible institutes have been founded in an attempt to train the ministry for the Bolivian Church. Until recently these institutions had very little contact with each other and concern for coordinating the programs had not been manifested by many. A nationwide consultation for theological education was held in Cochabamba in 1963, however, brining together directors and professors from virtually all of the nation's institutions. General papers were presented, brief reports from each institution received and much helpful discussion was carried on. The two major decisions included the formation of an interdenominational graduate school to give advanced training to those already in the ministry, and the organization of a national theological education association.

In spite of subsequent efforts on the part of several leaders to form the graduate school, this was not successful. Opposition to it arose from several vocal and influential church leaders who feared that if the school included professors from the more liberal groups, the Bolivian ministry would be corrupted rather than helped. When the idea was finally given up, the Emmaus Bible Institute inaugurated a graduate program for the Evangelical Christian Union, and the Berea Bible Institute of Santa Cruz set up one for such holiness denominations as the World Gospel Mission and INELA (Oregon Friends).

The proposed association, later named Asociación Evangélica Boliviana de Educación Teológica (AEBET), fared somewhat better. Those who were influential in promoting it were careful in distinguishing between an organization which would stress academic aspects of ministerial training, rather than theological aspects. A doctrinal statement purposely was omitted from the constitution. Such possible functions as the publication of a joint theological journal or interchange of professors were avoided, whereas the possibility of establishing a system of accreditation, interchange of information, and raising the academic levels of the institutions were emphasized. As a result, eight institutions became charter members, and annual assemblies of the AEBET have been held ever since. Little positive action has been taken on the stated goals, however, with the exception of exchange of information. Some talk of forming an international association with Peru, Chile and Ecuador is in the air.

COOPERATION IN SOCIAL SERVICE: COMBASE AND ALFALIT

As a result of the growing awareness among evangelicals as to the need of the Church to express its love for fellow men through social action, several Protestant denominations joined together in another task-oriented association. In 1963 the Bolivian Commission for Evangelical Social Action (Comisión Boliviana de Acción Social Evangélica or COMBASE) was formed. COMBASE is now the agency which coordinates the distribution of resources from such disparate sources as Church World Service, World Vision, Christian Children's Fund, USAID, etc. Again, since COMBASE is a task-oriented type of cooperation, its constitution contains no doctrinal statement. Social service is rendered in the name of the Protestant community as a whole in spite of the fact that some of the more conservative denominations officially have not yet joined. Membership in COMBASE does not carry the public implication that any cooperation denomination either endorses or repudiates the theological position of fellow members. It simply means that in the realm of social service they have combined their efforts.

COMBASE has helped the Protestant community through flood relief, the establishment of cooperatives, direct help to needy children, evangelical clinics, colonization programs, medical supplies, and many other avenues of service that would have been out of the reach of individual denominations.

The ALFALIT (Alfabetización y Literatura) program has also enjoyed rather wide success in Bolivia. This is sponsored by the Lit-Lit Department of the National Council of Churches of the USA, but like the Bible Society, has the active support of many who otherwise would not wish to be associated with the NCC. ALFALIT was introduced to Bolivia as a part of the Evangelism-in-Depth program in 1965. It is not a grass-roots Bolivian organization, but a service-centered foreign organization aiding the Bolivian Church. Teaching Christians to read their Bibles is one of the most urgent tasks for those who would see the Church grow.

HYMNOLOGY

In February, 1964, a group of interested leaders in Cochabamba formed the ad hoc National Hymnology Committee (Comité de Himnología Nacional) with the purpose of encouraging talented Bolivians to compose hymns in a musical idiom which reflected the Bolivian culture. The committee entered into an agreement with the interdenominational Protestant magazine, *Visión Evangélica*, so that a hymn would be published each month in the magazine. Words and music of the qualifying hymns had to be written by Bolivians, although technical help on the committee was furnished by missionaries as well as nationals. A total of 34 hymns have now been published with 42 composers participating. Additional hymns totaling 91 have been accepted by the committee for future publication (Heredia 1968:11).

The potential value of the hymnology committee for future church growth is evident. The more the music of the Church is expressed in a native Bolivian idiom, the more its message will be able to penetrate into the hearts of those who hear it and the more the Protestant Church will be accepted as a legitimate and permanent part of Bolivian life and culture.

The CALA committee, which works among Aymaras of all denominations, has recently published an Aymara hymnal, which ran to 35,000 copies in the first edition. In 1968 a group interested in publishing a new Quechua hymnal was organized.

9

Denominational Comparisons

Table 24 shows the current membership of all the Bolivian denominations, establishing the total number of members at 53,084. Probably the total Protestant community of Bolivia, including unbaptized children and adherents, would reach some 150,000, about 3.8 percent of Bolivia's population of 3,900,000.

TABLE 24

Current Denominational Membership

Denomination	Members
Pioneer Church-planters	
Brethren Assemblies (1895)	500
Bolivian Baptist Union (1898)	3435
Methodist Church (1901)	3480
Evangelical Christian Union (1903)	9229
Seventh-day Adventists (1907)	14955
Total	31599
Second Sowing of Missions	
Union Bible Seminary (1919)	868
Bolivian Friends Holiness (1919)	500*
Swedish Free Mission (1920)	343
Salvation Army (1920)	150*
Oregon Yearly Meeting (INELA) (1924)	5000
South America Indian Mission (1926)	225*

TABLE 24, cont.

Denomination	Members
New Testament Missionary Union (1926)	200*
International Church of the Foursquare Gospel (1929)	100
German Lutherans (1930?)	70
Total	7456
Between the Wars	
United World Mission (1936)	300
World Mission Prayer League (1937)	2000
Total	2300
Third Sowing of Missions	
New Tribes Mission (1942)	200
World Gospel Mission (1944)	950
Church of the Nazarene (1944)	1398
Church of God (Holiness) (1945)	2100
Brazilian Baptists (1946)	400
Assemblies of God (1946)	4255
Bolivian Holiness Mission	1006
Bethesda Missions (1950)	300
Iglesia Evangélica Nacional (1957)	60
Midnight Call Mission (1960)	100
Maranatha Baptists (1962)	60*
Latvian Baptists (1950)	100*
German Mennonites (1954)	200*
Church of the Open Door (1955)	50*
Seattle Bible Union (1952)	60*
Brazilian Pentecostals	150*
Chilean Pentecostals	150*
Norwegian Pentecostals	80*
Church of God (Cleveland)	40*
World Wide Missions	50*
International Baptist Missions	20*
Total	11,729
Grand Total	53,084

*Educated guess

Table 25 estimates the annual Protestant growth rate in Bolivia at 17.4 percent (1960-1967), while the Population Reference Bureau (1968) gives the population growth rate at 2.4 percent. From this we calculate that the Protestant Church in Bolivia is growing at a rate of about eight times that of

Denominational Comparisons 181

the population as a whole (see Figure 26).

TABLE 25

Church Growth According to Ecclesiastical Tradition

Tradition	1950	1960	1967	Per decade growth 1960-1967
EFMA-IFMA-Faith Missions	2,910	11,980	26,331	208%
WCC - NCC	1,295	3,630	9,065	268%
SDA	3,100	8,200	14,955	135%
Others	100	120	2,733	(60,000%)
Totals	7,405	23,930	53,084	211%

The Seventh-day Adventists have shown the most numerical growth according to Table 24 and Figure 27. They now have 30 percent of Bolivian Protestant Church members. As we have seen, much of this growth has taken place among the Aymaras, but the exact ethnic breakdown is not available. Their school approach seems to have been used to good advantage, but more research is needed before any safe conclusion can be drawn.

Fifty-nine percent of the total church membership is found in the five pioneer missions described in Chapter 3. Of them, only the Brethren have not grown well over the years, although Figure 27 indicates that their current growth rate is one of the highest in the country. This is rather deceptive, however, since with their low figures just the winning of a couple of extended families could push the rate fairly high. The other pioneer missions occupy four of the first six places in absolute membership statistics (See Figure 28).

The two denominations which started later but now appear in the first six are the Oregon Friends and the Assemblies of God, both of them deeply involved in the Aymara areas. The only denomination among the first six which has not depended largely upon Aymara growth is the Evangelical Christian Union. Figure 27 shows, however, that the present growth rates for INELA (Oregon Friends), Assemblies of God, Methodists, and Bolivian Baptist Union, all are higher than those of the leaders, Seventh-day Adventists and Evangelical Christian Union.

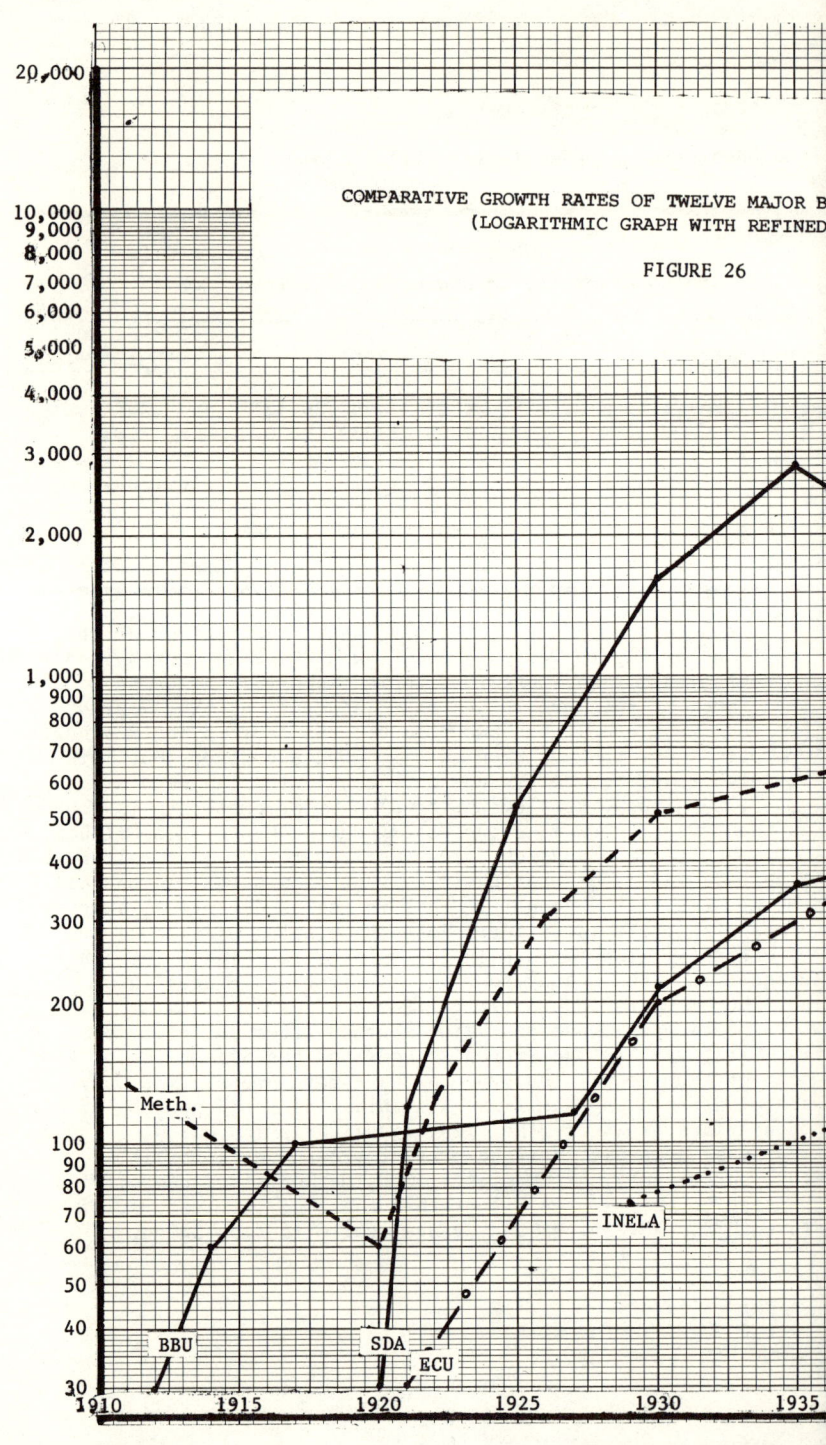

COMPARATIVE GROWTH RATES OF TWELVE MAJOR B
(LOGARITHMIC GRAPH WITH REFINED

FIGURE 26

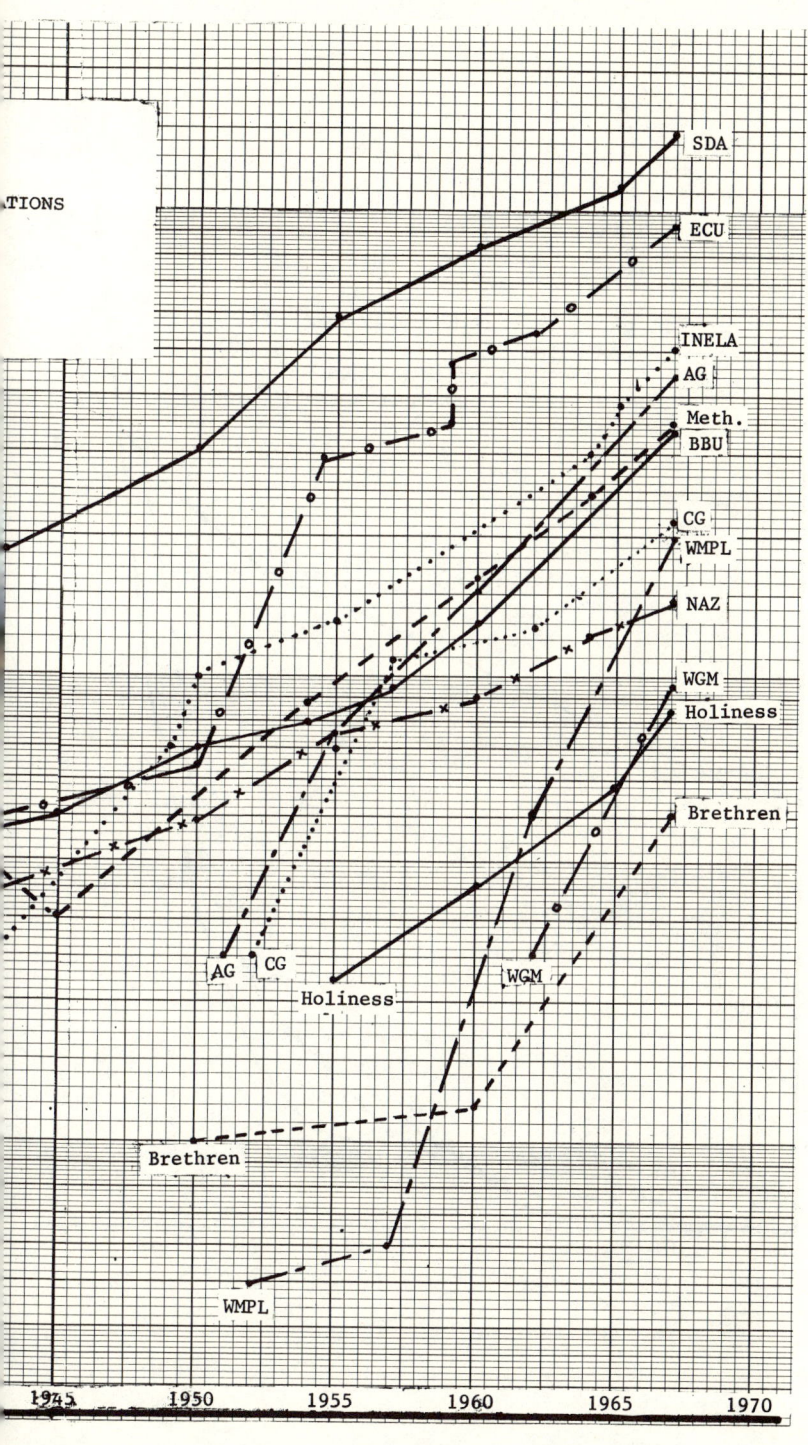

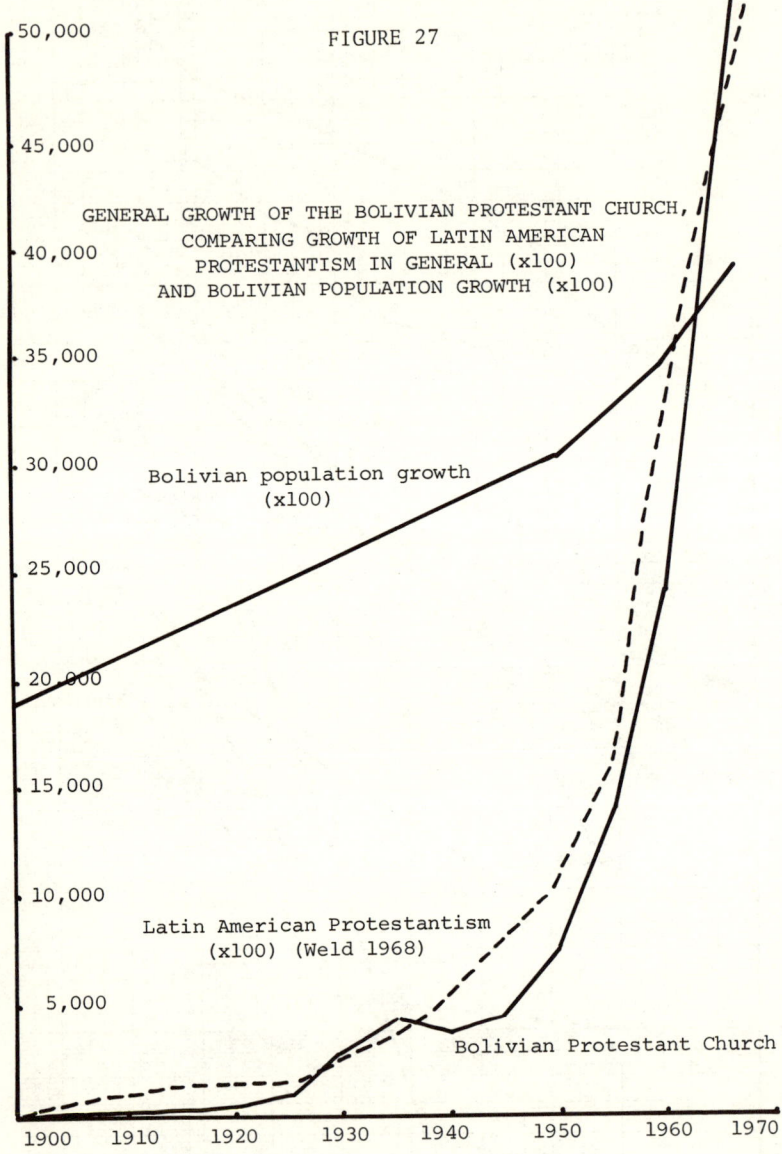

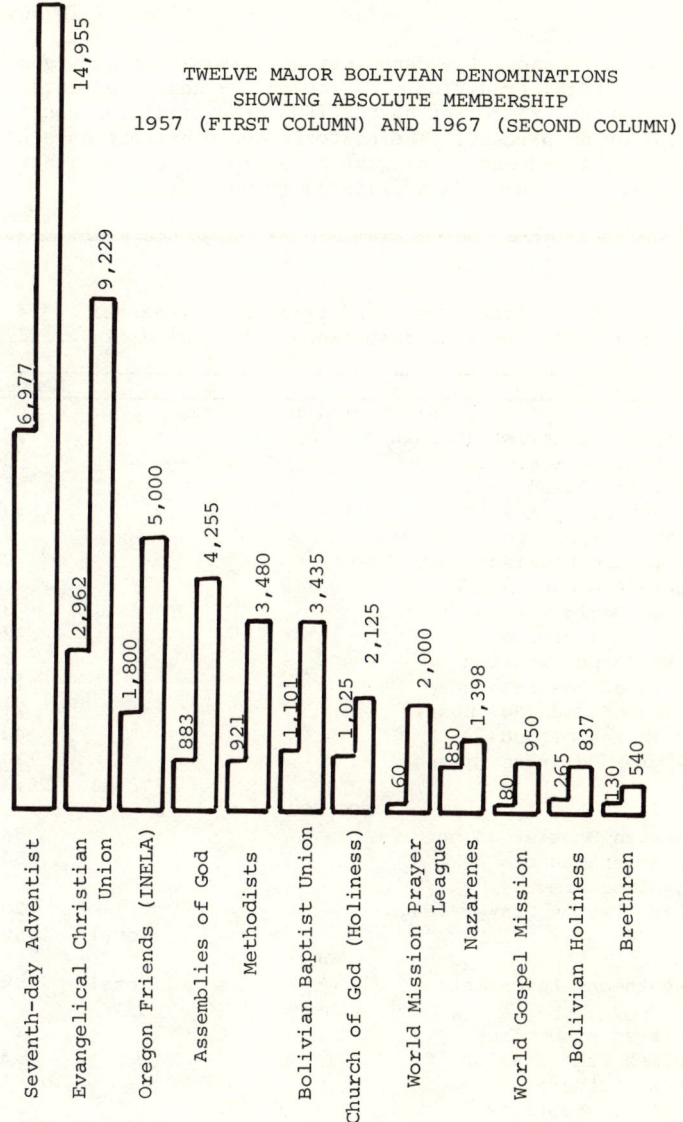

FIGURE 28

Table 26 shows the denominations grouped according to ecclesiastical tradition. Of the 38,129 non-Adventists, the denominations representing the IFMA-EFMA tradition count for 26,331 or 69 percent. The historic denominations have only 9,065 or 24 percent. The remaining 7 percent are either separatists or non-USA affiliated groups.

TABLE 26

Ecclesiastical Groupings of Bolivian Denominations
(Showing ecclesiastical tradition, not necessarily affiliation)

Denomination		Members
IFMA-EFMA-Faith Missions		
Evangelical Christian Union		9229
Union Bible Seminary		868
Bolivian Friends Holiness		500
Oregon Yearly Meeting of Friends		5000
South America Indian Mission		225
New Testament Missionary Union		200
Foursquare Church		100
United World Mission		300
New Tribes Mission		200
World Gospel Mission		950
Church of the Nazarene		1398
Church of God (Holiness)		2100
Assemblies of God		4255
Bolivian Holiness Mission		1006
	Total	26,331
WCC-NCC		
Bolivian Baptist Union		3435
Methodist Church		3480
Salvation Army		150
World Mission Prayer League		2000
	Total	9,065
SDA		
Seventh-day Adventists	Total	14,955
Others		
Brethren Assemblies		500
Swedish Free Mission		343
German Lutherans		70
Brazilian Baptists		400
Bethesda Missions		300
Iglesia Evangélica Nacional		60

TABLE 26, cont.

Denomination	Members
Midnight Call Mission	100
Maranatha Baptists	60
Latvian Baptists	100
German Mennonites	200
Church of the Open Door	50
Seattle Bible Union	60
Brazilian Pentecostals	150
Chilean Pentecostals	150
Norwegian Pentecostals	80
Church of God (Cleveland)	40
International Baptist Missions	20
World Wide Missions	50
Total	2,733
Grand Total	53,084

Table 27 compares the membership of the representatives of the several theological emphases. The surprising fact here is

TABLE 27

Theological Groupings

Theological Tradition	Number of Denominations	Current Membership
Calvinist	16	15,239
Arminian	11	15,702
Pentecostal	7	5,118
Lutheran	2	2,070
Seventh-day Adventist	1	14,955
Total		53,084

the low figure for the Pentecostal groups as compared not only to the others in Bolivia but also to the Pentecostal movement in general in Latin America. In Bolivia less than 10 percent of the Protestants are Pentecostals. This contrasts to such figures as 82.8 percent in Chile, 69.1 percent in El Salvador, and 66.3 percent in Brazil (CGRILA 1967). It seems as if the Andean Indians have not responded as well as other peoples to the Pentecostal appeal. In Peru only 10.4 percent of the Protestants are Pentecostals. In Ecuador the figure rises to 28.0 percent, perhaps not so much due to Pentecostal strength as to non-Pentecostal weakness. Further study on this point would be helpful to church leaders.

GROWTH RATES

Tables 25 and 28, with their accompanying bar graphs (Figures 29 and 30), show the perspective of comparative rates of growth. This type of comparison runs the risk of meaningless figures at the very low levels (e.g., the 3100 percent decadal growth for "Others") but is very revealing when the figures go higher. The denominations in the tradition of the World Council of Churches are presently growing faster (214 percent) than those of the faith missions and newer denominations (171 percent per decade), although the latter through the years have accumulated almost three times the total number of members. Undoubtedly the recent growth of the Methodist Church among the Aymaras has much to do with this high rate. The relatively low rate of growth of the Seventh-day Adventists (117 percent per decade) is rather surprising.

TABLE 28

Church Growth According to CGRILA Classification

CGRILA Classification	1950	1960	1967	Per decade growth 1960-1967
Faith missions	650	5,000	11,784	240%
Pentecostals	200	1,550	5,118	450%
Non-traditional den.	1,260	3,150	6,392	175%
Traditional denom.	2,295	6,030	14,835	262%
SDA	3,000	8,200	14,955	135%
Totals	7,405	23,930	53,084	211%

When all Pentecostals are grouped together (Table 28),

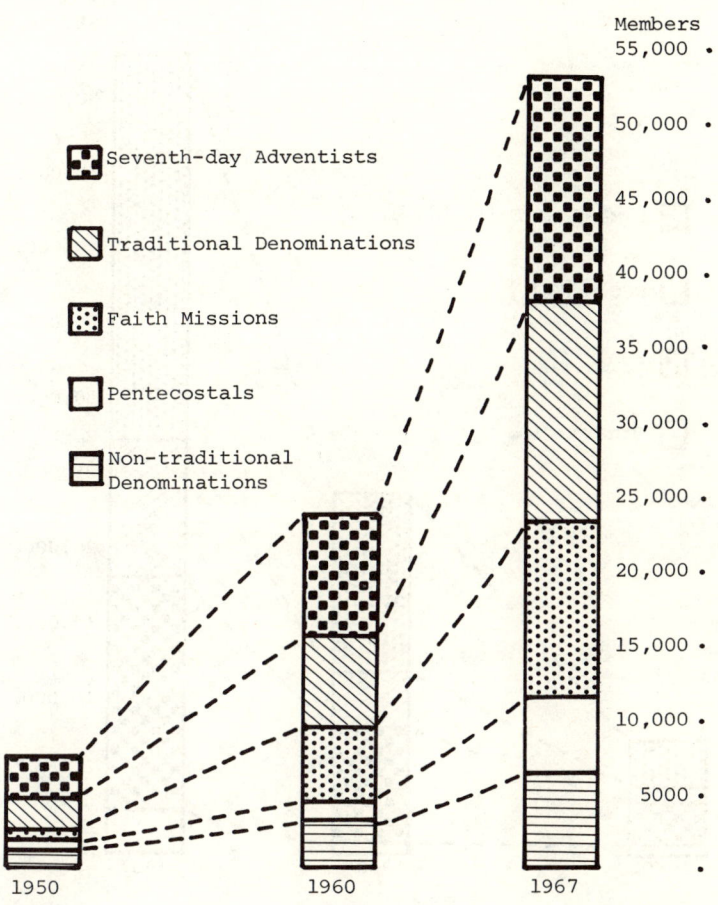

FIGURE 29

CHURCH GROWTH ACCORDING TO ECCLESIASTICAL TRADITION

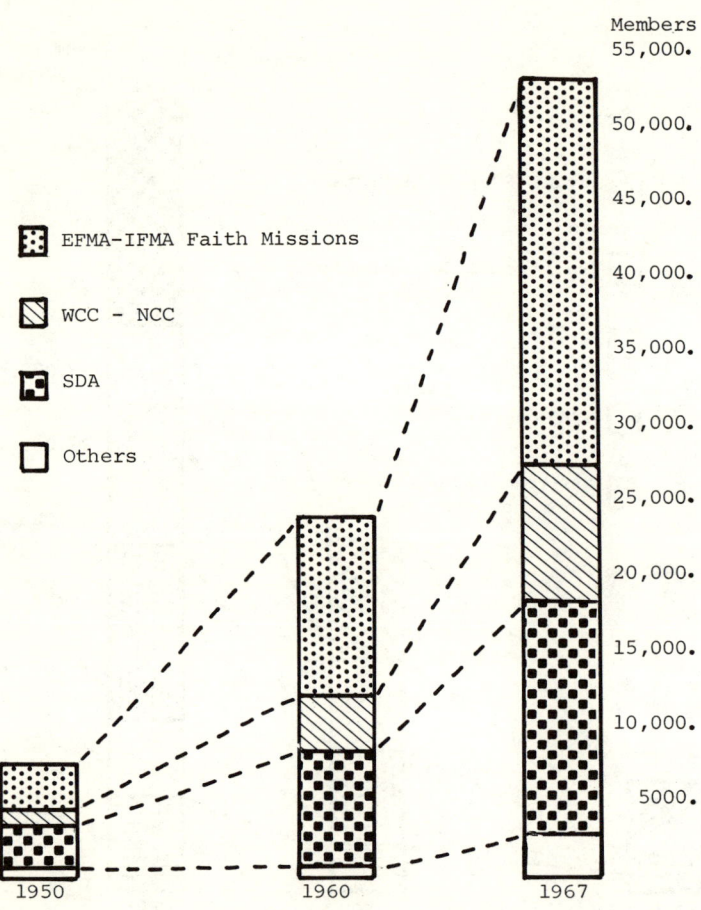

FIGURE 30

their combined growth rate of 328 percent per decade is extremely revealing. Whereas their growth in Bolivia has been somewhat retarded up to now, the present trend might indicate that a breakthrough has begun. One problem is that the statistics for several of the Pentecostal denominations are unknown at this writing, and the guesses (Table 24) have little basis in known facts.

When grouped together, the faith missions have shown a very low rate of growth (114 percent per decade). This is partially due to the rate of 128 percent per decade for the Evangelical Christian Union, which on this comparison suffers like the Seventh-day Adventists from relatively large size. Some faith missions, however, must be below the ECU. Although this statistic might be disturbing to some in the faith missions, it should encourage them to keep more accurate statistics, for faith missions, unlike denominations, have been notoriously lax in this area.

One heartening fact is that all the groups are growing at a rate of over 100 percent per decade. The 174 percent general figure is good. The Church, however, should not be content with this. A rate of 300 percent would not be beyond immediate possibilities, and every effort should be made to reach it. God is pleased when multitudes are won to Himself. As the Bolivian Protestant Church continues to increase, not only the total number of individuals who are reconciled to God through Christ and baptized into the Church, but also the rate at which this is being done, God will be proportionately pleased with what His children are accomplishing in Bolivia.

10

Regional Church Growth

Statistical information available to the author does not permit the type of meaningful regional comparison of church growth that might be desired. Since Bolivia is so clearly divided into geographical regions, each denomination should keep a statistical breakdown for the Altiplano, the mountain valley regions, the tropical yungas, and the lowlands of Pando, Beni and Santa Cruz. A further breakdown for urban and rural churches and for new colonization projects would also be helpful. This chapter necessarily will be limited to three or four significant segments of Bolivian church development.

THE LOWLANDS AND THE JESUIT REDUCTIONS

The departments of Beni and Santa Cruz were colonized in the seventeenth and eighteenth centuries by the Jesuits. Although the order was expelled from Bolivia in 1767, the imprint left by the black-robed padres is clear even today. When the Jesuits turned their work over to the Franciscans, they left behind in Santa Cruz twenty-two organized towns called "reductions," with 23,936 "Christians" living in them (López Menendez 1965:85), and in the Beni nineteen reductions with 31,000 Christians (López Menendez 1965:75). With few exceptions, the former Jesuit reductions are today the key centers of population in the Bolivian lowlands. Towns such as San Javier, San José, Concepción, San Ignacio, Trinidad, Santa

Ana, San Joaquín, and Magdalena were designed and engineered by the priests and inhabited by the friendly Indians whom they coaxed out of their jungle habitat.

These reductions were highly successful cultural innovations in their own right. Attracted to the promises of protection from slavery and a peaceful life, the nomadic Indians willingly settled down under the paternal benevolence of the padres. Only two priests were assigned to each reduction which usually had 1000 to 2000 inhabitants. When the supply of priests increased, the extra ones moved out to begin new reductions. Within the reductions, money was unknown. The Jesuits handled all of the commerce and the contact with the outside world. Each family had its own plot of farmland, and all worked together on the church lands. The Jesuits were the uncontested supreme rulers. Perhaps this is where the term "great white father" originated. The priests were strict, employing spies and inflicting hard punishment on those who disobeyed their laws. Few ran away - there was nowhere to go. The jungle is no place for individual survival and any contact with non-Jesuit civilization would almost inevitably have brought with it being placed on the slave market.

Dependence upon the priests and thus the Church was complete in almost every area of existence. Bolivian historian René Moreno writes:

> No one was lazy here; everyone worked; they worked communally under the tutelage of the priests, ... They received everything from the hands of the priests; from their food and clothing for their families to the blessing of religious instruction ... they wove, tanned leather, carved wood, melted and forged metal, boiled sugar cane, sewed, spun, made shoes, played instruments, sang, cultivated and worked the cacao, and herded three species of cattle (1965:151-152).

This full identification of the society with the Church is very important as a negative factor in the subsequent planting of Protestant churches.

The inhabitants of the towns had been saved from the degradation of tribal life. They lived well and were content, with all their needs provided by their benefactors. But the Jesuits trained the Indians only to be good servants, nothing more. Bishop Neill observes that the people lived a dull, submissive life with no training for independence, leadership, or the ability to make individual decisions (1966:64).

This way of life can clearly be seen in the psychology of the inhabitants of the lowlands to this day. In spite of the inability of the Franciscans to maintain the high standards of discipline and organization that the Jesuits did, the cultural patterns of the reduction had become so deeply rooted that the people were almost impervious to innovations of any kind. Protestant missionaries have attempted to evangelize the Jesuit reductions through the years, but with scant success. When the Gospel seemed to threaten the umbilical-like relationship of the Catholic Church to the society in general, it encountered immediate resistance.

Churches have been planted in a number of towns, such as San José, San Ignacio de Velasco, San Joaquín and Santa Ana, with similar results. After a period of resistance and even persecution, one or two are won to Christ. Often they have had a run-in with the priest or for some other reason are disenchanted with the Catholic Church. Strong social pressures are exerted by the others to make them recant. Some, unable to stand, yield to the pressure. Some are so protected by the Protestant missionary that they do not have to yield. Others are able to gain the personal victory and even win relatives to Christ. Family relationships, including the compadrazgo (godparent) bond, are very important in these villages. When Protestantism becomes identified with a particular family, the rest of the town seems to regard it as almost a private possession, or an idiosyncrasy of that household, but hardly ever as a valid alternative to the Catholicism of the village. As a result, churches in the reductions have usually grown to around thirty members and have been sealed off. The conversion pattern was one-by-one-against-the-social-tide. This helps explain why the Protestant churches in the lowlands have not grown well. Even Evangelism-in-Depth was not able to help much and some of the blame for this unjustly fell upon the regional EID coordinators.

There were two exceptions to this general rule. The first was George Haight of the SAIM, who settled in Santiago and was able to disciple at least 10 percent of the population. The second was the renowned missionary, Walter Herron of the AEM, known now as the "Condor of the Jungle" (Wagner 1966). His Magdalena church is without doubt the outstanding Protestant church in the Jesuit reductions of Bolivia. Haight and Herron had much in common. Both of them became functional alternatives to the Jesuit or Franciscan padre. Haight established a school, a large agricultural project, a transportation service with the town's first truck, a tile factory, a cattle ranch, and a firewood industry which supplied the railroad. Herron pioneered the air taxi service for the Beni, founded a leprosarium, started a school, served as doctor, operated a cattle ranch, and opened a canal. Both mixed freely with the local politicians, and both were deeply involved with the social and economic life of their villages. Both had strong personalities and were stern disciplinarians, maintained a formality in most social relationships and were accepted as community leaders. Both handled large sums of local money, which in turn were used to support their projects. Scores of other missionaries have worked in the Jesuit reductions through the years but none with the same results. Only when the missionary was able to participate in the secular life of the village would a significant segment of the population accept his message. Not every missionary has the gifts to do this successfully. The Protestant picture in the Bolivian lowlands would have been, in all probability, quite different if a dozen or more Haights and Herrons had been available.

The Jesuit reductions are not the only villages presently in the Bolivian lowlands. Roboré has grown recently as a railroad town. Guayaramerín and Riberalta have developed as river ports. These new towns are generally more receptive to the Gospel than the reductions. The Roboré church is the largest in Eastern Bolivia, outside of Santa Cruz. Guayaramerín has three Protestant churches. Riberalta is another story, since the Maryknoll priests from the USA have made it a center of operations, and have virtually won ecclesiastical control of the town, using procedures not unlike those of the old Jesuits. No Protestant church has grown well in Riberalta in spite of the fact that it is a new and growing community and people should be responsive to the Gospel.

URBANIZATION AND THE CHURCH

From the worldwide perspective, Bolivia is considered a country of moderate urbanization, falling into the category of 10 percent to 20 percent of the population in cities over 100,000. But Bolivia is the least urbanized of all Latin American countries except Haiti. As Herrick says,

> Bolivia seems to be the only South American exception to this generalization about rapid urban growth. La Paz grew at a rate less than Bolivia's between 1942 and 1957. The violence and economic disorganization following the

Bolivian revolution in 1952 probably triggered the same
back-to-the-farm movement experienced in other countries
during similar periods of social unrest (1965:28).

Undoubtedly the revolution has influenced Bolivia's low rate
of urbanization somewhat, but my own observation would lead me
to assign more weight to two other factors. The first is the
very high rural infant mortality rate said by some to be the
highest in the world, at 60 percent. With a negligible
increase in rural population, the "push factor" from the
country experienced by other republics is not so strong in
Bolivia. The second is the unusual amount of emigration from
Bolivia. Some 600,000 farm workers now live in Northern
Argentina, and a large chunk of Bolivia's middle and professional class can be found in Peru, Brazil and the USA.
Whereas other countries struggle with the powerful "pull
factor" exerted by their own capital cities, Bolivia's strong
and perplexing "pull factor" seems to be outside of the country.

To be specific, whereas Bolivia's total population grew
14.6 percent in the decade 1950-1960, the eight largest cities
grew only 18 percent, much slower than in other Latin American
countries. Her two largest cities, La Paz and Cochabamba, grew
slower than the population, but the next three all grew faster.
This means that Bolivia does not suffer from the "one city
complex" of neighboring countries, but her urbanization is
distributed over several cities (Alonzo 1962:159). This is a
social and economic advantage.

Although the rate is slow, Bolivia's cities are growing.
Santa Cruz is the leader, and the closest that Bolivia comes
to a population explosion. Whereas Santa Cruz was a provincial
and introverted city of 25,000 just two decades ago, it is now
cosmopolitan, progressive and approaching the 100,000 mark. It
will soon pass Cochabamba and if the area continues to develop
as it is now, may eventually become Bolivia's largest city.
Although accurate statistics are not yet available, the
churches in Santa Cruz are reported to be growing well and as
new sections of the city are formed into barrios or neighborhoods, opportunities continue to present themselves for church
planting. If a Protestant church could be planted every five
or six blocks throughout the city, thousands undoubtedly would
be won to Christ.

As people move from the country to the city, they break
with old traditions and become receptive to new ideas. How
long urban migrants are receptive to Protestantism in Bolivia,
or elsewhere in Latin America, is not known, but should be the

Regional Church Growth

subject of future research. Some have guessed that if they are not reached within ten years that they will lose most of their responsiveness. The Church should not wait for ten years, however. Wherever a new migrant enters the city, the Church should be waiting for him. As William Wonderly says,

> The clear implication of this situation is that the church today has a responsibility as never before in its history to meet these culturally "displaced persons" in their place of need and help them in their hour of transition to discover those values which alone can enable them to keep a sense of human dignity and to weather the storm of cultural change (1960:206).

Specific suggestions for strategy to reach Bolivia's cities may be found in Chapter 12.

MIGRATION FROM THE MOUNTAINS TO THE TROPICAL LOWLANDS

Undoubtedly the most significant sociological phenomenon in Bolivia today is the massive program to shift the population from the arid wastes of the Andes to the fertile lands of the Amazon basin. The Bolivian government, along with several private agencies, is promoting this internal migration vigorously. Three areas have been selected for colonization: the Alto Beni area north of La Paz. the Chapare region northeast of Cochabamba, and the provinces to the north of Santa Cruz. Thousands of families have already moved, and thousands more will soon go. In some of the regions the pioneers have been predominantly Protestants. This is not surprising since they are usually the innovative type, and ready to make beneficial changes when the opportunity presents itself. Churches such as the Evangelical Christian Union, the Methodist Church, and the INELA (Oregon Friends) which have made an effort to minister in the colonies have grown well. Exact statistics of church growth in the colonies are badly needed. Life in the Bolivian colonies is reminiscent of that of our own Wild West. The debate about the involvement of the Church in social problems there is parochial. No individual or institution can exist in such an environment without becoming involved. But because making disciples of the colonists implies involvement in the social problems, Protestants should not shy away. The new colonies probably constitute the ripest harvest field in Bolivia today with the possible exception of the Aymaras around Lake Titicaca. All available resources should be freed for ministry in the colonies.

11

Ethnic Church Growth

The ethnic composition of Bolivia was briefly described in Chapter 1. A further word would be in order to describe church growth within the various ethnic segments such as Aymara, Quechua, Guaraní and mestizo. Unfortunately, such statistics are not available. The extended discussion of the growth of the Assemblies of God in different ethnic units (pp. 141-146) was made possible through the good record-keeping of their leaders. How churches have grown in each of the ethnic divisions will, consequently, have to become a subject for further research. Keith Hamilton's book, *Church Growth in the High Andes*, includes much helpful preliminary information on this subject.

QUECHUAS AND AYMARAS

One of the more obvious conclusions which can be drawn from the available statistics is that the Protestant Church has grown more rapidly among the Aymaras than the Quechuas. Subsequent research will be able to indicate more precisely the reasons for this. Even Kessler, in his thorough work, *A Study of the Older Protestant Missions and Churches in Peru and Chile*, does not discuss this to any great extent, although he recognizes the problem in Peru. He simply cites an observation from Herbert Money:

it seems in general that the Quechuas are less persevering
than the Aymaras. The freeholding Aymaras enjoy a better
standard of living than the Quechuas, and it may be that
the prohibition of alcohol and festivities which characterizes the Adventist work as well as that of other
Protestant missions, robs the Quechua Indian of a highlight
in his dreary existence that the Aymara can more easily
compensate in other ways (Kessler 1967:240).

The difference between freedom and serfdom is an important one, not only in the contrast between Aymaras and Quechuas, but among Aymaras themselves. We have already sensed this as it applied to the Canadian Baptist Guatajata farm project (pp. 42-44). Since the 1952 Revolution made virtually all Bolivian Indians free land holders, it would have been expected that this factor would by now have been neutralized. This apparently did not happen in any dramatic way, however, since the Aymaras sixteen years after the Revolution still appear more receptive. Even before the Revolution, a people movement occurred among the Aymaras when the Seventh-day Adventist membership rose from 30 to almost 3000 between 1920 and 1935.

My own observation leads me to suspect that two other factors have contributed to greater Aymara growth. The first is a stronger ethnic selfconsciousness and identity among the Aymaras than the Quechuas. It will be remembered that previous to the massive consolidation of the Andean Indians under the Inca empire, numerous separate tribes populated the region. The Incas were successful in superimposing a uniform language, that of Quechua, upon all the tribes except two, the Aymara and the Uru-Chipaya. Since this change was brought about under the pressures of political conquest, it is to be expected that while the Quechua language was adopted, the cultures of all the tribes did not become homogeneous in every respect. Probably the further the conquered tribes were from Cuzco, the Inca capital, the less they would have identified with the pure Inca culture. Bolivian Quechuas were separated from Peruvian Quechuas by a broad band of Aymaras.

The Aymaras were conquered politically, but not linguistically. They had enough inner vitality to resist this innovation in spite of what no doubt must have been tremendous pressure to change. Their joint resistance to the Incas, as well as their common culture and language, have produced a strong people-consciousness among them. The Quechuas retained a loyalty to their sub-tribes, but this did not necessarily carry over to neighboring Quechua-speaking tribes, some of which were rivals or enemies. Therefore, in Bolivia, it is more accurate to refer to the Aymaras as a fairly homogeneous piece of the Bolivian ethnic mosaic (although the existence of distinctive sub-tribal groups is recognized), than the Quechuas. Much more attention should be paid to Quechua tribal structure, and strategy for church growth should be projected on this basis rather than on the assumption that Quechuas are a homogeneous ethnic unit.

This people-consciousness is probably the main reason why the interdenominational Committee for Aymara Literature and Literacy (CALA) has been so successful. The production of large volumes of evangelical literature for semi-literates in the Aymara language, widespread literacy programs, and an excellent Aymara-Spanish hymnal containing many hymns written originally in Aymara and subsequently translated into Spanish, have all made a valuable contribution to the growing Aymara Church. Ellen Ross, for many years head of this excellent committee, deserves much credit for its success.

On the other hand, several attempts have been made to form a parallel committee for the Bolivian Quechuas, but with notable lack of success. Perhaps the lack of a pan-Quechua sense of unity is at the root of this. It may also have been the basic reason why Evangelism-in-Depth as a movement was successful among the Aymaras, but not so much among the Quechuas.

The second Aymara characteristic that would tend to make them responsive to the Gospel is their aggressive, sensitive, ambitious, and impatient personality. Aymaras are open to new ideas, and do not tend to conform for conformity's sake. When they have entered in many of Bolivia's political revolutions, they have been successful. In almost every recent revolution, Aymara La Paz sees much more bloodshed than Quechua Cochabamba. It would seem that Quechua-speaking people are more passive, fatalistic and indifferent to change. Innovation comes to them very reluctantly.

THE CHIPAYAS

As has been mentioned, the Uru-Chipayas, located in the Carangas district of the department of Oruro, were the only other tribe besides the Aymaras to resist the imposition of the Quechua language by the Incas. They number 700 (Olson 1968:1). According to La Barre, they are divided into two sub-tribes, each endogamous, rivals and antagonistic. He says:

All Chipaya, without exception, are bilingual and speak Aymara fluently; indeed ordinarily the speak Uru only among themselves at home (La Barre 1963:583).

The Chipayas were first visited by Andes Evangelical missionary Minnie Myers. Later Ron Olson of the Summer Institute of Linguistics moved into their village near the Chilean border. Together with his wife, Fran, Olson adopted native dress and identified himself with the Chipayas as much as possible. A small people movement began there under his ministry, after ECU pastor, Saturnino Copa, led a Chipaya leader to the Lord. Olson, a careful observer and good correspondent, has given a fascinating first hand account of how this happened. Here is his story.

> Ceferino López was the first believer. He is on the fringe of the tribe in many ways, and this perhaps is an important factor in his becoming the first convert. He lost his father and didn't get along well with his stepfather, so he went to Chile to work. There he even forgot some of his Chipaya.
> Next was Eugenio Paredes. He became a believer when he was sick. I believe that, from the human standpoint, this was a large factor in his decision. Both Ceferino and Eugenio were from the eastern ayllu.
> Eulogio Felipe and Zenobio Huarachi came next, together with their wives. After much spiritual battle, Ceferino and Eugenio were also able to win their wives. Zenobio's wife is Eulogio's sister. Gospel Recordings records and personal chats [with Olson] were important factors in several of these conversions.
> Then Máximo Felipe and his wife came. Our medicine plus chats with Eulogio, Zenobio and Ceferino were crucial factors.
> Augustín Huarachi, Zenobio's brother, and his wife came.
> At the same time a single fellow made a profession but family pressures forced him to retract his profession.
> Miguel and his wife came. She is Zenobio's sister.
> Albino and his wife came. She is Máximo's sister. Then two of Albino's uncles came ...
> You can see the importance of family ties in the spread of the Gospel ... Generally the family has come as a unit. Often one was ready and wanting to become a believer before the other, but usually the husband or wife would wait until

the spouse was also ready. Four different single men made professions, but each of them was forced back to the old life by family and community pressures. One of these came back to the Lord two years after getting married, together with his wife (Olson 1968).

The Chipaya church became affiliated with the Evangelical Christian Union because of its location in their old comity district, the former visits of Minnie Myers, and Ron Olson's own inclination. Ceferino López was the functional pastor of the church because of his seniority in the things of the Lord. But then the Chilean Pentecostals came upon the scene and offered USA surplus goods to the believers if they would become Pentecostals. Some of them accepted, and a tension developed between the leader of that group, Zenobio, and Ceferino, who remained loyal to the ECU. Ceferino, because of his time in Chile, was considered less "Chipaya" than Zenobio, and was not able to carry the majority with him. Because of his distaste for the methods the Pentecostals were using to gain control, Olson tended to side with Ceferino. He now says, "perhaps we did not handle the ball quite right" (1968:2). He then explains:

> for a time Zenobio was very strongly against us, in fact he tried to get the community to throw us out because we were a hindrance to his gaining control of the believers. At the present, we are working with both groups of believers. Zenobio has once again showed his desire to use the Chipaya materials: the songs, the Gospel of Mark, and the literacy materials. Zenobio also has made several strong statements giving us support in our work and saying how wonderful it was that we brought the Gospel to Chipaya and were giving them the Scriptures in their language (1968:2).

At the present time, the Chipaya Protestants, thirty-seven in all, are divided into two congregations, the largest being the Pentecostal group. Whether the people movement will continue is not known. Some 600 Chipayas have yet to leave their Christo-paganism and believe in Christ.

THE OKINAWANS

Immigration into Bolivia is not common, but a number of colonies of Japanese have been established in the Santa Cruz district in the past few years. These people in all probability would be receptive to the message of Christ, but the opportunity for ministry to them has not been evident to all. Church growth statistics are not yet available, but the fact that both the Catholic Church and the Methodists have attempted to disciple them is worthy of mention. With the world population explosion, it would not be surprising if immigration into Bolivia began to increase greatly in the near future, and those with church growth eyes will want to be ready to buy up the opportunities to reach these communities.

The Methodists were able to enlist the services of a young Japanese minister, Katsumi Yamahata, to work in the 245-family Okinawan colony, north of the city of Santa Cruz. The international and ecumenical aspects of the project are unusual. A Japanese minister was sent half way around the world to a colony of Okinawans, who speak Okinawan instead of Japanese (Patch 1962:6). He was commissioned by the United Church of Christ of Japan, with his salary underwritten by the Swiss Methodist Church, and the budget for mission expenses paid by a Methodist congregation in New Jersey (Yamahata 1964:173; Derby and Ellis 1961:139,140).

Apparently a strong tension developed between the Methodists and the Catholics as they both attempted to bring the Okinawans into their churches. Yamahata says, "I was an unwanted man here, since they were taught to believe that conversion to Catholicism would be to their advantage in Bolivian society" (1964:171,172). The Catholics won out, for "sixty percent of them are Catholics and attend Mass in a new church attended by a Maryknoll father from Boston" (Patch 1962: 6). In 1964 Yamahata wrote, "Even now we are oppressed both materially and spiritually by the community, of which the leadership is still in the hands of the Catholics" (1964:172).

These immigrants were ready to change from their former religion to Christianity. They probably had not premeditated what form of Christianity they would adopt. Curiously, the Catholic from Boston was able to win more than the Methodist from Japan. Was his Japanese nationality a disadvantage to Yamahata? Those with church growth eyes will be alert to future opportunities to win these immigrants. The Maryknolls, who Patch says are "omnipotent in the *oriente*" (Eastern Bolivia), have already determined their course of action.

12

Strategy for Future Harvest

If the Bolivian Protestant community numbers 150,000, this is something for which to thank God. Payne, Reekie, Allan, and Harrington scarcely dared dream of such a wide movement of the Spirit of God in Bolivia. They sowed the seed amidst tears, sacrifice and persecution. The harvest now is being reaped in abundance.

But God is concerned for those who yet are to believe. Just for the sake of argument, let us make the questionable assumption that the Catholic Church has successfully discipled 15 percent of Bolivia's population. This, added to Protestantism's 3.8 percent would total 18.8 percent, leaving a pagan - or perhaps more accurately a Christo-pagan - reservoir of 81.2 percent or 3,166,800 souls. Thousands upon thousands of these will cordially receive the Gospel if they hear it in terms that they can understand. They are ripened fruit ready to be gathered in. God wills that His harvest fields be reaped (Matthew 9:37) thirty-, sixty-, and one hundredfold (Matthew 13:23). Faithfulness to God requires that the winnable be won. The Master's banquet table must be filled. If some resist, excusing themselves on the basis of buying land, proving five yoke of oxen, or getting married, others in the "lanes of the city" and in the "highways and hedges" will gladly come (Lunk 14:16-24).

The most immediate and urgent task for God's people in Bolivia is to find the lost and bring them back to the fold. If some have been invited but will not come, there are others who will. Who are these people? Where do they live? How can the message of light be communicated in cultural and linguistic terms that they will understand? These are the burning questions that must be answered and must be acted upon decisively.

If the average annual growth rate over the past seven years has been 12.1 percent (derived from Tables 25 and 28), this is good. It undoubtedly could be increased, however. Definite goals must be set. If the 1967 church membership is 53,084, increase at 12.1 percent annually will mean roughly 75,000 members by 1970. Is such growth possible? It undoubtedly is, if the Protestant Church makes a determined effort to win those who will believe and, like the woman who lost a piece of silver, "light a lamp, sweep the house, and seek diligently" (Luke 15:8) until they are found and become responsible members of the Church of Jesus Christ.

How can this be done? Undoubtedly through prayer and careful rethinking of our missionary and evangelistic strategy, the Holy Spirit will give many of the answers. As a result of this study, some suggestions will be offered here. No claim is made that these conclusions provide some gimmick, which when mechanically applied will cause the Bolivian Church to grow. They should, however, be prayerfully considered as possible starting points for new evaluation of what foreign missions and the national Church in partnership are attempting to accomplish.

FURTHER RESEARCH IS NEEDED

Keith Hamilton's *Church Growth in the High Andes* was the first study of this area from the church growth perspective. This present thesis moves on from there specifically concentrating on the Republic of Bolivia. J. B. A. Kessler's recent book, *A Study of the Older Protestant Missions and Churches in Peru and Chile* as well as Wayne Weld's M.A. thesis on Ecuador (School of World Mission 1968) add to the growing body of literature for the area.

More specific study is needed, however. The reader will have noticed that many basic gaps in the statistics of each denomination in Bolivia will have to be filled. The "educated guesses" of Table 24 need to be changed into hard facts. Historical data will have to be supplied to fill in many vacant places.

Breakdowns for the data for each church according to ethnic, social, economic, occupational, and geographic categories is needed. A series of twenty-four graphs should be

Strategy for Future Harvest

drawn to show the comparison of the various possible combinations of regional ethnic church growth on the pattern found in Table 29.

TABLE 29

Possible Regional-Ethnic Combinations

	Europeans	Mestizos	Quechuas	Aymaras	Guaraní	Tribes
Highland Urban	1	2	3	4	XXX	XXX
Lowland Urban	5	6	XXX	XXX	7	XXX
Urban Migrants	8	9	10	11	12	XXX
Highland Rural	XXX	13	14	15	XXX	XXX
Lowland Rural	16	17	XXX	XXX	18	19
Rural Migrants	20	21	22	23	24	XXX

    A complete study should be written comparing the Aymaras to the Quechuas, delving into their history, culture, psychology and religion, as well as the growth of both the Catholic and Protestant churches in each ethnic segment. A complete study of the sub-tribes for each language group might unlock much information that could be used to plan for the strategy for evangelization. We need to know how best to win the more than one million Quechuas and Aymaras who are not yet committed Christians.

    A study of Protestant schools in Bolivia needs to be made to determine their past and present effect on church growth. Another thesis could be written on youth, treating the university students, high school students, children, peasant youth and young working people in the cities. Theological education across the board, would also furnish the topic for a valuable study which might help draw a new blueprint for the future.

The goal of all of this research is to discover where the ripened harvest fields are and how they can best be reaped. In Chapter 3 were listed four factors of resistance in the early days of Protestant missions to Bolivia. The ecclesiastical factor, or the strong opposition of the Catholic Church, has been drastically reduced since Vatican II. The sociological factor which tied the Catholic Church into the feudal social structure was changed by the Revolution of 1952. The power of the political conservatives was broken by the Chaco War. The anthropological factor involving community structures has not changed, but this has been, and can be used positively for the spread of the Gospel. These facts would indicate that the former strong resistance should be melted away by now, and that responsiveness to Protestantism should continue to increase in the near future.

COMPLETING THE AYMARA HARVEST

Missions working with the Aymaras should increase their efforts, since it is known that they presently are turning to Christ in large numbers. Groups on the fringe of the Aymara areas should move in as possible. Denominations, such as the Evangelical Christian Union, which already have a few Aymara churches, should give top priority to helping them reach out and win the neighboring ayllus. As the section on the Bolivian Holiness Mission indicated (pp. 147-151), the most successful approach is to plant the greatest number of churches even if they are small at the beginning. Emphasis should be given to quantity of churches planted rather than a disproportionate concern on perfecting the churches already planted. New converts certainly need proper shepherding but the greater danger is that some of the lost will not be found until it is too late.

In order to aid Aymara growth, several techniques learned by the denominations experienced in working with them should be adapted. The family lines, including the compadrazgo or godparent relationship, should be followed wherever possible, hence the evangelist should expect to win families rather than individuals. The multi-individual conversion pattern should be encouraged. When an individual wishes to move out against the social tide, the question must be asked whether he should be baptized until a more representative segment of his group

Strategy for Future Harvest 209

is also ready. The example set by the Oregon Friends in the use of Christian fiestas should be followed by all denominations.

William Wonderly suggests more use of "liturgy" or congregational participation. Rather than just running the services by a select group which has had some sort of special training, he feels that in a communal society the wider the participation by the congregation in the services, the better (Hamilton 1963:3).

Very few missionaries have made the effort to become fluent in Aymara. It is time, however, that those working with the Aymaras learn the language well, in spite of its great difficulty. An interdenominational language school for Aymara should be established in La Paz. Since the Aymara responsiveness will in all probability continue for some time, language learning would be time well spent.

SATURATING THE COLONIES WITH CHURCHES

Missions already working in the areas of new colonization in the tropical regions should give high priority to increasing their efforts. Some entire colonies are already considered Protestant and the potentiality of others following suit should not be overlooked. A church should be planted in each colony using the Protestant colonists as spiritual bridges. Since distances are great the churches should be located within easy walking distance of the surrounding farms. Inexpensive mud-and-wattle structures should be used for church buildings during this pioneer interval. When the colonies become criss-crossed with good roads and public transportation serves the areas, the churches then can be located further apart and buildings made more permanent.

Church leaders should be aware of the new highways which are projected or presently under construction. Wherever a new road penetrates, people will begin to settle and they should be relatively open to the Gospel for a period of time. A new road from Cochabamba to the colonies in the Chapare, for example, will soon be opened. All the villages along the new route will grow, while those on the old road will not. Good planning would lead denominations already in the area to plant churches in every one of the towns of 500 inhabitants or more, through which the road will pass. What McGavran has written about the great new "Marginal Highway" bears repeating here. La Marginal is the highway, already under construction,

which will run through the eastern foothills of the Andes from
Venezuela to Bolivia. He writes:

> Mobility in missions is demanded. Those missions which
> have been quietly "serving the Indians" who have stead-
> fastly rejected the Gospel, should make provision for the
> supervision of whatever congregations they may have in the
> high country, and shift their major forces to La Marginal.
> These people moving down there need help. They will be
> doubly unchurched down there. If they needed the Gospel
> up on top, where they could not "hear" it, they need it
> all the more down on La Marginal where they can "hear" it.
> The experience of the Oregon Friends in their tent cam-
> paigns and of all other missions which have already been
> planting churches in the high yungas, should be pooled and
> made available to the churchmen, nationals and missionaries
> who will be planting churches on the eastern shelf
> (McGavran 1967:10).

MULTIPLYING CONGREGATIONS IN URBAN AREAS

Even though Bolivia's cities are not growing at the
dramatic rates of Buenos Aires, Lima, Caracas, or Sao Paulo,
they nevertheless present similar opportunities for church
planting to those of the other cities. The reasons for this
are iven in Chapter 10 (pp. 195-197). Protestants have been
relatively successful in Latin America's cities in general.
Much good work is being done in Bolivia's urban areas, but the
momentum needs to be continued and increased. Five suggestions
could be made as to how to accomplish this:

*1. Large numbers of churches should be planted in the
cities.* Whenever a new barrio (neighborhood) begins to spring
up, Protestants should be alert enough to secure a parcel of
the relatively inexpensive land. This could be loaned to a
Protestant family where an inexpensive home could be built.
Here the nucleus of the church will begin. When the congregation grows, a church building can later be constructed. Having
a permanent building tends to communicate the image of
stability in a world of bustle, change and uncertainty.
Planning a large number of smaller neighborhood churches is
better strategy than concentrating on a few large churches.
The new urbanite needs the social intimacy that a smaller
congregation provides. This lack may be one reason why the

Catholic Church has not enjoyed success in the growing Latin American cities proportionate to that of the Protestant. Some tangible evidence of church membership, such as a wall certificate, should be provided, since "joining" is a characteristic of migrant people.

2. *Congregations should be developed along familiar cultural patterns.* New members should be involved in church activity as soon as possible. Each barrio congregation should have as much autonomy as possible, with the individual believer feeling that he is a vital part of the group. The large inner-city churches should continually be reproducing themselves on the growing fringes of the cities, but they should avoid the temptation of exercising too much paternal control over their smaller offspring. Urban substitutes for key rural cultural elements should be incorporated into the church. Fiestas and compadrazgo relationships, adapted to Protestant norms, should be encouraged. Worship services should draw out congregational participation.

3. *The ministry should be adapted to the needs of the new city churches.* An academically multilevel ministry is one of Bolivia's facts of life. The Chilean Pentecostals have shown that formal training is not necessarily a prerequisite for a successful urban ministry. Extension theological training can and should be used to good advantage in urban areas. Night Bible institutes will succeed better in the cities than in the country and should be exploited.

Ministers of the larger and older city churches should be good preachers. The more stable city dwellers will be able to select their churches and may choose the one offering the most helpful pulpit ministry.

4. *Each congregation should be evangelistic in nature.* Each church member should be active in winning others in his neighborhood to Christ. Then each congregation should make plans as soon as possible for reproducing itself in nearby barrios. In the cities, Protestant churches should be about as ubiquitous as houseflies.

5. *Each congregation should show tangible concern for the social problems of the barrio.* Action in practical areas of immediate concern is more important than involvement in theoretical aspects of long-term politics. One common problem of new urban residents is finding a job. If the Protestant

church could form an employment agency for its members, it would render a very important service both to them and to the surrounding employers.

RENEWED EFFORTS TO WIN THE QUECHUAS

Probably a key to reaching the Quechuas who have not yet believed is to discover the exact tribal mosaic into which they are fragmented. Each of these should be thought of, not as Quechuas, but as Jucumanis, Tarabuqueños, or what have you. Attempts should be made to disciple entire tribal units, working through the familiar patterns of social structure that exist in each.

In order to do this, a large number of missionaries should dedicate themselves to Quechua learning. At least two generations more will need to be reached in the Quechua tongue. The Andes Evangelical Mission, with the cooperation and direction of Henry Spenst of the Summer Institute of Linguistics, runs a small Quechua language school for missionaries. This should be intensified and more younger workers encouraged to attend. The AEM in the early years required only Quechua of its missionaries. For some time the swing was more toward Spanish, but now more are learning Quechua and ministering in that tongue. Now that Bolivia has a President who makes nationwide speeches in Quechua, and Quechua is being taught in the universities, the language is gaining rather than losing prestige. The current project of the Bible Societies to translate the New Testament into a popular form of Quechua (parallel to *Good News for Modern Man*) is a creative and valuable step.

MISSIONARY AND NATIONAL WORKERS SHOULD BE MOBILE

When fertile soil and ripened harvest fields are located, missions and churches should be flexible enough to pull workers from the resistant areas and use them for areas where greater church growth is possible. Perhaps some of the Bolivian denominations have become overly concerned with the "quality" of their congregations rather than with obeying the Great Commission. This has been carefully, but not successfully, rationalized by some groups. Where this centripetal attitude still exists, churches will not grow as they should. The church should be thought of as a fire. The more new fuel a fire consumes, the hotter it gets within its own interior.

Strategy for Future Harvest 213

Likewise, the more active a church is in winning new members, the more her inner vitality will increase. The highest quality church is almost invariably the church that is active in finding the lost and giving them the bread of life.

TRAINING THE MINISTRY FOR A GROWING CHURCH

Although a separate study needs to be done on this, as a preliminary observation, it seems as if the best method for training the ministry for the Bolivian Church, which is multicultural and academically multilevel, is to inaugurate vast programs of extension education in conjunction with existing theological institutions. Many Bolivian churches have functional pastors who are called "laymen" and thus relegated to a somewhat secondary ministerial category. Because they have families, jobs and community responsibilities, few of these natural leaders can break from their home environments and attend a three-year program of studies in one of the institutions for theological education. They need to receive first-class accredited training without having to move to an institution. Their training has to be accommodated to their levels of previous secular training and recognized by their denominations for ordination. Although the Andean area presents the special problem of a semi-literate ministry, steps should be taken to introduce the kind of training so successfully employed by the Presbyterian Seminary in Guatemala in "taking the Seminary to the students."

ALLOWING REGIONAL AND ETHNIC AUTONOMY

This study has shown that being monocultural is often an advantage for church growth. The INELA (Oregon Friends) has been very conscious of this and has determined to maintain the monocultural Aymara nature of their denomination. The Assemblies of God began with the principle of regional autonomy but later became integrated, probably to their own disadvantage. The Bolivian Baptist Union, probably one of the most broadly integrated multicultural denominations in the country, bears careful watching. The Methodists are making a strong attempt to integrate their Aymara and mestizo churches. The Evangelical Christian Union, with its decentralized structure and nine regional sub-committees, is taking important steps toward solving the problems of a multicultural Church. As each denomination faces and handles these problems, it should bear in mind that every people will feel more comfortable in a church that is "their own" in the sense of adaptation to their own cultural expectations and values. If Aymaras think that they have to become mestizos in order to be Christians or vice-versa, proportionately fewer will come to Christ.

Decentralization in itself, however, may not be enough. The importance of making certain that the leaders of each presbytery or each synod be members of the ethnic group being discipled should not be taken for granted. Whereas, for example, often mestizos attempted to become members of the Oregon Friends Aymara churches, they were never permitted to do so. This may have seemed rather heartless to some, but the result has been one of the fastest growing indigenous churches in Bolivia. The mestizos would have become leaders because of their social status, not necessarily because of their spiritual gifts. This would have retarded the growth of the Church.

MAINTAINING A SOCIAL WITNESS

When a developing country is undergoing rapid social change, the Church cannot be indifferent to the legitimate social aspirations of not only its own members but of the nation as a whole. Involvement in these aspects of life is highly important. Unfortunately some Latin American Protestants have so emphasized this aspect of Christian testimony that they have negated the important factor of individual conversion, baptism into the Body of Christ, and church growth. This understandably has caused a contrary reaction on the part of evangelicals and caused a tension in the Church. There is no easy answer, but when two good and legitimate aspects of the Church's ministry come into conflict, biblical priorities must necessarily be established. The New Testament is clear that both the nature of God and the nature of the Church demand that highest priority be given to finding those who are lost because they have not believed in Christ as Savior and Lord, and bringing them to faith and life. All other good Christian activities must take second place. As they begin to dilute or hinder the evangelistic effectiveness they to this degree become no longer good.

Christians, then, should show their love to their neighbor through social service wherever and whenever possible. The Church should become known to those outside as a fellow-participant in the struggle for social justice. COMBASE has been a good agency for this, and should be encouraged.

DEVELOPING BOLIVIAN HYMNOLOGY

The final suggestion is that the efforts to develop a Bolivian hymnology previously described in Chapter 8, be continued and that the Bolivian hymnal be published in its first edition as soon as possible. This will be an important step in the process of further identifying the Bolivian Protestant Church with the Bolivian culture. The Aymara hymnal should be revised and continued; a hymnal of original Quechua hymns (not hymns which have been translated) should be projected.

CONCLUSION

Bolivia is one of the world's ripe harvest fields today. The Protestant Church is growing and prospects for more accelerated growth seem good for the near future. God's will is that all Bolivians from Illimani to Tunari to the Gran Chaco be reconciled to Himself through Jesus and be baptized into the Church. There are 3,166,800 yet to come. His final judgment on today's Bolivian Church will be based largely on how they have accomplished this vast and challenging task.

Appendix

A DIRECTORY
OF THE PROTESTANT DENOMINATIONS
CURRENTLY IN BOLIVIA

This is an alphabetical listing according to the Spanish name of the denomination, followed by the English name which is associated with each, either by virtue of being the sponsoring denomination or the English translation of its Spanish name. Where available, dates of entrance into the country of the denomination or missions are given.

ADVENTISTAS DEL SEPTIMO DIA. Seventh-day Adventists General Conference (USA) 1907. Casilla 355, La Paz, Bolivia.

ASAMBLEAS DE DIOS. General Council of the Assemblies of God (USA) 1946. Casilla 112, Santa Cruz.

ASAMBLEAS DE DIOS NORUEGA. Norwegian Assemblies of God (Norway). Casilla 64, Riberalta, Beni.

BAUTISTAS MARANATA. Maranatha Baptists (USA) 1962. Casilla 1309, Cochabamba.

CONVENCION BAUTISTA BOLIVIANA. Brazilian Baptists 1946. Casilla 181, Santa Cruz.

EJERCITO DE SALVACION. Salvation Army (England) 1941.
    Casilla 926, La Paz.

HERMANOS LIBRES. Christian Missions in Many Lands (England,
    Australia, New Zealand, USA) 1895. Casilla 680, Cochabamba.

IGLESIA BOLIVIANA DE SANTIDAD. Bolivian Holiness Mission or
    Holiness Methodist Church (USA) 1948. Casilla 1119, La Paz.

IGLESIA CUADRANGULAR. International Church of the Foursquare
    Gospel (USA) 1929. Casilla 6, Trinidad, Beni.

IGLESIA DE DIOS. Church of God, Cleveland (USA). Casilla 303,
    Sucre.

IGLESIA DE DIOS BOLIVIANA. Church of God, Holiness (USA) 1945.
    Casilla 2371, La Paz.

IGLESIA DE LA PUERTA ABIERTA. Church of the Open Door (USA)
    1955. Casilla 953, Cochabamba.

IGLESIA EVANGELICA LOS AMIGOS. Bolivian Friends! Holiness
    Mission (USA) 1933. Casilla 922, La Paz.

IGLESIA DEL NAZARENO. Church of the Nazarene (USA) 1945.
    Casilla 407, Oruro.

IGLESIA EVANGELICA LUTERANA BOLIVIANA. World Mission Prayer
    League (USA) 1938. Casilla 266, La Paz.

IGLESIA EVANGELICA MUNDIAL. World Gospel Mission (USA) 1944.
    Casilla 55, Santa Cruz.

IGLESIA EVANGELICA NACIONAL. National Evangelical Church
    (Bolivia) 1957. Casilla 578, Santa Cruz.

IGLESIA LUTERANA ALEMANA. German Lutheran Church. La Paz.

IGLESIA MENONITA. Mennonite Church (Paraguay) 1954.

IGLESIA METODISTA EN BOLIVIA. Methodist Church (USA) 1901.
    Casilla 356, La Paz.

IGLESIA NACIONAL BETHESDA. Bethesda Missions (USA) 1951.
    Casilla 290, Santa Cruz.

Appendix

IGLESIA NACIONAL EVANGELICA LOS AMIGOS. Oregon Yearly Meeting of Friends Church (USA) 1924. Casilla 544, La Paz.

MISION BAUTISTA INTERNATIONAL. International Baptist Missions (USA).

MISION BAUTISTA LETA. Latvian Baptist Mission (Brazil) 1950. Rincón del Tigre, via Puerto Suárez.

MISION DEL SEMINARIO BIBLICO. Union Bible Seminary (USA) 1919. Casilla 1422, La Paz.

MISION LLAMAMIENTO DE MEDIANOCHE. Midnight Call Mission (Switzerland) 1960. Casilla 62, Riberalta, Beni.

MISION NEOTESTAMENTARIA. New Testament Missionary Union (USA, Canada) 1926. Puerto Suárez.

MISION NUEVAS TRIBUS. New Tribes Mission (USA) 1942. Casilla 522, Cochabamba.

MISION UNIDA MUNDIAL. United World Mission (USA) 1936. Casilla 7, Santa Cruz.

PENTECOSTAL BRAZILERA. Brazilian Pentecostals.

PENTECOSTAL CHILENA. Chilean Pentecostals.

PENTECOSTAL NACIONAL. National Pentecostal Church. Casilla 51, Trinidad.

PENTECOSTAL SUECA. Swedish Free Mission (Sweden) 1920. Casilla 1627, Cochabamba.

SOUTH AMERICA INDIAN MISSION. (USA) 1926. Casilla 843, Santa Cruz.

UNION BAUTISTA BOLIVIANA. Canadian Baptist Foreign Mission Board (Canada) 1898. Casilla 86, Cochabamba.

UNION BIBLICA. Seattle Bible Union (USA) 1952. Casilla 3, Camiri.

UNION CRISTIANA EVANGELICA. Casilla 1196, Cochabamba.
  Andes Evangelical Mission (New Zealand, Australia, England,
    USA, Canada) 1903. Cajón 514, Cochabamba.
  Evangelical Union of South America (USA) 1937. Casilla 88,
    Camiri.

WORLDWIDE MISSIONS (USA). Casilla 758, Cochabamba.

Bibliography

ALEXANDER, Robert Jackson
1958   *Bolivian National Revolution*. Washington, The Savile Book Shop.

ALLAN, George
1920   *The Bolivian Indian Mission*. No place or publisher. Pamphlet.

1936   *Reminiscences being Incidents from Missionary Experience*. Dunedin, New Zealand, Bolivian Indian Mission.

ALONSO, Isidoro
1964   *La Iglesia en América Latina, estructuras eclesiásticas*. Bogotá, FERES.

ALONSO, Isidoro, GARRIDO, Gines, BELLIDO, Dammert, TUMIRI, Julio
1962   *La Iglesia en Perú y Bolivia: estructuras eclesiásticas*. Bogotá, FERES.

AMUNDSEN, Wesley
1944   *Sons of the Incas*. Washington, Review and Herald.

ANDEAN OUTLOOK
1967   Quarterly publication of the Andes Evangelical Mission, Cochabamba, Bolivia, 57:3; July-September.

ARCINIEGAS, German
    1966   *Latin America: A Cultural History.* New York,
            A. Knopf.

ARMAS MEDINA, Fernanco de
    1953   *Cristinización del Perú (1532-1600).* Sevilla,
            Escuela de Estudios Hispano-americanos.

ARMS, Goodsil F.
    1921   *History of the William Taylor Self-Supporting Missions
            in South America.* New York, Methodist Book Concern.

ARNADE, Charles W.
    1957   *The Emergence of the Republic of Bolivia.*
            Gainesville, University of Florida.

ASSEMBLIES OF GOD
    1960   "Bolivia." Springfield, Missouri, Foreign Missions
            Department, Assemblies of God. Pamphlet.

AYARRAGARY, Lucas
    1935   *La Iglesia en América, Estudio de la Epoca Colonial.*
            2a edición. Buenos Aires, Rosso.

BANNON, John Francis, SJ
    1963   *History of the Americas.* New York, McGraw-Hill.

BANNON, John Francis, SJ and DUNNE, Peter Maston, SJ
    1958   *Latin America: An Historical Survey.* Milwaukie,
            Bruce.

BARBER, Natalie
    1965   "The Methodist Church Completes 60 Years in Bolivia,"
            La Paz News Letter. December, pp. 12-14. La Paz,
            U. S. Embassy.

BARCLAY, Wade Crawford
    1957   *History of Methodist Missions.* Vol. III. New York,
            The Board of Missions of the Methodist Church.

BEACH, Harlan P.
    1916   *Renaissant Latin America: An Outline and Interpretation of the Congress on Christian Work in Latin America, Held at Panama, February 10-19, 1916.*
            New York, Missionary Education Movement.

Bibliography

BEACH, Harlan P. and FAHS, Charles H.
1925   *World Missionary Atlas.* New York, Institute of Social and Religious Research.

BECK, Bessie Dunn
1938   *A Study of Changing Social Attitudes in the American Institutes of Bolivia.* Chicago, University of Chicago.

BENNETT, Wendell C.
1963   "The Andean Highlands: An Introduction," *Handbook of South American Indians.* II:1-60, New York.

BENNETT, Wendell C. and BIRD, Junius B.
1960   *Andean Culture History.* New York, American Museum of Natural History.

BILBAO, Francisco
1943   *El evangelio americano; estudio preliminar.* Buenos Aires, Ed. Americalee.

BINGLE, E. J. and GRUBB, Kenneth G.
1952   *World Christian Handbook 1952.* London, World Dominion Press.

1957   *World Christian Handbook 1957.* London, World Dominion Press.

BOLIVAR, Simón
1950   *Obras completas, compilación y notas de Vicente Lecuna con la colaboración de la senorita Esther Barret de Nazaria.* Vol. III. La Havana, Editorial Lex.

BRITISH AND FOREIGN BIBLE SOCIETY
1828   *The Twenty-Fourth Report of the British and Foreign Bible Society with an Appendix.* London, J. Moyes.

1829   *The Twenty-Fifth Report of the British and Foreign Bible Society with an Appendix.* London, J. Moyes.

BROWN, Roger H.
1965   "Obra evangélica de los hermanos," unpublished answer to questionnaire sent out by David B. Phillips, June 14, 1965.

BROWNE, George
  1859 *The History of the British and Foreign Bible Society from its Institution in 1804 to the Close of its Jubilee in 1854.* Vol. II. London, Bagster and Sons.

BROWNING, Webster E., RITCHIE, John and GRUBB, Kenneth G.
  1930 *The West Coast Republics of South America, Chile, Peru and Bolivia.* London, World Dominion Press.

BRUNDAGE, Burr Cartwright
  1967 *Lords of Cuzco: A History and Description of the Inca People in Their Final Days.* Norman, University of Oklahoma Press.

BUCK, Mary and HILLYER, H. S.
  c. 1949 *Fifty Years of Christian Witness in Bolivia, 1898-1948.* No place or publisher. Mimeographed drama.

BUECHLER, Hans Christian
  1966 *Agrarian Reform and Migration on the Bolivian Altiplano.* New York, Columbia University. (Ph.D., University Microfilms 67.786)

CAMMACK, Phyllis
  1966 *Missionary Moments, Sixty Diverse "Moments" in the Life of a South American Missionary.* Newberg, Oregon, Barclay Press.

CANADIAN BAPTIST FOREIGN MISSION BOARD
  1914, 1915, 1916. *Annual Reports.* Toronto, Baptist Church House. (1914 is third annual report of work July 1, 1913 to June 30, 1914.)

  1917-1921 *Annual Reports.* Toronto, Standard Publishing Co.

  1922-1957 *Annual Reports.* Toronto, Wilson Printing Co.

  1950-1962 *Canadian Baptists Overseas, Missionary Digest.* Toronto, CBFMB.

  1963 *The Church Overseas.* Toronto, CBFMB.

CARTER, William E.
  1965 *Aymara Communities and the Bolivian Agrarian Reform.* Gainesville, University of Florida Press.

CENTRAL YEARLY MEETING OF FRIENDS
1946-1958 *Minutes*. No place or publisher.

CGRILA
1967 See Read 1967

CHAPMAN, Ralph
1964a *Análisis de su programa de obras benificiosas ofrecido por la Misión Evangélica Los Amigos a la INELA*. La Paz. Mimeographed paper.

1964b Letter written to OYM Board of Missions. La Paz, January 20.

CHURCH OF THE NAZARENE
1944, 1948, 1952 *Journal of the General Assembly*. Kansas City, Missouri, Church of the Nazarene.

CLARK, Francis E. and CLARK, Harriet A.
1909 *The Gospel in Latin Lands*. New York, The MacMillan Company.

CLISSOLD, Stephen
1966 *Latin America, A Cultural Outline*. New York, Harper and Row.

COLLIER, John
1947 *Indians of the Americas*. New York, New American Library.

COMAS, Juan
1962 "Bolivia," *Indianist Yearbook*. pp. 13-22. (Supercedes *Boletín indigenista*, 1941-1961) Mexico, Inter-American Indian Institute.

COMIBOL
1967 "Comibol Progress Report," *New York Times*. March 18.

CONRAD, W. Howard
1967 *A Report to the Department of World Missions of the Church of the Nazarene Concerning Growth on Its Mission Fields*. An unpublished M. A. thesis, Fuller Theological Seminary.

COPPLESTONE, J. Tremayne
1967 "The Methodist Church, Board of Missions of," *Encyclopedia of Modern Christian Missions*. Burton Goddard, ed. pp. 407-418. New York, Nelson.

COXILL, H. Wakelin and GRUBB, Kenneth G.
1962 *World Christian Handbook 1962*. London, World Dominion Press.

1967 *World Christian Handbook 1967*. Nashville, Abingdon.

CRIVELLI, P. Camilo, SJ
1933 *Directorio Protestante de la America Latina*. Isola del Liri, Italy, Soc. Tip. A. Macioci & Pesani.

DABBS, Norman H.
1952 *Dawn Over the Bolivian Hills*. Toronto, Canadian Baptist Foreign Mission Board.

DANIELS, Margarette
1916 *Makers of South America*. New York, Missionary Education Movement.

DEBRAY, Régis
1967 *Revolution in the Revolution? Armed Struggle and Political Struggle in Latin America*. New York, Monthly Review Press.

DENNIS, James S., BEACH, Harlan P. and FAHS, Charles H.
1911 *World Atlas of Christian Missions*. New York, Student Volunteer Movement for Foreign Missions.

DERBY, Marian and ELLIS, James E.
1961 *Latin American Lands in Focus*. New York, Board of Missions of the Methodist Church.

DIFFENDORFER, Ralph E., ed.
1923 *The World Service of the Methodist Episcopal Church*. Chicago, Methodist Episcopal Church.

DIVISION OF EVANGELISM, LATIN AMERICA MISSION
c. 1967 *New Dimension in Evangelism*. Bogota, New Jersey Latin America Mission. Pamphlet.

ECHOES OF SERVICE
1900-1966 See Stunt, William T.

   1965 "Spotlight on Bolivia," *Echoes of Service*. XCIV:1441,
January, pp. 16-19.

ELLIOT, Elizabeth
   1968 *Who Shall Ascend, The Life of R. Kenneth Strachan of
Costa Rica*. New York, Harper and Row.

ENNS, Arno W.
   1967 *Profiles of Argentine Church Growth*. An unpublished
M.A. thesis, Fuller Theological Seminary.

EYZAGUIRRE, José Ignacio Victor
   1859 *Los intereses católicos en América*. Tomos I y II.
Paris, Librería de Garnier Hermanos.

FAGG, John Edwin
   1963 *Latin America, A General History*. New York, Macmillan
Company.

FELIMAN VELARDE, José
   1961 *Los Imperios Andinos*. La Paz, Editorial Don Bosco.

FRAMPTON, Keith
   1968 Personal letter to author, Guayaramerín, February 17.

GEYER, Robert Raine
   1963 *Death Trails in Bolivia to Faith Triumphant*. New York,
Vantage Press.

GLOVER, Robert Hall and KANE, J. Herbert
   1960 *The Progress of World-Wide Missions*. New York, Harper
and Brothers.

GODDARD, Burton L., ed.
   1967 *The Encyclopedia of Modern Christian Missions*. Camden,
Thomas Nelson and Sons.

GOSLIN, Thomas S.
   1956 *Los evangélicos en la América Latina, siglo XIX, los
comienzos*. Buenos Aires, La Aurora.

GRAMS, Monroe D.
　1968a　Personal letter to author, La Paz, March 12.

　1968b　Personal letter to author, La Paz, April 1.

GROCOTT, Horace D.
　1960　*Bolivian Episode: Impressions and experiences of pioneer missionaries in Bolivia, South America, on service with the Bolivian Indian Mission, 1909-1914.* No place, An unpublished bound typescript.

　1962　*Bolivian Indian Mission, Manuscript Diary in Correspondence, 1909-1914.* Wellington, Bound manuscript.

GRUBB, Kenneth G.
　1927　*The Lowland Indians of Amazonia.* World Dominion Survey Series, London, World Dominion Press.

　1938　*The West Coast Republics of South America, Review of Ten Years Evangelical Progress to 1938.* London, World Dominion Press. (Bound with Browning 1930)

GRUBB, Kenneth G. and BINGLE, E.J.
　1949　*World Christian Handbook 1949.* London, World Dominion Press.

GUNTHER, John
　1967　*Inside South America.* New York, Harper and Row.

HAINES, Marie H.
　c. 1955　*Friends in Aymara Land, 1930-1955.* Portland, Oregon Yearly Meeting.

HAMILTON, Keith
　1962　*Church Growth in the High Andes.* India, Lucknow.

　1963　"Consultation on Andean Indian Work." Unpublished mimeographed report.

HANKE, Lewis
　1967　*Modern Latin America: Continent in Ferment, Vol. 2, South America.* Revised edition. Princeton, Van Nostrand.

HARLOW, R. E. and SMART, John
   1960   *Who Is My Neighbor? Assembly Missionaries in Latin America.* New York, The Fields, Inc.

HARRIS, Marvin
   1964   *Patterns of Race in the Americas.* New York, Walker and Company.

HAWTHORNE, Sally Reese
   n.d.   *Cloud Country Sojourn, Missionaries in the South American Andes.* London, Bolivian Indian Mission.

HEREDIA, Cornelio
   1968   "Himnología Nacional de Bolivia," *Visión Evangélica.* 10:3 Marzo, pp. 10-11.

HERRICK, Bruce H.
   1965   *Urban Migration and Economic Development in Chile.* Cambridge, Massachusetts, MIT Press.

HERRING, Hubert
   1961   *A History of Latin America.* New York, Alfred Knopf.

HISTORICAL SOCIETY OF THE METHODIST CHURCH IN BOLIVIA
   1961   *The Methodist Church in Bolivia, La Iglesia Metodista en Bolivia.* Diglot. Cochabamba, Imprenta Icthus.

HORTON, Arthur G.
   1966   *An Outline of Latin American History.* Dubuque, Brown.

HOWARD, George P.
   1944   *Religious Liberty in Latin America?* Philadelphia, Westminster.

HUDSPITH, Margarita Allan
   1958   *Ripening Fruit.* Plainfield, N. J., Bolivian Indian Mission.

HYAMS, Edward and ORDISH, George
   1963   *The Last of the Incas. The Rise and Fall of an American Empire.* New York, Simon and Schuster.

IGLESIA DE DIOS BOLIVIANA
   1968   *Reglamento Interno.* La Paz, Iglesia de Dios Boliviana.

IGLESIA METODISTA EN BOLIVIA
1916-1919   *Actas de la Conferencia Anual Provisional.*
         La Paz and Cochabamba.

INTERNATIONAL CHURCH OF THE FOURSQUARE GOSPEL
  1937   *Yearbook.* Los Angeles, International Church of the
          Foursquare Gospel.

ISIAS, Juan M.
  1968   "Personal Reflections on Evangelism-in-Depth,"
          Mimeographed. Office of Worldwide Evangelism-in-
          Depth, Bogota, N.J., Latin America Mission.

ISAL,
  1967a   "Informe de la Sección IV Migraciones Internas,"
          Mimeographed report of committee at ISAL meeting in
          Pirapolis, Uruguay, December.

  1967b   *El Indigena de los Andes, de la comunidad a la ciudad.*
          Montevideo, ISAL.

JAUREGUI ROSQUELLAS, Alfredo
  1924   *La Ciudad de Cuatro Nombres.* Sucre, La Glorieta.

JOHNSON, Jean Dye
  1967   *God Planted Five Seeds.* New York, Harper and Row.

KESSLER, J. B. A.
  1967   *A Study of the older Protestant missions and churches
          in Peru and Chile with special reference to the
          problems of division, nationalism and native ministry.*
          Goes, Oosterbaan & le Cointre.

KNIGHT, Roscoe
  1966   "Don't Send Money," *World Vision Magazine.* July-
          August, p. 4.

KNUTSON, J. B.
  1968a   Personal letter to author, Woodworth, Wisconsin,
          February 2.

  1968b   Personal letter to author, Woodworth, Wisconsin,
          February 21.

KUBLER, George
  1963   "The Quechua in the Colonial World," *Handbook of South American Indians.* II:331-409.

LA BARRE, Weston
  1963   "The Uru-Chipaya," *Handbook of South American Indians.* II: 575-586.

LATOURETTE, Kenneth Scott
  1939   *A History of the Expansion of Christianity, Vol. III, Three Centuries of Advance, AD 1500 - AD 1800.* New York, Harper and Brothers.

LEAR, Gilberto M. J.
  1951   *Un explorador valiente, Pequena biografía de la vida del infaligable don Guillermo S. Payne.* Lanus, Argentina, Librería Editorial Cristiana.

LEE, John
  1907   *Religious Liberty in South America, With Special Reference to Recent Legislation in Peru, Ecuador and Bolivia.* New York, Eaton and Mains.

LEONS, Madeline Barbara
  1966   *Changing Patterns of Social Stratification in an Emergent Bolivian Community.* An unpublished Ph.D. dissertation, UCLA, Los Angeles. (University microfilms 67.4502)

LEWIS, Barbara H., ed.
  1960   *Methodist Overseas Missions 1960, Gazeteer and Statistics.* New York, Women's Division of Christian Service of the Board of Missions of the Methodist Church.

LISSON CHAVES, Emilio
  1943   *La Iglesia de España en el Perú, Colección de documentos para la historia de la iglesia en el Perú, que se encuentran en varios archivos.* Tomos I-V. Sevilla.

LLOSA M., José Antonio
  1966   *René Barrientos Ortuno, Paladín de la Bolivianidad.* La Paz, Empresa Editorial "Novedades."

LOPETEGUI, León and ZUBILLAGA, Felix
    1965   *Historia de la Iglesia en la América espanola Desde el Descubrimiento hasta comienzos del siglo XIX, México, América Central, Antillas.* Madrid, Editorial Católica.

LOPEZ DE LAMA, Jesús A.
    1967   "The Aymara," *Worldmission.* 18:4; Winter 1967-1968: pp. 25-28.

LOPEZ MENENDEZ, Felipe
    1965   *Compendio de historia eclesiástica de Bolivia.* La Paz, Imprenta El Progresso.

LORES, Rubén
    1967   "Evangelism-in-Depth," *One Race, One Gospel, One Task.* Vol. II:495-497. Minneapolis, World Wide.

LOWDEN, C. H.
    1912   *The Doors of Bolivia.* Auckland, New Zealand, BIM.

MCBRIDE, George McCutchen
    1921   *The Agrarian Indian Communities of Highland Bolivia.* New York, Oxford University Press.

MCCLEARY, Paul
    1965   "The Methodist Church in Bolivia," Mimeographed paper. Also published in Spanish in *Avance,* XI:2,3; XII:1. La Paz, Iglesia Metodista en Bolivia.

    1968   Personal letter to author, La Paz, March 26.

MCGAVRAN, Donald A.
    1967   "Church Growth Eyes on La Marginal," *Church Growth Bulletin.* IV:2 November, pp. 9,10.

MCGAVRAN, Donald A., HUEGEL, John and TAYLOR, James
    1963   *Church Growth in Mexico.* Grand Rapids, Eerdmans.

MECHAM, J. Lloyd
    1966   *Church and State in Latin America.* Chapel Hill, University of North Carolina Press. (First edition 1934).

METHODIST CHURCH, BOARD OF MISSIONS
  1966 *Partnership in Missions, A Guide to Second Mile Giving Through Advance Special Projects*. New York, Board of Missions of the Methodist Church.

METHODIST EPISCOPAL CHURCH
  1883ss *Annual Reports*.

MILLARD, E. C. and GUINNESS, Lucy E.
  1893 *South America: The Neglected Continent*. London, E. Marlborough.

MISHKIN, Bernard
  1963 "The Contemporary Quechua," *Handbook of South American Indians*. II: 411-470.

MISSIONARY RESEARCH LIBRARY
  1966 *North American Protestant Foreign Mission Agencies*. New York, Missionary Research Library.

MISSIONARY SOCIETY OF THE METHODIST EPISCOPAL CHURCH
  1887-1906 *Annual Reports*. New York, Methodist Episcopal Church.

MORNER, Magnus, ed.
  1965 *The Expulsion of the Jesuits from Latin America*. New York, Alfred A. Knopf.

NEELY, Thomas B.
  1906 *South America: A Mission Field*. New York, Eaton and Mains.

  1909 *South America: Its Missionary Problems*. New York, Missionary Education Movement.

NEILL, Stephen Charles
  1964 *A History of Christian Missions*. Harmondsworth, Pelican.

  1966 *Colonialism and Christian Missions*. New York, McGraw-Hill.

OLSON, Ron
  1968 Personal letter to author, Cochabamba, April 11.

OSBORNE, Harold
1952   *Indians of the Andes: Aymaras and Quechuas*. London, Routledge and Paul.

1964   *Bolivia, A Land Divided*. London, Royal Institute of International Affairs. (Third edition)

OSTRIA GUTIERREZ, Alberto
1961   *The Tragedy of Bolivia: A People Crucified*. (Translated by Eithne Golden) Belmont, Massachusetts, American Opinion.

PARKER, Joseph I.
1938   *Interpretative Statistical Survey of the World Mission of the Christian Church*. New York, International Missionary Council.

PATCH, Richard W.
1962   *Bolivia's Developing Interior*. New York, American Universities Field Staff, 366 Madison Ave., N. Y., 10017.

1964   *Bolivia's Experiments in Development Without Aid*. New York American Universities Field Staff.

1965   *A Note on Bolivia and Peru*. New York, American Universities Field Staff.

1967   "Peasantry and National Revolution: Bolivia," in *Expectant Peoples*. K. H. Silvert, ed. New York, Vintage.

PATTEE, Richard, ed.
1951   *El Catolicismo contemporáneo en Hispanoamérica*. Buenos Aires, Fides. Chapter "Bolivia" by Raimundo Grigorin Sánchez de Lozada.

PAYNE, Will and WILSON, Charles T. W.
1904   *Missionary Pioneering in Bolivia, with some Account of Work in Argentina*. London, H. A. Raymond.

PENZOTTI, Francis G.
1916   *Spiritual Victories in Latin America, Autobiography*. New York, American Bible Society.

Bibliography

PHILLIPS, David
n.d. "El Evangelio en la America Latina." Unpublished lecture notes. Cochabamba, Seminario Teológico Bautista.

POHL, Irmgard and ZEPP, Josef
1967 *Latin America: A Geographical Commentary*. New York, Dutton.

POPULATION REFERENCE BUREAU
1968 "World Population Data Sheet - 1968." Washington, Population Reference Bureau.

READ, William R., JOHNSON, Harmon A., MONTERROSSO, Victor M.
1967 *Evangelical Church Growth in Latin America*. Mimeographed report. Pasadena.

ROBERTS, W. Dayton
1967 *Revolution in Evangelism: The Story of Evangelism-in-Depth in Latin America*. Chicago, Moody.

ROWE, John Howard
1963 "Inca Culture at the Time of the Spanish Conquest," *Handbook of South American Indians*. II:183-330.

RYAN, Edwin
1932 *The Church in the South American Republics*. New York, Bruce.

RYCROFT, W. Stanley and CLEMMER, Myrtle
1963 *A Factual Study of Latin America*. New York, United Presbyterian Church USA.

SALLES, Edson
1966 "Histórico de la obra misionera desarrollada por los bautistas brasileños en el oriente de la República Boliviana." Unpublished paper in author's files.

SANDSTROM, D. J.
1968 Personal letter to author, Lima, Peru, April 9.

SARMIENTO, Domingo F.
1915 *Conflicto y armonías de las razas en América*. Buenos Aires, La Cultura Argentina.

SCHURZ, William Lytle
   1954   *This New World, The Civilization of Latin America.*
           New York, E. P. Dutton and Company.

SEVENTH-DAY ADVENTISTS
   1908-1967 *Yearbook.* Washington, Review and Herald
           Publishing Association.

   1966   *Encyclopedia of Seventh-day Adventists.* Vol. 1.
           Takoma Park, Washington, D.C., Review and Herald
           Publishing Association.

   1967   *Seventh-day Adventist Yearbook 1967.* Washington,
           D.C., General Conference of the Seventh-day Adventists.

SHAULL, Richard
   1968   "Toward a Reformation of Objectives," *Protestant
           Crosscurrents in Mission, The Ecumenical-Conservative
           Encounter.* Nashville, Abingdon.

SHEREDA, Edith
   1934   *Among the Bolivian Indians.* Chicago, Moody Church.

SINCLAIR, John, ed.
   1967   *Protestantism in Latin America: A Bibliographical
           Guide.* Austin, Hispanic American Institute.

SMITH, Mildred F.
   1961   *The Methodist Church in Bolivia 1906-1961; La Iglesia
           Metodista en Bolivia.* Diglot. Cochabamba, Editorial
           Icthus.

SPEER, Robert
   1915   *South American Problems.* New York, Student Volunteer
           Movement.

STAHL, F. A.
   1920   *In the Land of the Incas.* Mountain View, Calif.,
           Pacific Press Publishing Association.

STATISTICAL SECRETARY, GENERAL CONFERENCE OF SEVENTH-DAY ADV.
   1905-1965 *Annual Statistical Reports of Seventh-day Adven-
           tists.* Washington, General Conference of Seventh-
           day Adventists.

STEWARD, Julian H., ed.
1963   Handbook of South American Indians. Six volumes.
        New York, Cooper Square.

STEWARD, Julian H. and FARON, Louis C.
1959   Native Peoples of South America. New York, McGraw-Hill.

STILLWELL, H. E.
1924   Pioneering in Bolivia. Toronto, CBFMB.

STRONG, Esther Boorman and WARNSHUIS, A. L.
1933   Directory of Foreign Missions. New York, International Missionary Council.

STUNT, William T, PULLENG, Alexander, PICKERING, Arnold, eds.
1900-1966   Echoes of Service. 1 Widcombe Crescent, Bath, Somerset, England, Pitman Press.

THE FIELDS
1968   Missionary Prayer Handbook for Daily Use Listing Some Missionaries Commended by American and Canadian Assemblies. New York, The Fields.

TIME
1968   "The Benefits of Subversion," January 19, p. 25.

TORMO, Leandro and AIZPURU, Pilar Gonzalbo
1961   La historia de la iglesia en la América Latina, Tomo II, La iglesia en la crisis de la independencia. Bogota, FERES.

TORRES, Ezequiel
1965   "La Obra Nacional de la UCE," Essay written in response to a questionnaire, July 12.

1967   Personal letter to author, Cochabamba, October 9.

TRACHSEL, Laura
1961   Kindled Fires in Latin America. Marion, Indiana, World Gospel Mission.

TSCHOPIK, Harry
1963   "The Aymara," Handbook of South American Indians. II:501-573.

VARETTO, Juan
　1918　*Diego Thomson.* Buenos Aires, Casa Bautista de
　　　　Publicaciones.

VARGAS UGARTE, Rubén, SJ
　1953　*Historia de la Iglesia en el Perú.* Lima, Imprenta
　　　　Santa María, 5 tomos.

VERGARA, Ignacio
　1962　*El Protestantismo en Chile.* Santiago, Ed. del
　　　　Pacifico.

VON HAGEN, Victor Wolfgang
　1961　*The Ancient Sun Kingdoms of the Americas: Aztec,
　　　　Maya, Inca.* Cleveland, World Publishing Company.

WAGNER, C. Peter
　1967　*Defeat of the Bird God.* Grand Rapids, Zondervan.

WAGNER, C. Peter and MCCULLOUGH, Joseph S.
　1966　*The Condor of the Jungle.* Westwood, New Jersey,
　　　　Revell.

WARNECK, Gustav
　1906　*Outline of a History of Protestant Missions from the
　　　　Reformation to the Present Time with an Appendix
　　　　Concerning Roman Catholic Missions.* New York,
　　　　Fleming H. Revell Company.

WELD, Wayne
　1968　A graph of growth for Latin American Protestantism.
　　　　Unpublished.

WELLS, Henry, ed.
　1966　*Bolivia Election Factbook, July 3, 1966.* Washington,
　　　　Institute for the Comparative Study of Political
　　　　Systems, a Division of Operations and Policy Research,
　　　　Inc.

WHITAKER, Arthur P. and JORDAN, David C.
　1966　*Nationalism and Contemporary Latin America.* New
　　　　York, Free Press.

WILLCUTS, Clare and GREGORY, Dean
　1963　"Missionary Prayer Bulletin: Urgent," La Paz, Oct. 19.

WILLCUTS, Jack L.
  1965 "Together Again," *World Vision Magazine*. Oct., p. 22.

  1968a Personal letter to author, Newberg, Oregon, Jan. 3.

  1968b Personal letter to author, Newberg, Oregon, Feb. 5.

WINTER, Ralph D.
  1968 Unpublished lecture notes taken by author in class.

WONDERLY, William L.
  1960 "Urbanization: The Challenge of Latin America in Transition," *Practical Anthropology*. Sept.-Oct.:205-209.

WORCESTER, Donald E.
  1963 *The Three Worlds of Latin America*. New York, Dutton.

WORLD CHRISTIAN HANDBOOK (*WCH*)
  1949, 1952, 1957, 1962, 1967 Each edition is listed separately under editor.

WORLD MISSION PRAYER LEAGUE
  1965 Unsigned response to D. Phillips' research questionnaire.

WYMA, Richard
  1965 Response to David Phillips' research questionnaire.

  1968 Personal letter to author, Cochabamba, February 29.

YAMAHATA, Katsumi
  1964 "The Lost Sheep of Bolivia," *Japan Christian Quarterly*. July: 170-173.

YBOT LEON, Antonio
  1954 *La Iglesia y los eclesiásticos espenoles en la empresa de Indias, Los ideas y los hechos*. Barcelona, Salvat Editores, S. A.

YODER, Howard W.
  1948 "Bolivian Evangelical Union," Published minutes, November 15, La Paz.

ZEA, Leopoldo
   1963   *The Latin American Mind*. Norman, University of Oklahoma Press.

ZOOK, David H.
   1960   *The Conduct of the Chaco War*. New Haven, Bookman Associates.

William Carey Library
PUBLICATIONS

Africa

PEOPLES OF SOUTHWEST ETHIOPIA, by A. R. Tippett, Ph.D.
   A recent, penetrating evaluation by a professional anthropologist of the cultural complexities faced by Peace Corps workers and missionaries in a rapidly changing intersection of African states.
   1970: 320 pp, $3.95.   ISBN 0-87808-103-8

PROFILE FOR VICTORY: NEW PROPOSALS FOR MISSIONS IN ZAMBIA, by Max Ward Randall.
   "In a remarkably objective manner the author has analyzed contemporary political, social educational and religious trends, which demand a reexamination of traditional missionary methods and the creation of daring new strategies...his conclusions constitute a challenge for the future of Christian missions, not only in Zambia, but around the world."
   1970:   224 pp, Cloth, $3.95. ISBN 0-87808-403-7

THE CHURCH OF THE UNITED BRETHREN OF CHRIST IN SIERRA LEONE, by Emmett D. Cox, Executive Secretary, United Brethren in Christ Board of Missions.
   A readable account of the relevant historical, demographic and anthropological data as they relate to the development of the United Brethren in Christ Church in the Mende and Creole communities. Includes a reformation of objectives.
   1970:   184 pp, $2.95.   ISBN 0-87808-301-4

APPROACHING THE NUER OF AFRICA THROUGH THE OLD TESTAMENT, by Ernest A. McFall.
   The author examines in detail the similarities between the Nuer and the Hebrews of the Old Testament and suggests a novel Christian approach that does not make initial use of the New Testament.
   1970: 104 pp, 8 1/2 x 11, $1.95.
ISBN 0-87808-310-3

Asia

TAIWAN: MAINLINE VERSUS INDEPENDENT CHURCH GROWTH, A STUDY IN CONTRASTS, by Allen J. Swanson.
    A provocative comparison between the older, historical Protestant churches in Taiwan and the new indigenous Chinese churches; suggests staggering implications for missions everywhere that intend to promote the development of truly indigenous expressions of Christianity.
    1970: 216 pp, $2.95. ISBN 0-87808-404-5

NEW PATTERNS FOR DISCIPLING HINDUS: THE NEXT STEP IN ANDHRA PRADESH, INDIA, by B.V. Subbamma.
    Proposes the development of a Christian movement that is as well adapted culturally to the Hindu tradition as the present movement is to the Harijan tradition. Nothing could be more crucial for the future of 400 million Hindus in India today.
    1970: 212 pp, $3.45. ISBN 0-87808-306-5

GOD'S MIRACLES: INDONESIAN CHURCH GROWTH, by Ebbie C. Smith, Th.D.
    The fascinating details of the penetration of Christianity into the Indonesian archipelago make for intensely interesting reading, as the anthropological context and the growth of the Christian movement are highlighted.
    1970: 224 pp, $3.45. ISBN 0-87808-302-2

NOTES ON CHRISTIAN OUTREACH IN A PHILIPPINE COMMUNITY, by Marvin K. Mayers, Ph.D.
    The fresh observations of an anthropologist coming from the outside provide a valuable, however preliminary, check list of social and historical factors in the context of missionary endeavors in a Tagalog province.
    1970: 71 pp, 8 1/2 x 11, $1.45. ISBN 0-87808-104-6

Latin America

THE PROTESTANT MOVEMENT IN BOLIVIA, by C. Peter Wagner.
    An excitingly-told account of the gradual build-up and present vitality of Protestantism. A cogent analysis of the various subcultures and the organizations working most effectively, including a striking evaluation of Bolivia's momentous Evangelism-in-Depth year and the possibilities of Evangelism-in-Depth for other parts of the world.
    1970: 264 pp, $3.95. ISBN 0-87808-402-9

LA SERPIENTE Y LA PALOMA, by Manuel Gaxiola.
The impressive success story of the Apostolic Church of Mexico, (an indigenous denomination that never had the help of any foreign missionary), told by a professional scholar now the director of research for that church. (Spanish)
1970: 200 pp, $2.95. ISBN 0-87808-802-4

THE EMERGENCE OF A MEXICAN CHURCH: THE ASSOCIATE REFORMED PRESBYTERIAN CHURCH OF MEXICO, by James Erskine Mitchell.
Tells the ninety-year story of the Associate Reformed Presbyterian Mission in Mexico, the trials and hardships as well as the bright side of the work. Eminently practical and helpful regarding the changing relationship of mission and church in the next decade.
1970: 184 pp, $2.95. ISBN 0-87808-303-0

FRIENDS IN CENTRAL AMERICA, by Paul C. Enyart.
This book describes the results of faithful and effective labors of the California Friends Yearly Meeting, giving an analysis of the growth of one of the most virile, national evangelical churches in Central America, comparing its growth to other evangelical churches in Guatemala, Honduras, and El Salvador.
1970: 224 pp, $3.45. ISBN 0-87808-405-3

Europe

THE CHALLENGE FOR EVANGELICAL MISSIONS TO EUROPE: A SCANDINAVIAN CASE STUDY, by Hilkka Malaska.
Graphically presents the state of Christianity in Scandinavia with an evaluation of the pros and cons and possible contributions that existing or additional Evangelical missions can make in Europe today.
1970: 192 pp, $2.95. ISBN 0-87808-308-1

THE PROTESTANT MOVEMENT IN ITALY: ITS PROGRESS, PROBLEMS, AND PROSPECTS, by Roger Hedlund.
A carefully wrought summary of preliminary data; perceptively develops issues faced by Evangelical Protestants in all Roman Catholic areas of Europe. Excellent graphs.
1970: 266 pp, $3.95. ISBN 0-87808-307-3

U.S.A.

THE YOUNG LIFE CAMPAIGN AND THE CHURCH, by Warren Simandle.

If 70 per cent of young people drop out of the church between the ages of 12 and 20, is there room for a nationwide Christian organization working on high school campuses? After a quarter of a century, what is the record of Young Life and how has its work with teens affected the church? *"A careful analysis based on a statistical survey; full of insight and challenging proposals for both Young Life and the church."*

1970: 216 pp, $3.45. ISBN 0-87808-304-9

THE RELIGIOUS DIMENSION IN SPANISH LOS ANGELES: A PROTESTANT CASE STUDY, by Clifton L. Holland.

A through analysis of the origin, development and present extent of this vital, often unnoticed element in Southern California.

1970: 304 pp, $3.95. ISBN 0-87808-309-X

General

THEOLOGICAL EDUCATION BY EXTENSION, edited by Ralph D. Winter, Ph.D.

A husky handbook on a new approach to the education of pastoral leadership for the church. Gives both theory and practice and the exciting historical development in Latin America of the *"Largest non-governmental voluntary educational development project in the world today."* Ted Ward, Prof. of Education, Michigan State University.

1969: 648 pp, Library Buckram $7.95, Kivar $4.95. ISBN 0-87808-101-1

THE CHURCH GROWTH BULLETIN, VOL. I-V, edited by Donald A. McGavran, Ph.D.

The first five years of issues of a now-famous bulletin which probes past foibles and present opportunities facing the 100,000 Protestant and Catholic missionaries in the world today. No periodical edited for this audience has a larger readership.

1969: 408 pp, Library Buckram $6.95, Kivar $4.45. ISBN 0-87808-701-X

CHURCH GROWTH THROUGH EVANGELISM-IN-DEPTH, by
Malcolm R. Bradshaw.
"*Examines the history of Evangelism-in-Depth
and other total mobilization approaches to evangelism. Also presents concisely the 'Church
Growth' approach to mission and proposes a
wedding between the two...a great blessing to the
church at work in the world.*" WORLD VISION
MAGAZINE.
    1969: 152 pp, $2.45. ISBN 0-87808-401-0

THE TWENTY FIVE UNBELIEVABLE YEARS, 1945-1969, by
Ralph D. Winter, Ph.D.
    A terse, exciting analysis of the most significant transition in human history in this millenium and its impact upon the Christian movement. "*Packed with insight and otherwise unobtainable statistical data...a brilliant piece of work.*" C. Peter Wagner.
    1970: 120 pp, $1.95. ISBN 0-87808-102-X

EL SEMINARIO DE EXTENSION: UN MANUAL, by James H.
Emery, F. Ross Kinsler, Louise J. Walker, Ralph D.
Winter.
    Gives the reasons for the extension approach to the training of ministers, as well as the concrete, practical details of establishing and operating such a program. A Spanish translation of the third section of *THEOLOGICAL EDUCATION BY EXTENSION*.
    1969: 256 pp, $3.45. ISBN 0-87808-801-6

ABOUT THE WILLIAM CAREY LIBRARY

William Carey is widely considered the "Father of Modern Missions" partly because many people think he was the first Protestant missionary. Even though there was a trickle of others before him, he deserves very special honor for many valiant accomplishments in his heroic career, but most particularly because of three things he did before he ever left England, things no one else in history before him had combined together:

1) he had an authentic, personal, evangelical passion to serve God and acknowledged this as obligating him to fulfill God's interests in the redemption of all men on the face of the earth.

2) he actually proposed a structure for the accomplishment of that aim - he did indeed, more than anyone else, set off the movement among Protestants for the creation of "voluntary societies" for foreign missions, and

3) he added to all of this a strategic literary and research achievement: shaky those statistics may have been, but he put together the very best possible estimate of the number of unreached peoples in every part of the globe, and summarized previous, relatively ineffective attempts to reach them. His burning conclusion was that existing efforts were not proportional to the opportunities and the scope of Christian obligation in Mission.

Today, a little over 150 years later, the situation is not wholly different. In the past five years, for example, experienced missionaries from all corners of the earth (53 countries) have brought to the Fuller School of World Mission and Institute of Church Growth well over 800 years of missionary experience. Twenty-six scholarly books have resulted from the research of faculty and students. The best statistics available have at times been shaky -though far superior to Carey's - but vision has been clear and the mandate is as urgent as ever. The printing press is still the right arm of Christians active in the Christian world mission.

The William Carey Library is a new publishing house dedicated to books related to this mission. There are many publishers, both secular and religious, that occasionally publish books of this kind. We believe there is no other devoted exclusively to the production and distribution of books for career missionaries and their home churches.

ABOUT THE AUTHOR

Rev. C. Peter Wagner has been the Associate General Director of the Andes Evangelical Mission since 1968. He began his missionary career in Bolivia in 1956 under the South American Indian Mission, engaging in general missionary work in the tropical regions. Subsequently under the A.E.M. he became professor of theology and Director of the Emmaus Bible Institute, now the George Allan Theological Seminary, where he continues to teach part time. Active in Bolivian interdenominational activities, he was a founding officer of the Bolivian Commission for Evangelical Social Action (COMBASE), the Bolivian Theological Education Association (AEBET), and the Bolivian Evangelical Fellowship (ANDEB). Among books he has published are *Defeat of the Bird God*, *Condor of the Jungle* (with Joseph S. McCullough), and *Latin American Theology*. Wagner, who holds the B.S. Rutgers University), M.A. (Fuller School of World Mission), B.D. (Fuller Seminary), and Th.M. (Princeton Seminary) degrees, resides in Cochabamba, Bolivia with his wife and three girls.